THE FOODS OF
GREECE

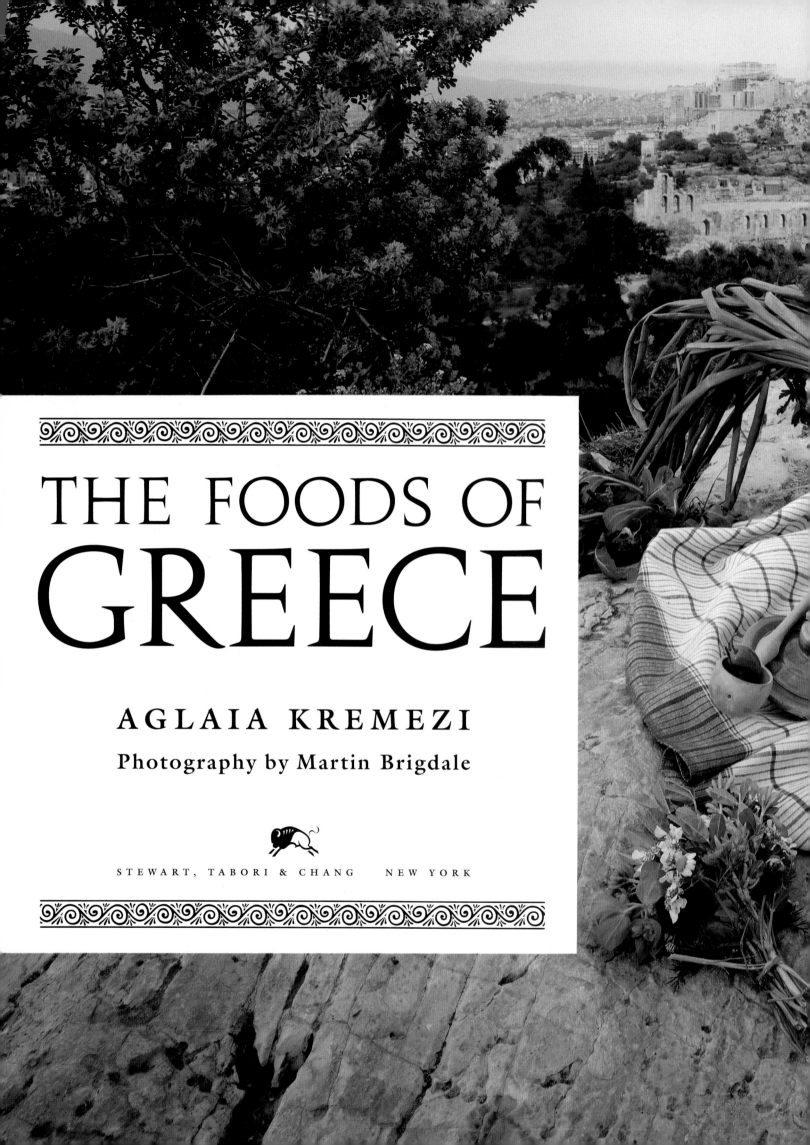

THE FOODS OF GREECE

AGLAIA KREMEZI

Photography by Martin Brigdale

STEWART, TABORI & CHANG   NEW YORK

Left: SMALL CHURCH IN CASTRO, THE CAPITAL OF ASTYPALAIA.
Opposite page: WINE JUG, CHANIA, CRETE.
Page 1: HYDRA HARBOR AT SUNRISE.
Pages 2–3: THE TRADITIONAL PICNIC HELD ON FILOPAPPOU HILL IN ATHENS ON CLEAN MONDAY, THE FIRST DAY OF LENT. ON THE PLATE ARE EGGPLANT CAVIAR (page 50) AND OLIVES; IN THE GREEN AND BLUE BOWL IS CARP ROE SPREAD (page 56) AND NEXT TO IT IS GARLIC SAUCE (page 54). BEHIND THEM IS SMOKED HERRING SPREAD (page 57). THESE TRADITIONAL DISHES ARE SERVED WITH *LAGANA* (FLAT BREAD), RETSINA, ARUGULA, AND FRESH GARLIC.
Pages 6–7: ASTYPALAIA: VIEW OF YIALOS—THE HARBOR—AND CASTRO.

Text copyright © 1993 Aglaia Kremezi
Photographs copyright © 1993 Martin Brigdale
Photographs on pages 16, 22, 153, and 187
copyright © 1993 Aglaia Kremezi ·

Map and border art by Jim Cozza
Edited by Ann ffolliott

Published in 1993 by
Stewart, Tabori & Chang, Inc.
575 Broadway, New York, New York 10012

Library of Congress Cataloging-in-Publication Data
Kremezi, Aglaia.
    The foods of Greece / Aglaia Kremezi : photography by Martin Brigdale.
    Includes bibliographical references and index.
    ISBN 1-55670-204-3
    1. Cookery, Greek.   I. Title.
TX723.5.G8K65   1993
641.59495—dc20   93-18562
                                  CIP

Distributed in the U.S. by Workman Publishing,
708 Broadway, New York, New York 10003
Distributed in Canada by Canadian Manda Group,
P.O. Box 920 Station U, Toronto, Ontario M8Z 5P9
Distributed in all other territories (except Central and South America) by Melia Publishing Services,
P.O. Box 1639, Maidenhead, Berkshire SL6 6YZ England
Central and South American accounts should contact
Export Sales Manager, Stewart, Tabori & Chang.

Printed in Japan
10 9 8 7 6 5 4 3 2 1

To Niko Kyriazidis,
my life's companion and my food taster

CONTENTS

APPETIZERS, SALADS, AND EGG DISHES

SIMPLE FISH AND SEAFOOD

MEATLESS MEALS AND VEGETABLE DISHES

MAKING THE MOST OF MEAT

BREADS, BISCUITS, PHYLLO, AND PASTA

DESSERTS AND SWEETS

PREFACE

This book is by no means a complete account of the full range of Greek cooking. It is a personal selection and adaptation of recipes—some classic and some nearly forgotten—from the rich Greek culinary tradition. This tradition, unfortunately, is disappearing rapidly in Greece, along with the last generation of women who were its guardians and who can find few interested young people willing to master and sustain it for future generations.

For many reasons, cooking in Greece has lost much of its original taste. Even women who still cook the traditional dishes they learned from their mothers and grandmothers believe these foods are not worthy to serve to special guests. They think *souvlaki,* pizza, hamburgers, *moussaka,* and a bad version of *horiatiki salata* (Greek salad) are the dishes most esteemed. So these are the ones visitors to Greece are most likely to find in the country's tavernas and restaurants.

The irony is that just as the world has discovered the benefits of the Mediterranean diet—with its reliance on olive oil, vegetables, grains, and dried beans—we in Greece are running away from it, without even looking back. The only hope lies in this strong trend from abroad. Scientists and other influential people from all parts of the Western world are telling us we have reason to be proud of our culinary heritage. So, now some young Greek women have started asking their mothers and grandmothers to take their faded, handwritten ledgers out of dusty boxes stacked in the attic and to teach them the secrets of phyllo pastry or *trahana,* to give them their versions of stuffed vegetables, and to explain the different qualities of the wild greens needed for the perfect *hortopita* (wild greens pie).

This was the hope that guided me through the long and difficult research that led to this book. I know that I have not found all the recipes worth writing about, so my search continues.

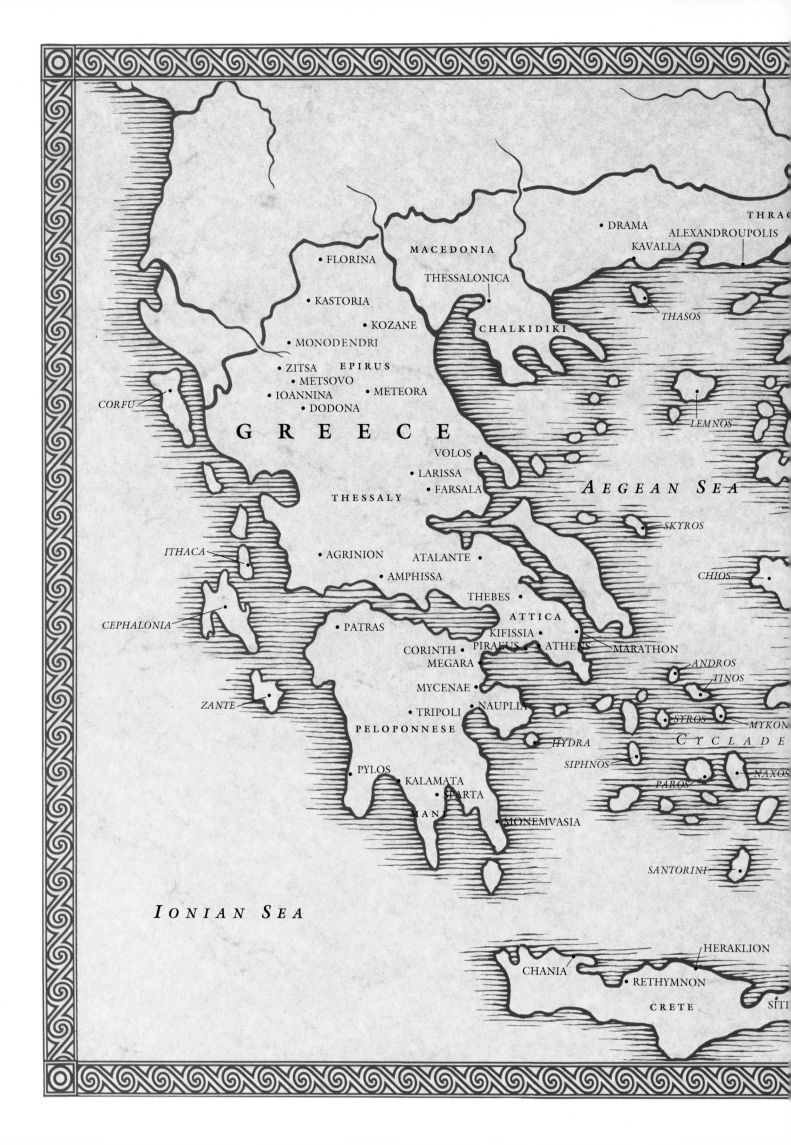

EDESMATA
THE FOODS OF GREECE

It's the middle of the night when the boat, after a twelve-hour trip from Piraeus, starts to sail parallel to the rocky, uninhabited side of Astypalaia, about an hour from the port. In the darkness, one can barely distinguish the shape of the island, although it is so near. But nobody can miss its fragrance. This combination of thyme and sage, oleander and ligaria that mixes with the sea air is, for me, the quintessence of Greece.

In the 1990s, you need to go far from the overcivilized and built-up Greek towns to find that idyllic place we often dream of. It still exists—who knows for how long. Astypalaia, the first island of the Dodecanese (or the last of the Cyclades, as some scholars claim), is our adopted second home. Niko, my companion, and I went there for a ten-day vacation some years ago, and we ended up buying one of the sixteenth-century stone houses on the hill, above the old castle.

We couldn't quite put our finger on what made us do such a foolish thing as buy a house that needed a lot of work to become habitable, on an island thirteen boat hours away from our home in Athens. It was obvious that we could not visit the place often, or stay very long. But we felt we needed to become part of this island. Its beauty was not the main reason. More important was the way of life in Astypalaia—the calm manner of its inhabitants, their way of taking real pleasure from a glass of ouzo at midday or from coffee served in a tumbler in the afternoon. They were never in a hurry, taking their time to narrate extraordinary stories, savoring every moment, mostly doing very little in terms of work.

I must admit that, at first, trying to restore the house with local workers was a nightmare. These people had a particular rhythm of their own and could not be coerced to work faster. Gradually, I adapted to their way of doing things: working when it was not cold or raining, or when it was not windy—which is only about one day in seven in the winter and one in eight in the summer. But then, it might be too hot, or a cousin might have given a party for his name day, the night before, and the next day—after so much wine and dancing—nobody felt like

PREPARING CRACKED GREEN OLIVES, MARATHON.

working. Instead, the master builder and his workers sat in a coffeehouse discussing the events of the previous evening.

In the few tavernas of the island, the women cooks still pride themselves on their cooking, asking for the

CHURCH BELLS, SANTORINI.

customers' comments, mainly seeking approval for their *dolmadakia* (stuffed vine leaves) or their *kakavia* (a simple and delicious fish soup). It is very rare in Greece these days to find a restaurant cook (who is usually the owner's wife) who really cares.

There is Popy, in Maltezana, at whose vegetable garden I buy whatever seasonal produce she has to offer. "Let's go and see if there are any ripe tomatoes," she says, taking me to the plants to pick my own. Or she climbs up a ladder to collect figs or plums. "You are never here to taste our tangerines," she complains, while she offers me slices of the bread she and her sister bake every Saturday. If I want a chicken, I ask her to slaughter one (they are tough but very tasty), and the same goes for lamb or kid. "Just tell me one day in advance," Popy asks, and the next morning the skinned animal hangs from a tree, while Popy asks what part of it I want to buy. She also sells some homemade cheese and, of course, marvelous thyme honey. My wanderings in this vegetable garden are the highlight of the days I spend in Astypalaia.

The rest of the year, as I sit behind my desk in Athens, so far from Popy's Garden of Eden, I dream of these few days on the island each year; and I find myself acting like some of my friends, who are often

compelled to talk about their fantastic childhoods, living among goats and hens in remote villages.

Nearly half of all the baby-boomers who live in the big cities—Athens and Thessalonica—came from agricultural areas. Even living in ugly cement apartment houses of the gray and smoggy city of Athens, our ties to Mother Earth remain strong. For instance, those who have moved to big cities during the last forty years have brought with them traditional village cooking and culinary habits. They maintain close ties with their place of birth and visit the villages for long weekends, summer holidays, as well as every Christmas and Easter. There are many factors that drive all these new inhabitants of the cities back to the land. Surely one of the most important is the taste of food of the village, which evokes memories of a happier time in their lives. City people often feel the need to describe in detail the delicious dishes that their mothers and grandmothers used to make; also, many Athenians receive food parcels from relatives in the villages. My brother-in-law still gets parcels from his mother, who lives in Volos, Thessaly, containing not only fantastic baklava and squash pie made with hand-rolled phyllo pastry, but also *katsamaki,* a kind of cornmeal porridge. *Katsamaki* is something that most of us would not like to eat unless we had been starved for a couple of days. But what for most of us is tasteless mush is, for him, a reminder of happy, although difficult, childhood years.

People from one region of Greece frequently choose to live together in the same neighborhood in Athens. In these neighborhoods are small grocery stores and coffeehouses that sell all the special products of that particular region. It is in these humble places—and not in the fancy, expensive delicatessens of Kolonaki or Kifissia—that people who appreciate good food can find the delicious mizithra cheese from Naxos; the thick and aromatic honey from Astypalaia; the small, fruity olives of Crete; or the giant beans from Kastoria. In these neighborhoods, regional customs for weddings and local saints' days are upheld. Celebratory foods are often brought, together with the musicians, from the village, because without these two key elements there can be no real celebration.

But how do these many and varied regional eating habits combine to form Greek cooking? I believe

Greek cooking is, foremost, the product of great ingenuity. Every day the Greek cook manages to create a new dish from the same few, humble, seasonal ingredients. Take, for example, the various wild greens and comestible weeds that Greeks gather from the hills and fields. In many parts of the country, wild greens (*horta*) fulfill an important role in people's diets. The greens are boiled and made into salad, or sautéed with onions or garlic and supplemented with homemade pasta or cheese to make a more substantial meal. Greens are also added to a flour-based soup or porridge, or mixed with a batter and fried to make patties. When meat or poultry is available, the greens can be added and finished with *avgolemono*, the delicious Greek egg-and-lemon sauce, to create a Sunday feast. And, of course, wild greens are the basis of many pies, flat and coiled. Today, we try to recreate these exquisite pies with spinach and other cultivated greens, but we will never come close to the taste of the pies cooked in Metsovo, which often contain seven or more different kinds of *horta*, each complementing the other in flavor and aroma.

Greek food is not sophisticated or refined. It is simple and down to earth, tied to and making the most of the seasonal produce of each region. Greek cooks don't make stuffed tomatoes or eggplant spread in the winter, although these vegetables are now available year-round.

Unfortunately, many Greek dishes, closely related to religious holidays and traditions, are tending to disappear as pizza and hamburgers—as well as the infamous *souvlaki*—take over, making much of Greek food as banal as the food in the rest of the industrialized world.

FOODS OF
THE ANCIENT GREEKS

Greek-style ingredient-based cooking can be traced back to ancient times. Greece always had flour, honey, almonds, and walnuts, so it is only natural that in Aristophanes's comedies, written in the fifth century B.C., we find descriptions of sweets very similar to the simple, fried batter puffs we call *loukoumades,* or to the fried phyllo *diples* or *kserotigana,* sprinkled with chopped nuts and cinnamon.

The portrayal of a constant roasting of meat described by Homer in *The Iliad* and *The Odyssey* gives a false picture of what ancient Greeks really ate. Athenaeus, a Greek author who lived in Rome between A.D. 170 and 230, gave a very good explanation for that. He suggested that roasted meat was the food everyone expected male heroes to eat, while fish, which requires considerable preparation, was more often associated with women cooks.

Athenaeus is an important source of information about the food of the ancient Greeks. He collected references to food and drink in earlier Greek texts, including comments from well-known writers and philosophers such as Aristotle, Plato, and Aristophanes. His references also include many minor poets and playwrights whose work has survived only through him. Athenaeus's work resulted in the *Deipnosophistai,* fifteen books written in the form of a conversation that took place during a dinner, in which the participants quoted earlier writers about all kinds of wines and foods.

From Athenaeus's work and the writings of many other ancient authors, it is clear that the common man of ancient Greece consumed very little meat—only after sacrifices during big feasts. He ate a lot of fish and many vegetables, but his mainstay was either a gruel—similar to my brother-in-law's *katsamaki*—made of cereal or legumes, or barley bread. That meager meal was made more palatable by adding a

THE TEMPLE OF POSEIDON, SOUNION.

fermented fish sauce called *garos* (later called *garum* by the Romans), which also played an important role later during the Byzantine era. Ancient Greeks also ate a lot of garlic and onions with their bread or gruel, while fish was an important source of protein, especially for Athenians and the other Greeks living near the sea. The fish was salted or smoked to preserve it throughout the year.

Ancient Greeks ate a lot of cheese, but drank hardly any milk. Their favorite drinks, apart from wine, were *hydromeli* (water mixed with some honey) and *kykeon* (the water in which barley was boiled), scented with sage, mint, or thyme, which was also considered very nutritious.

A VEGETARIAN TRADITION

While vegetarianism and the abstinence from meat as a way of life was introduced by Pythagoras in the sixth to fifth century B.C., until very recently Greeks have been largely vegetarian—not by choice, but by necessity. In this mountainous country it was not possible to pasture large herds to provide meat for everybody. Village people, like my friend Popy in Astypalaia, still try to be self-sufficient. They have one or two goats or sheep to give them milk, from which they make yogurt and cheese, and some hens for eggs. Garden vegetables are plentiful in summer, and some vegetables, such as tomatoes, are dried for winter use. Legumes and the year's supply of wheat are either bought or cultivated on small plots of land.

With the wheat, villagers prepare *trahana,* the traditional Greek homemade pasta. The grain is stone-ground in hand mills and then boiled in milk or mixed with sour milk. In early summer, one can see pieces of *trahana* drying on the rooftops of village houses.

Up until forty years ago, meat was a rare, festive dish in most parts of the country, consumed on Sundays, at Easter and Christmas, and on important saint's days. I come from a middle-class Athenian family and in the late 1940s and early 1950s—after the hard days of World War II and the civil war—we ate meat only twice a week, always on Sunday and once during the week.

Apart from poverty, there was another reason for this largely meatless habit: the knowledge that had been gained over the years and codified in the form of religious custom. Greeks never ate foodstuffs derived from animals on Wednesdays and Fridays, or for the forty days before Easter and Christmas, or on many other occasions. These customs were strictly obeyed. Indeed, travelers to Greece in the seventeenth century wrote about people going to bed on an empty stomach because the only food they had to eat—bread—had been touched by meat. This is also the reason why many of our traditional dishes—stuffed vegetables, pies, and so forth—come in two versions: one with meat (sometimes called the festive version) and one without, for fasting days.

OUR DAILY BREAD

Until recently, the staple food in Greece was bread, as it had been in ancient times. Although nowadays Greek people can afford a great variety of foods, we still consume enormous quantities of bread. Even stale bread is not wasted. Cotton sacks with pieces of dried bread hang from the rafters in village dwellings. Pieces of dried bread are soaked and mixed with ground meat to make *keftedes* or *soutzoukakia,* or dipped in vegetable soup to make it more substantial.

In classical Athens, according to the laws of Solon, the ruler of the city in the sixth century B.C., *maza*—a kind of barley rusk—was the basic food;

BLESSING THE BREAD, ASTYPALAIA.

wheat bread was eaten only on festive days. Twenty-two centuries later, little seemed to have changed in rural Greece. In the seventeenth century, a French priest named François Richard, who visited the island of Santorini, wrote that people subsisted on dark barley rusks that they prepared two or three times a year. These rusks, briefly dipped in water and consumed with vegetables and fish, were the main food for the island's inhabitants. Richard writes that the rusks were so black that in France even the dogs would refuse to eat them; and that although the people seemed to enjoy them, for someone unused to such food they would result in hemorrhaging, even death! These rusks must have been very similar to the tasty barley *paximadia* we still find in Crete.

Greeks used to eat a lot of bread with their simple and meager meals, dipping large pieces in olive oil to abate hunger.

The olive is basic to our lives and our identity and olive oil is the basic fat used in Greek cooking. From the blessed olive tree Greeks not only use the fruit but also make charcoal from the branches, while olive pits left from the oil pressing are fuel for the stove. Olive wood is lovely and strong, used to make furniture, salad bowls, and spoons. In Crete and Lesbos, skilled popular craftsmen make wooden jewelry and the worry beads that men like to play with.

People of our parents' and grandparents' generations used to tell stories about the men and women of Crete who lived healthily past the age of one hundred, thanks to a diet rich in olive oil. Interestingly enough, those stories have been substantiated by scientific research. The irony is that these people—the very ones who told us of the longevity diet—have done exactly the opposite. During Nazi occupation and the civil war that followed, Greeks lived on beans and bread—that is, the lucky ones who did not starve to death. In the 1960s, when food was plentiful again, however, they ate to their hearts' content and also considered it their duty to stuff their children with lots of meat and butter.

Nevertheless, Greece still has one of the highest life expectancies in Europe. Certainly, traditional eating habits must contribute to this.

INFLUENCES, GOOD AND BAD

As Greece is situated at the eastern end of Europe, close to Asia, it is only natural that its cooking has been influenced by its eastern neighbors. One should also bear in mind that Greece was for roughly eleven hundred years part of the Byzantine empire (from A.D. 330 to about 1450) and spent four hundred years under Ottoman domination (from the mid-fifteenth century to the beginning of the nineteenth). Foreign influences have left their mark, although the influence was mutual.

People do not change their cooking habits quickly,

nor do they easily adopt foreign ideas. Peasant cooking is conservative, passed from one generation to the next, remaining remarkably unaltered for centuries. So it would be strange if Greeks living in Asia Minor—ancient Ionia—from the dawn of civilization, for example, suddenly changed their diet because they were conquered by the Turks. Rather, the contrary seems to have happened. The Turks, who were nomads and warriors, had loose ties to the earth and practically none to the sea and its products. So it's more likely that they adopted some of the cooking habits of some of the people they conquered, including the Greeks of Byzantium.

In the Byzantine courts, professional cooks had developed an elaborate cuisine with roots in ancient Greece, enriched by the many different foods and spices imported from all parts of the empire. Caviar—red and black—as well as the most esteemed Greek delicacy *avgotaraho* (smoked gray mullet eggs) were favorite gourmet foods. That culinary cornucopia was adopted later by the Ottoman rulers, who sent their cooks to study in Europe. When they came back, the cooks used the knowledge they gained to invent new dishes based on the traditional cooking of Byzantium. *Moussaka* is one example: French béchamel sauce was added to complement the eggplant and meat.

So it is not strange that many old Greek dishes have Turkish names. If you look closely, you can see, for example, that *kieftes* (meatball), which sounds Turkish, comes from *kopto,* the Byzantine term for minced meat. Also, the Turkish word *yahni,* which defines food sautéed with onions, might have its roots in the Greek verb *ahnizo,* which means to sauté. The latter term is still used, especially in the north of Greece.

Greeks have a tendency to view even their food in ideologic or nationalist terms. For that reason, they came to despise Turkish-sounding foods and renamed many of them. An extreme example was the renaming of Turkish coffee to "Greek" coffee or even "Byzantine" coffee (for the more patriotic) after Turkey invaded Cyprus in 1974. But of course this coffee, which came to the West around 1550, from the Arab world through the courts of the Ottoman sultans, has nothing to do with Byzantium or Greece.

The most influential cookbook in Greece appeared in the late 1920s. It was written by Nicolas Tselementes, a Greek from Siphnos who grew up in Constantinople and was an esteemed professional cook. He had worked in such places as the St. Moritz Hotel in New York, and the Sacher in Vienna. In his book, Tselementes assembled French, Italian, American, and other recipes, along with the Greek ones he considered important. This book had an enormous impact on the rising Athenian middle and upper classes. To this day, "Tselementes" is synonymous with "cookbook" in Greece; and his beliefs and ideas influenced not only home cooking but also professional cooking, because he was the principal teacher in all the important schools of cooking.

Tselementes tried to refine Greek peasant cooking, making it more suitable for the tastes of Europeans and Americans. He believed that French cooking had its origins in ancient Greece, and that under Turkish rule, Greek cooking became more Eastern—something he was determined to correct. So in his book, Tselementes urges educated chefs to free Greek recipes of all spices that might have been added by Eastern rulers. He probably had never read any description of ancient or Byzantine Greek food, and had only a vague notion of the supposedly pure dishes our ancestors consumed, in contrast to the "barbaric" spiced cooking of our Eastern neighbors.

These ideas have marked Greek cooking from that time on. Greek cooks gradually stopped using spices, thinking that in this way the food would be more European. So our dishes, especially the ones served in big hotels and restaurants, became insipid. Fortunately, some of the original tastes of Byzantium have survived in the cooking of *prosfyges,* Greeks who came back to the mainland as refugees from Asia Minor after the Greek defeat by the Turks in 1922. In this cooking, we can trace better, tastier Greek food.

It was not until the end of the 1960s that Greece stopped being one of the underdeveloped countries and joined Europe as an equal partner. No longer a poor relation, Greece became more prosperous, and its people felt that they had to remove any vestiges of a difficult past. So the old, handmade copper pots and pans, the wooden troughs in which bread was kneaded, and the lovely, handwoven curtains and blankets were sold to traveling merchants for a song,

replaced by plastic tablecloths and aluminum kitchenware. With the passing of these traditional utensils and furnishings we also lost many of our old eating habits, our culinary heritage.

Greece has never had great chefs to record its cooking traditions. My mother's generation, which came of age before World War II, and especially women who have lived in the countryside most of their lives, are the last remaining link with a rich culinary past. In remote villages—and especially on the islands, where traditions are more important—one can still find the crude and tasty peasant cooking of our great-grandmothers. But one has to search hard for it. In the tavernas, in the holiday resorts, hardly anyone cooks dishes typical of the region. *Souvlaki*, hamburgers, veal or pork chops, spaghetti, and pizza are everywhere in Greece, often served with badly cooked *moussaka*.

What most Greeks of my age and younger have known as "Greek" food is the "neither Eastern nor European" dishes that Tselementes promoted—food that cannot compete with French or Italian cooking. To a certain extent, it is understandable why Greek and Mediterranean cooking is not very "fashionable" in Athens. Dozens of Chinese, Thai, German, Indian, and other ethnic restaurants, together with a lot of French and Italian ones, have opened recently. Last year we also got our first McDonald's and Wendy's; both have been extremely successful. Alas, as of now, we have hardly any restaurants that serve good-quality Greek dishes in a pleasant atmosphere.

But things seem to be changing. People are growing tired of sophisticated "foreign" foods and processed ingredients, and they are feeling a need to go back to the source. In addition, the traditional Mediterranean diet based on olive oil and vegetables has captured the attention of nutritionists and scientists. Now Americans—who introduced us to a lot of meat and processed foods—are turning to our food traditions. Cookbook authors, journalists, and chefs from all over the Western world are looking at old Greek recipes. I don't think it unrealistically optimistic to foresee the day when young Greek chefs start using almost-forgotten recipes to create the next chapter of our age-old cooking.

SUNRISE AT A SHEEP AND GOAT FARM, ASTYPALAIA.

THE ELEMENTS OF GREEK FOOD

Greek cooking is heavily dependent on fresh, tasty vegetables, herbs, cheeses, and fruits. Fortunately, most of these can be found in supermarkets and greengrocers throughout the United States. Because Greek and Mediterranean cooking, in general, uses seasonal produce that is at its best when ripened by the sun, I suggest you shop at local farmers' markets whenever possible. Dishes made with ripe, seasonal vegetables taste so much better!

Here is a description of the key ingredients you will find in many recipes in this book. Some of them, such as olives, are served by themselves as appetizers.

OLIVES
(ELIES)

No one knows how and when man figured out how to make the bitter, inedible fruit of the olive tree into one of our favorite foods. But we can speculate that one day, olives happened to fall into the sea, and the salted water washed away their bitterness. From then on, people couldn't stop eating olives.

Ancient Greeks preferred black ripe olives, believing that they—not green olives—were better for one's health. They also considered olives preserved in vinegar to be good for the digestion. Athenaeus wrote that the ancient Athenians used to offer "cheese and barley cakes, ripe olives and leeks, in memory of their ancient discipline" to the Dioscuri (the twin sons of Zeus, gods of light). These foods were the Athenians' traditional, everyday diet. In the same text we read: "In pious memory of Marathon (where Athenians defeated the Persians) for all time, they all put 'mara-

SUN-DRIED TOMATO SLICES, CHOPPED TOMATOES READY TO BE COOKED AND FROZEN (page 32), PICKLED HOT GREEN PEPPERS (page 34) AND CAPERS IN VINEGAR. VINE LEAVES IN BRINE, AND GRILLED GREEN AND RED BELL PEPPERS PRESERVED IN GARLIC VINAIGRETTE (page 52), IN CHANIA, CRETE.

thon' [fennel] in the briny olives." Greeks still put fennel in their olives. In the open-air markets all over Athens, in November, the month table olives are usually harvested, one finds little pieces of wild fennel stems tied together, ready to be added to olive brine. In Aristophanes's comedies we read about cracked olives, and in other ancient texts we find *elaies colymvades,* or olives preserved in olive oil, which are still called by the same name.

In the house I grew up, in Patissia—a neighborhood of Athens that was full of gardens until the early 1960s—we had a big, old olive tree just outside the window of my room. From that tree my grandfather used to make two kinds of olives: cracked green olives (*tsakistes*) in early fall, and later—when the fruit ripened and turned dark purple—he slit the olives with a very sharp knife and placed them in brine to make olives similar to those called *Kalamata*.

My cousins, my sister, and I all helped him prepare the cracked olives. Each of us took a clean, flat stone in hand and banged the olives, one by one, on a piece of broken marble that once was the top of my grandmother's kitchen table. "Don't hit very hard,"

my grandfather used to say, "because you may break the pit, and the olives will be inedible."

The cracked olives were placed in water, which was changed every day for about a week to rinse away their bitterness. Then a brine was made with plenty of salt. To test if the brine was right, a whole egg was thrown in, and if a part of it about the size of a small coin called a *dekara,* roughly the size of a quarter, floated above the surface, the brine contained the right amount of salt.

Cracked olives are kept in this brine throughout the year. Wild fennel stems and lemons are also added to give fragrance. You can use a less salty brine, but then you must keep the olives in the refrigerator.

Cracked Green Olives in Oil and Vinegar Cracked olives are stored in their brine until they are consumed. After two to three weeks, you can take out a

GREEN OLIVES, ASTYPALAIA.

portion, rinse them in cold water, and marinate them in *ladoxido* (vinaigrette made with two parts oil to one part vinegar) with savory or oregano, lemon pieces, garlic, chili pepper, and whatever other spices you like. Leave them in this marinade for one to two

days before serving, but do not let them stay in it for more than a week.

Olives in Coarse Salt (*Elies Throumbes*) with Herbs
The ripe, round black olives that are usually harvested in Greece in November are placed in a basket or colander and generously sprinkled with coarse salt. For best results use unprocessed sea-salt crystals. The olives are tossed and turned at least twice every day to reduce some of their juices, together with their bitterness. On some islands, people prepare their *throumbes* by dipping the olive basket into the sea every day, and then hanging it to drain. After six or seven days, when their skins begin to wrinkle and the inner flesh turns dark brown, they are ready to be eaten.

These olives have an excellent taste if eaten fresh, but they may dry out if kept too long.

To give more flavor to your *throumbes,* after their flesh has turned dark, place them on paper towels to dry, then transfer them to a large bowl and drizzle some virgin olive oil over them. Sprinkle with dried oregano, savory, thyme, and rosemary; toss well so that all the olives are coated with the oil. Place in a colander to drain off excess oil and transfer them to jars and store in the refrigerator.

Other Varieties of Olives Unlike olives prepared in other countries, Greek olives are always what they appear to be: green olives are unripe and black olives are ones that were left to ripen on the trees—not green olives dyed to look black. This is why Greek black olives are not always perfectly shaped. But rest assured that they taste great, because theirs is the natural taste of olive.

The most well-known Greek olives are the ones that come from Kalamata, the southern part of the Peloponnese. Firm, with a pungent acidic taste from the vinegar in which they are kept, Kalamata olives are a perfect *meze,* eaten right out of the jar or seasoned with oregano and chopped garlic.

For people who prefer sweeter olives, the round, black ones from Amfissa are the best choice. There are also giant olives, a late addition to the Greek repertoire, which come mainly from Atalante, in central mainland Greece.

CURING *THROUMBES* OLIVES WITH COARSE SALT, LESBOS.

But the olives I find irresistible are the tiny *lianolia* from Crete. Mainly home-cured in the region of Chania, these olives have an unforgettable fruity flavor. Unfortunately, most of them are consumed in Crete, and very seldom can one find them in the central market of Athens.

OLIVE OIL
(*LADI*)

As with most Greek delicacies that are not easily found everywhere, Greek olive oil is not widely available outside Greece. But connoisseurs like the French specifically ask for it because of its high quality and fair price. Once you try it, you will become hooked on its mellow taste and rich aroma.

Olive oil was specified, with honey and wine, for *spondai*, the ancient Greek libations. Scholars find it difficult to explain why something that is not a drink is used in libations. Walter Burkert, in his magnificent book *Greek Religion*, explains that our forefathers marked with olive oil the places where libations had taken place. They also marked some special stones in sanctuaries and crossroads by rubbing them with oil.

According to the Greek Orthodox religion, the priest and godfather anoint babies with olive oil at christening.

Olives and olive oil are mentioned in the earliest written Greek texts, the clay tablets found in the palaces of Knossos, Pylos, and Mycenae, which date to the fifteenth century B.C. On the recently deciphered tablets from the palace of Knossos, in Crete (circa 1375 B.C.), one of the inscriptions reads: "Olive oil to all the gods of Amnissos."

Olive oil was and still is the main fat used in Greek cooking and baking. Greece consumes more olive oil, per capita, than any other country in the world: about 20 quarts per person each year.

Olive oil is so much a part of our everyday life that in modern Greek, a language that is strangely limited in words for colors and their shades, there is the color *ladi*, the color of olive oil.

The oil-producing olive harvest usually starts in late November, depending on the weather and the amount of rain in previous months.

People of all ages help collect the fruit, and Greek civil servants can get a special paid leave of absence to go to their villages and help harvest olives. Most of the olive trees are very old, with marvelously twisted trunks. They often grow in the hills and the mountains, even next to the sea. These trees, with their extensive network of roots, keep the precious soil on the steep slopes of the islands from being washed away. The majority of Greek olive trees are not irrigated, which makes the taste of Greek olive oil richer than that produced in countries where the trees are regularly watered.

The olives from tall, age-old trees in densely planted groves are still harvested, in most areas, in the same way as was done in ancient times: either by hand or with the help of a cane. A man standing on a tall ladder beats the branches of each tree with a cane, so the ripe olives fall onto large nets that have been laid out to collect them. Kneeling down, the rest of the team—usually women—collect the fallen olives and place them in large baskets or sacks, which are taken to the oil press.

Virgin Olive Oil Large baskets, filled with shiny dark purple olives, are brought to the nearest oil press. There, the olives are separated from the leaves and small branches, rinsed to remove dust and dirt, and then crushed and milled to produce olive paste.

In some old presses that still operated in remote villages and on islands of the Cyclades up until the mid-1970s, olives were pressed with primitive methods that I'm sure differed little from those ancient Greeks used to extract their olive oil. These presses were powered by blindfolded donkeys or mules, who were forced to walk in circles to operate the stone mills. That paste was then placed in envelopes of special mats, either woven with goat hair or made of jute, which were piled up on the base of the press. Warm water was often thrown on the pile to make squeezing easier. Then the press was operated by two, three, or even four men, who helped turn the huge wooden screw to bring the weight down and squeeze the piled sacks with the olive paste to extract the oil. The extracted juice was channeled into two stone cisterns built on different levels in the floor. They had small drain pipes in their base to take the heavier water—contained in the pressed juice—out of the press, while the lighter oil stayed in the cistern.

These old presses later were powered by electricity. Then, the oil was separated from the water by centrifuging. In recent years a lot of the hydraulic presses have been replaced by new high-speed centrifugal machines that extract the oil without applying pressure on the olive paste.

In any case, the newly extracted oil has little resemblance to the clear transparent stuff we buy in bottles. It looks more like a greenish paint or gravy, and needs to be left to stand, in stainless-steel tanks, so that it clarifies before consumption. Olive oil is often filtered to ensure clarity before it is bottled. It is at its best one year after pressing.

Olive oil extracted by purely mechanical means, as described above, is called virgin olive oil. Its quality and taste depend on the olives from which it was extracted. The adaptations of the olive tree to the soil and climate of the region are factors that determine the quality of the virgin olive oil. It is very important that the olives be unblemished and free of insect bites, and that they are pressed as soon as they are collected. Roughly five pounds of olives are needed to produce one pint of virgin olive oil.

The color of virgin olive oil ranges from intense green to yellow gold, and depends on the ripeness of the olives that were pressed to produce it. Green olive oil is the product of unripe green olives, while the yellow comes from ripe ones. The color is not necessarily an indication of the strength or quality of the oil's flavor.

Greeks, before the classification of the best olive oil as virgin or extra virgin (top quality), used to call the best olive oil *agoureleo*. The word literally means "oil from unripe olives," and that was the case if it came from the Peloponnese. But the term also meant "olive oil from the first pressing." The old presses could separate the different pressings, and the oil from the first was the best, while the second and third pressings produced inferior oils. In Lesbos, where the oil is produced by ripe olives, people call *agoureleo* the freshly pressed oil, which they like to consume young, one to two months after pressing.

Ancient Greeks also distinguished between the olive oil extracted from unripe olives—calling it *homotribes*—and the oil that came from the over-ripe ones—which was often called *sabinon*, as the best came from southern Italy, a part of Greece at that time. It was believed by some that the latter tasted better and was also healthier, although the different ancient writers didn't always agree on the matter.

Refined and Pure Olive Oil The virgin olive oils that are of inferior quality or have an elevated acidic level (more than 3.3 percent) are refined. They are heated at high temperatures or processed with chemicals (but never with benzene and other solvents, as are various other vegetable oils). Refined olive oil is pale yellow in color and quite bland in taste. Only 25 to

30 percent of Greek olive oil is refined because the bulk is of excellent quality, and so consumed as virgin olive oil.

Refined olive oil is mixed with a certain amount of virgin to give it taste. This blend is called pure olive oil. In Greece, the larger quantity of olive oil sold in the market falls into this category and contains a large amount of virgin olive oil.

Virgin and extra-virgin olive oil, which is so popular in Europe and the United States, is exported from Greece, but only recently has appeared in Greek supermarkets. It accounts for a little less than half the total amount of the bottled olive oil sold. But you must bear in mind that roughly two out of three Greek families either come from oil-producing regions or have a friend or relative who does.

Throughout December each oil-producing family waits patiently for its turn at the local olive press, so as to get its olives pressed and collect the oil for the family's use. If there is more oil than the family can use,

CLOUDY YELLOW-GREEN OLIVE OIL, AS IT COMES OUT OF AN OLIVE PRESS, LESBOS.

they sell it to friends and relations. Even the aged who own only a few trees feel compelled to produce their own oil, which to them is superior to any other. Most Athenians get their year's supply from friends and relatives who produce it in Amphissa, Mani, Crete, or Lesbos, to name but a few of the regions known for high-quality virgin olive oil.

Since Greeks grow up eating olive oil, our taste for it is very different from that of people who have recently discovered it. For example, a friend of mine grew up in Messara, Crete, and likes the heavy, acidy oil his family produced, which for me is inedible. Eating my food cooked with lighter oil, he always complains, "Did you fry the potatoes in water?"

This is an extreme example, but there are Greeks —especially people who grew up in oil-producing regions—who prefer virgin olive oil even if its acidity level is 2.5 or 3 percent. In general, we prefer olive oils with a rich, sweet, fruity taste and aroma.

Which Olive Oil Should You Use? If you are thinking of switching to olive oil from butter or other oils with less flavor, start by using pure and light olive oil, which contain more refined and less virgin olive oil and is milder in flavor. As you get used to its taste, you will be able to start appreciating the rich flavor of the best-quality Greek virgin olive oil.

Virgin olive oil is best raw, in salads and spreads or drizzled on grilled meat and fish. Pure olive oil, especially Greek, which contains a fair amount of virgin oil, is good for any kind of cooking.

Raw Olive Oil Sauces In salads of cooked or uncooked vegetables and greens, for grilled fish or meat, and on many other occasions, two basic olive oil sauces—the Greek versions of vinaigrette—are used.

LADOLEMONO
(Olive Oil and Lemon)

2 parts virgin or extra-virgin olive oil
1 part fresh lemon juice
Sea salt and freshly ground pepper to taste
Optional: dry mustard, dried oregano, dried savory,
    chopped fresh dill, chopped flat-leaf parsley,
    chopped scallions, chopped capers

Combine the oil, lemon juice, and salt and pepper. To this, you may add one or more of the optional items. Place all the ingredients in a jar with a lid and shake well.

LADOXIDO
(Olive Oil and Vinegar)

2 1/3 parts virgin or extra-virgin olive oil
1 part red wine or balsamic vinegar
Sea salt and freshly ground pepper to taste
Optional: dry mustard, dried oregano, dried savory, chopped fresh dill, chopped flat parsley, chopped scallions, chopped capers

Combine the oil, vinegar, and salt and pepper. To this, you may add one or more of the optional ingredients. Place all the ingredients in a jar with a lid and shake well.

VINEGAR

In Greek villages vinegar is made from homemade red wine, which is left to turn to vinegar. Since people are always afraid that their wine might turn to vinegar sooner than anticipated, and because they are unable to explain when and how their lovely wine turns sour, they have become highly superstitious. The word *xidi* (vinegar) used to be banned from households that kept wine, and the euphemism *glikadi* (the sweet one) was used instead. Homemade Greek vinegar is never very strong; the best substitute for it is Italian balsamic vinegar.

YOGURT
(GIAOURTI)

As a child, I remember the *yaourta* (the yogurt man) passing by our house every afternoon, on his rounds of the neighborhood. He carried a tin box resembling a small kitchen cupboard with shelves and two doors. In it, he carried larger and smaller shallow clay pots filled with yogurt. The pots were covered with oiled paper. We used to buy at least one pot each day, returning the empty cleaned pots from the previous day. This lovely sweet yogurt, made from sheep's milk, had a thin crust of cream on top.

Yogurt men disappeared in the 1960s, and the clay pots were abandoned in favor of disposable plastic ones. They were still covered with oiled paper up until the mid-1970s, when mass-produced yogurt appeared in sealed containers in every supermarket refrigerator.

But even the industrialized yogurt we buy in Athens today is better tasting than most of the yogurt found in Europe or the United States. Thick, creamy, and sweet, our yogurt is eaten throughout the day by itself, with fresh fruit, or more often with thyme honey and walnuts.

The best-tasting yogurt is full-fat, thick, strained yogurt. If you can't find it, place ordinary yogurt in a linen towel and hang it to drain for a few hours to make it thicker. This yogurt is served with *Dolmades* (Stuffed Vine Leaves, page 138) or with rice (page 135).

In the small tavernas of Crete, you will find yogurt served with French fries when they are offered as *meze*. When I tasted this combination for the first time some fifteen years ago, I liked it so much that I now always eat French fried potatoes with yogurt.

CHEESE
(TYRI)

It's not an exaggeration to say that every Greek village has its own variety of cheese. The problem is that some of the names mean completely different cheeses in different parts of the country. For example, in Athens and the islands we call a soft, creamy white cheese Manouri, but in Metsovo, Manouri is the hard, matured cheese other Greeks call Kefalotyri.

The majority of these often delicious regional cheeses—which seldom travel farther than the boundaries of the community that produces them—are made with a combination of goat's and sheep's milk. The animals wander the hilly landscape, and once or

VARIOUS CHEESES AND PIES PHOTOGRAPHED IN MR. PODOTAS' CHEESE CELLAR IN ASTYPALAIA: (from left to right) ON THE SHELVES, MATURING LOCAL GOAT CHEESE, HARD MYZITHRA, HANGING, FRESH CHEESE WITH GARLIC AND DILL HANGING IN A CHEESECLOTH, FRESH CHLORI SERVED WITH HONEY AND YELLOW SAFFRON BISCUITS, TRIANGLE-SHAPED CHEESE PIES (page 72), FRIED CHEESE SAGANAKI, TRADITIONAL GREENS PIE (page 148). IN FRONT, TWO VERSIONS OF LADOTYRI, A HARD CHEESE FROM LESBOS, RUBBED IN OLIVE OIL. IN THE CLAY JARS, AT THE BACK, IS *KOPANISTI*, MATURED GRATED CHEESE.

MAKING CHLORI CHEESE IN ASTYPALAIA: (top left and right) POURING MILK INTO A CAULDRON. (bottom left) PLACING THE CHEESE CURDS IN SMALL BASKETS AND SQUEEZING THEM TO DRAIN THE WHEY. (bottom right) UNMOLDING THE CHEESES ABOUT 45 MINUTES LATER. CHLORI IS USUALLY CONSUMED WHEN VERY FRESH.

twice a day are gathered at the farms to be milked. The cheeses are seasonal because the production of milk depends on the rains that help the grass grow that feeds the animals. The taste of these different cheeses depends on the quality of the milk, which in turn is closely related to the grass the animals eat.

The peak season is spring, which is why fresh cheese is used so much in traditional festive Easter sweets and pies. By late June, when the earth dries up

during the long sunny days, goats and sheep find just enough grass to stay alive and they produce very little milk. So the small farmers stop making cheese and only start again in the fall, after the first rains.

Cheese has been an important part of the everyday Greek diet since antiquity. The milky juice of the fig tree was originally used to coagulate the milk, as were the juices of other plants. But soon ancient Greeks discovered that using rennet from the stomachs of young ruminating animals produced better results. Aristotle wrote that the stomachs of hare and deer can also be used.

Making Cheese the Primitive Way To this day, small local farmers in the islands and in remote villages make their cheeses in exactly the same way the ancient Greeks did. On the island of Astypalaia, twenty minutes from the modern supermarket in the central square, is a goat farmer in a dilapidated shack. He has a magnificent view across the Aegean and to the islands, but no electricity or running water. Michelis, the father and master, his ten children, and his wife, Thimia, milk their goats and make cheese exactly as our ancestors did four thousand years ago.

To milk the goats and sheep, the men of the family assume a very awkward position: They lean across the animal's back while holding it in place by gripping the animal's head between their legs. Milking five hundred animals this way, twice a day, is quite an ordeal, but these semiwild animals cannot be milked in any other way.

To make the cheese, Michelis sits beside a cauldron, stirring the milk with a stick that has a bunch of rushes tied to its end. The little baskets in which the cheese will drain are woven from the same rushes. Thimia, his wife, works hard tending the fire, feeding it constantly, and at the right moment quickly removes the burning embers from the hearth so that the cheese will not spoil. Not to be wasted, the embers are transferred to a smaller stove where the day's meal is cooked.

Every Saturday Thimia bakes the week's bread for the family in the stone oven. The day starts at 4:30 A.M. for children and parents alike. The children work hard, helping their parents. Around 9 A.M., when the milking is finished, they eat the main meal of the day. Not all the children attend school. To us their life appears to be backbreaking and monotonous. Yet I would not be surprised if, when they take over the farm, they continue to make cheese in exactly the same way as their father—not for lack of money to invest in machinery that would make their lives easier, but because they feel it unnecessary.

Part of the freshly made farmer's cheese (called Anthotyro in Crete, Chlori in Astypalaia) is consumed the same day, often while still warm, with honey, or kept for up to seven days. Another part is left to drain further, then generously salted as it is unmolded from the small baskets and placed on the shelves of tiny rooms, with large openings usually facing the north. The dried and hardened cheeses are then dipped in liquid wax and stored in the house to be consumed throughout the year. The salty and pungent taste of this cheese makes it ideal for all kinds of pies. It is also grated and used with pasta, or fried to make *saganaki*, a delicious *meze* for wine or ouzo.

Oftentimes these hardened cheeses are grated and pressed into large clay jars, where they are left to mature. They become *kopanisti* ("the beaten one," as the word implies), a sharp cheese that is eaten as a *meze* with ouzo or mixed with sweeter cheeses and eggs to fill small pies.

Some of the most interesting Greek cheeses are:

Feta It is strange how feta, the regional cheese of Roumeli (central mainland Greece), has overshadowed all other Greek cheeses. Its popularity and low price (cheap feta made from cow's milk is imported to Greece from the Netherlands) tends to eliminate all the local cheeses.

The original feta is a "pickled" cheese, made from sheep's milk. To make it, the cheese curds are placed in

MILKING SHEEP, ASTYPALAIA.

a heavily salted brine, which kills all the microbes that would have made the cheese age to a tasty hard variety. In a sense, feta is a cheese forced to remain young.

It should be kept in brine because otherwise it spoils quickly. But if left in the brine too long, the cheese becomes too salty. In other words, feta should be eaten while relatively fresh. Its slightly acidic and chalky taste complements all vegetable dishes, and of course plays a very important role in Country Tomato Salad (page 82).

Although many Greeks use it in all their pies, I think that feta's flavor tends to make the pies too acidic. I prefer to use only a little, if any.

Feta can be a very tasty *meze,* served drizzled with olive oil and sprinkled with savory or oregano.

Kasseri A yellow, semihard, very oily cheese much loved by the Greeks; the quality varies greatly. Made mainly from sheep's milk, the curds are left to stand for about six days and then are kneaded before being placed in large molds. Kasseri is left to mature for about two months.

Kefalotyri The name comes from the word *kefali* ("head") and *tyri* ("cheese"). It was probably used to distinguish this large cheese from the more common small village cheeses. What we generally call Kefalotyri is a sharp, salty, hard cheese made from sheep's milk, which is left to mature at least three months. It is seldom eaten as such, but is mixed with feta in pies, grated and used with pasta, or fried to make *saganaki.* If you cannot find it, you can substitute pecorino.

DRIED MIZITHRA AND BARRELS OF FETA IN THE CENTRAL MARKET OF ATHENS.

Graviera The word comes from the French *gruyère,* and was originally used for the very tasty hard cheese from Crete, made from a combination of sheep's and goat's milk. That cheese is called Kefalotyri in Crete, and seems to be the first of its kind to appear in the markets all over the country. In Byzantine manuscripts we read about Kefalotyri from Crete and later—in what appears to be the first Greek-language cookbook, published on the island of Syros in 1827 (see also TOMATOES)—"cheese from Crete" is called for. There are many different kinds of Graviera, some made with just sheep's milk, as is the one from Metsovo. One can also find very tasty Graviera from the island of Naxos, a sweeter one from Corfu, and so forth.

Manouri and Mizithra These are two of the most common Greek fresh whey cheeses. Manouri is a soft cheese, made by adding up to 60 percent cream to the whey. It should be eaten fresh, and its quality varies greatly. The mass-produced ones can often be completely tasteless. Mizithra is made with or without the addition of milk in the whey. There is both a fat-free Mizithra and a full-fat one, the latter still containing much less fat than Manouri. Both cheeses can be rubbed well in salt and hanged to dry, to be used grated in pasta dishes. The hard salty variety is usually called Skliri Mizithra ("hard mizithra").

Goat Cheese from Metsovo An excellent hard white cheese made by the Baron Tositza Foundation in Epirus is made from the milk of semiwild goats, who feed on the rich and fragrant greens that grow in the Pindus Mountains. Coarsely ground peppercorns are added and the cheese is left to mature for three months. In short supply—only about 7 tons of it are produced yearly—the cheese can only be found in one or two Athenian stores, and it is seasonal, produced from March to June. Excellent eaten as a *meze* by itself, but also a great cheese for all kinds of pies.

Metsovone A very interesting smoked cheese made from cow's milk to which some goat's milk is added for fragrance and taste. This cheese is also produced in Metsovo by the Baron Tositza Foundation. Smoked cheese is not a recent invention; in Athenaeus is a description of a bread "that looked like smoked cheese."

HANGING WAXED AND LABELED METSOVONE CHEESES
TO DRY.

From that phrase one suspects that smoked cheeses were common in antiquity. The Metzovo cheese curds are kneaded before being placed in cylindrical tin molds, where they are left for three hours. The cheese is then dipped in brine and left for one or two days, according to the weight of each piece. After that, it matures for about two to three months. The matured cheeses are then smoked over a fire of vine cuttings, to which some special herbs from the Pindus Mountains have been added.

TOMATOES
(DOMATA)

If you tell somebody today that tomatoes came to Greece only in the nineteenth century, they would refuse to believe you. "But how could our ancestors cook with olive oil, without tomato?" they ask, favoring this marriage of acid tomato and pungent olive oil. It also explains why so many Greek cooks often use too much tomato, overwhelming the flavors of other ingredients in the dish.

The plant that produced "golden apples" (*chrissomila*, as tomatoes were called then) was introduced to mainland Greece in 1815; that year, the story goes, Paul d'Yvrai—the French father superior of the Capuchin monastery in the Plaka, the old Athenian neighborhood—brought tomato seeds, new grains, and flower bulbs for the beautiful garden of the famous monastery where Lord Byron had stayed in 1812. The round, red fruits of the plant were much admired, according to the story, and the seeds quickly found their way to a vegetable garden in Patissia, owned by a French family. According to another version of the story, the French family, who had connections with Marseilles, brought the seeds of the tomato plant to Athens and gave some to the Capuchin monks for their garden.

But these were difficult years. Greece was under Ottoman domination until 1821, when the revolution against the Turks started, so it is understandable that tomato cultivation did not quickly become general. In 1833, when Bavarian Prince Otto came to Greece as king—after the liberation and initial political unrest in the newly founded Greek state—a certain Mr. Fry, a high-ranking official, saw some "golden apples" on Poros, and suggested that this rare plant be immediately cultivated in Athens.

Keep in mind that at that time the Greek state ended about 125 miles north of Athens, and the only islands that belonged to it were the Cyclades. Friedrich Wilchelm Thiersch, a Bavarian scholar who first visited the country in 1831, soon published a detailed account "About the Greek Situation." He described the vast difference between the villagers in the mountainous parts of the mainland, "where families slept on the dirt floor of their homes by the fire," and the way of life in the houses of the merchants on the rich islands, "where the homes with the lovely Venetian furniture, although slightly outmoded in style, are a complete copy of our own." So it is not strange that, in 1827, the first Greek-language cookbook—a translation from an Italian one by a local doctor—was published on the island of Syros. In it, we find two recipes that use "golden apples": fried golden apples, in which tomatoes are halved, emptied of half of their flesh, stuffed with chopped liver and lots of spices, dipped in egg, dredged in bread crumbs, and fried; and a sauce for eggs, with salted sardines, onions, parsley, basil, and fish stock. We can therefore conclude that tomatoes were, by then, readily available in Syros. But of course, a rare few—if any—Greek women were able to read

GREENS AND VEGETABLES USED FOR A TRADITIONAL GREENS PIE IN METSOVO INCLUDE (clockwise, starting from center top) LEEKS, WILD SWISS CHARD (*SESKOULA*), WILD DANDELIONS, ZUCCHINI STALKS AND FLOWERS, SORREL, YELLOWISH *LOBODO* LEAVES (A REGIONAL GREEN FROM THE PINDUS MOUNTAINS), AMARANTH (*VLITA*), BEET GREENS, AND SOW THISTLE (*SOCHOS*).

that cookbook, so most cooks were trying to figure out what to do with the new fruit. Some thought it similar to the eggplant—they even called it "Frankish eggplant" for a time. In a manuscript of recipes by a lady from Ithaca, who lived in the early 1890s, I found a strange version of *moussaka* that uses sliced and fried tomatoes instead of eggplant.

Summer Greek tomatoes are not round and perfectly shaped, but they have a wonderful taste and texture. The small tomatoes produced in the islands—where the sun shines most of the year, and very little rain falls—are exceptional.

TOMATOES IN COOKING

In many Greek recipes, tomato pulp is specified. Although you can use good-quality canned crushed or diced tomatoes, I suggest that you prepare your own pulp and freeze it, in cup-size packages.

Buy tomatoes when they are at their best and cheapest, and never place them in the refrigerator. Keep them in a basket, stem side up, and add new ones if your basket begins to empty. Even the worst-quality tomatoes ripen and become flavorful that way. Use the firm ones for salads, and prepare tomato puree with the softer ones.

Tomato Puree If you have time and want to do it the right way, dip the tomatoes briefly in boiling water and peel them. Halve them and discard most of the seeds, if you like your tomato pulp absolutely pure. Greeks hardly ever do that; instead, we dice the flesh into a saucepan, letting all the juices drip in.

If you are too busy, pass the whole tomatoes through a food mill fitted with the coarse disk, or grate them with a hand grater after cutting off the stem. Then bring the diced tomatoes or tomato pulp to a boil, and let it bubble for ten to fifteen minutes to reduce some of the juice. Let the tomato pulp cool completely, and fill cups with it. Place the cups in the freezer, and leave to freeze overnight. The next day, dip each cup briefly in hot water, so that the frozen tomato pulp falls from the cup. Place each in a freezer bag in the freezer until needed.

Drying Tomatoes While sun-dried tomatoes only recently appeared in Greek markets, in many island households people used to dry their own plum tomatoes for winter use. Choose fleshy, ripe plum tomatoes in season. Cut them in half lengthwise, place them in a large pan, cut side up, and sprinkle coarse salt over them. You can place the pan in the sun to dry the

tomatoes naturally, or you can dry them in a 200° F. oven for six to eight hours.

Pack the dried tomatoes in a jar and fill with virgin olive oil. If you like, you can flavor it with halved cloves of garlic and branches of oregano and thyme.

ONIONS
(KREMYDIA)

Strong purple onions used to be the only ones found in Greece, and no shallots were available until recently. Instead of chopping onions, our mothers and grandmothers—who never had a decent knife in their kitchen—used to grate them, shedding streams of tears in the process. Onions are one of the most important Greek ingredients, giving flavor to salads, stews, soups, and pies. Pearl onions are used in *Stifado* (page 174), the best of our hearty stews.

GARLIC
(SKORDO)

The ancient Greeks considered garlic to be a delicious food, and the inhabitants of Athens suffered greatly during the Peloponnesian wars when they were unable to get enough garlic from Megara. Garlic was also believed to possess therapeutic powers. It was considered a remedy for many different diseases, and was prescribed as a cure for disorders ranging from kidney

WILD ASPARAGUS IN AN ATHENS STREET MARKET.

problems to gynecological ailments. To this day, garlic is thought to deter evil spirits, and in many villages a clove of garlic is sewn into children's clothes.

Modern science has now proved that our forebears were on to something. Garlic does, in fact, possess healing and preventive properties.

WILD GREENS
(HORTA)

The various *horta*, or wild greens, gathered from the hills and mountains, and the edible weeds gleaned from the fields, still fulfill an important role in Greek people's diet. As with fish, some of the names we use today—especially in Crete—are the same as the ancient Greeks used, and a few have roots in our very distant Indo-European past. Asparagus, which is still eaten in its wild form, is known worldwide by its ancient name.

The special properties and nutritional values of those wild greens are being rediscovered. It is interesting to learn that amaranth (*vlito* in both ancient and modern Greek) was cultivated in antiquity as it is today. It is from the same family as the amaranth that played such an important role for the Incas and Aztecs, who ate not only its shoots (as we do today), but also its seeds (as did the ancient Greeks). These seeds have been found by modern dieticians to contain even more protein than wheat.

According to the seasons and region of the country, wild greens are used as a salad, blanched in water and seasoned with olive oil and lemon, put in pies, stewed with meat and complemented with *avgolemono* sauce, or mixed with flour and fried as patties.

Sow thistle, the fresh shoots of poppies in early spring, nettles, and golden thistle with its fleshy root are some of the greens Greeks like to add to pies or eat as boiled salad. Although they are not widely available in the United States, if you have a garden you can grow them (see Mail-Order Sources).

CURRANTS AND RAISINS
(STAFIDES)

The small black seedless currants of Corinth, in the Peloponnese (known as Zante currants in the United States), were for many centuries the most important export of Greece. Their value was first appreciated by

the Venetians in the fourteenth century. Later, when Peloponnese was conquered by the Ottomans, the Venetians transplanted the vines to the Ionian islands, and continued to export the currants from there. It is often said that the money from this trade financed the whole Venetian fleet.

Currants, together with the more common golden raisins, are used in baking, in savory stuffings and pies, and also, instead of sugar, as a sweetener in tomato sauces.

CHILI PEPPERS
(KAFTERES PIPERIES)

Like tomatoes, chili peppers originated in the New World, but they have found their place in Greek cooking, mainly because their heat seems to add significantly to soups, stews, and tomato sauces.

In Macedonia and throughout the north of Greece, pounded hot red peppers made into a kind of red pepper flakes called *Boukovo* are used instead of black pepper. *Boukovo* is not as hot as the red pepper flakes available in supermarkets, and it has more flavor. If you can, use Near East or Alepo pepper (see Mail-Order Sources), which is very similar. Fresh green chilies are fried and served as *meze* with ouzo, as are pickled ones. And although there are people who hate their hot taste, there are a lot of aficionados as well.

You can make a paste from the pickled chilies, working them in a blender or food processor. Kept in a glass jar, the paste is a convenient seasoning for salad dressings or spreads, such as for *Melintzanosalata* (Eggplant Caviar, page 50).

Pickled Green Chilies (Kafteres Piperies Toursi) Wash and dry fresh chili peppers. Place them in glass jars, packing as many as you can into each jar. Place a bay leaf, some coriander seeds, and some halved cloves of garlic in each jar, and fill with boiling distilled white vinegar. Seal and store in a cool place for at least two weeks before using.

VINE LEAVES
(AMBELOFILA)

Greeks use a lot of vine leaves in cooking. The young leaves are gathered in the spring, and either packed in jars, with or without brine, or frozen in batches (see

PLACING SALTED CAPERS IN JARS WITH VINEGAR IN EKALI, AN ATHENS SUBURB.

page 138). These tender and very tasty leaves are used to wrap not only the famous *Dolmades* (page 138) but also fish (page 103). They can even take the place of phyllo pastry, in an unusual pie from Drama, in northern Greece (page 147).

Fresh vine shoots are also boiled and served as a salad, with lots of lemon or vinegar and olive oil, or are pickled, to be served as a *meze* for ouzo.

Ancient Greeks used fig leaves to wrap fish or meat that was to be baked over charcoal, a method completely abandoned by modern Greeks. But on some islands, fig leaves are still used to wrap fresh cheeses.

CAPERS
(KAPARI)

The best capers—the buds of the caper plant—come from the islands of the Cyclades. There, the plants with their superb flowers—some of the buds are always left to flourish on the plant—grow in the most unlikely places: over the sea, on steep rocks, or on the walls of the Venetian castle ruins.

In Paros, where excellent capers are prepared, the not very tiny buds are washed and then left in brine for about two weeks. After that they are drained and packed in jars, without any other liquid, or the jar is filled with mild homemade red wine vinegar. In Siphnos, capers are also dried in the sun, while fresh ones are sometimes cooked in tomato sauce, with lots of onions, and served as a *meze* for ouzo. In Santorini, a similar tomato sauce with capers accompanies "Mar-

ried Fava" (Mashed Yellow Split Peas, page 122), a specialty of the island.

Caper shoots—with or without some buds—are also pickled, to be served as *meze* for ouzo.

ALMONDS AND WALNUTS
(*AMIGDALA AND KARIDIA*)

Playing a very important role in Greek pastries and desserts, almonds and walnuts are also used in stuffings and to thicken sauces. You will find them in the traditional *Skordalia* (Garlic Sauce, page 54), in *Kotopoulo Maskouli* (Chicken in White Garlic Sauce, page 173), and in Rolled Eggplant Pie with Walnuts (page 150), among others.

Food historians believe that Europeans learned to use nuts as a sauce thickener from the Persians. In medieval cooking, almonds and walnuts were everywhere, but were later abandoned in northwestern Europe. They are still used a lot in Middle Eastern cooking.

HERBS

Although Greece is full of herbs growing wild, we use very few of them in our cooking.

Basil (**Vassilikos***)* Although pots of it are on every courtyard or balcony in the summer, basil is not used in traditional Greek cooking. Branches of basil are used by the Orthodox priests to spray the congregation with holy water during many church ceremonies.

THYME IN BLOOM, SANTORINI.

Sage (**Faskomilo***)* The scent of sage fills the arid hills of the Greek islands because even goats won't eat it. Sage is usually consumed as an herb tea; only one or two recipes from Crete call for it. Greek wild sage has a very strong flavor—very different from the sage Italians use in their cooking.

Rosemary (**Dendrolivano***)* Another very strong herb, rosemary has preserving properties. It is used only in *savori*, the vinegar sauce for fish (page 88), and to season olives.

Thyme (**Thimari***)* One more wild herb whose fragrance fills the hills of the islands, thyme is used sparingly to flavor roasted meat and also olives. Its main culinary contribution is indirect. Thyme's wonderful aroma flavors many of our sweets because it flavors the best Greek honey.

Mint (**Diosmos***)* Pots of mint sit on most Greek balconies and in gardens. The sweet-smelling herb—the modern Greek name *diosmos* derives from the ancient *idi-osmos*, which means "sweet smelling"—is used mainly fresh, but dried mint is used in meatballs, pies, and salads.

Oregano (**Rigani***)* In many English translations of ancient Greek texts, *origanon* (oregano, or *Origanum heracleoticum*) is mistakenly translated as marjoram (*Origanum manjorana*). The strong-smelling dried wild oregano is used a lot in Greek cooking. Sometimes, the even stronger aromatic wild savory (*throumbi*) is used instead of oregano.

Dill (**Anitho***) and Fennel (* **Maratho***)* Greeks use a lot of fresh dill in pies, as well as in salads, in *dolmades*, and in many other dishes. Fennel, which grows wild everywhere, is used much less frequently, but it can also be used as one of the greens in spinach or wild greens pies. Its long stems, cut into two-inch pieces and tied together, are used to flavor the brine in which olives are kept.

Parsley (**Maidanos***) and Celery (* **Selino***)* Fresh flat-leaf parsley is the only one used in Greece; it is added to many meat and vegetable dishes and stuffings. It is also used as a green, and accompanies Chicken in Egg-Lemon Sauce (page 170), a very interesting recipe from Macedonia. As food historian Charles Perry pointed out, the Arab word for parsley, *macadumi,* comes from Macedonia.

Celery leaves are used in boiled fish and soups, and also in the traditional *Fassolada* (Lima Bean Soup, page 128).

Bay Leaves (Dafnofila) Fresh or dried bay laurel leaves, from the bush that was considered to be Apollo's creation, are used in Lentil Soup (page 125), as well as in some meat dishes and for pickling. The small black berries of the bay laurel were used by my grandmother, and many other women of her age, to make hair lotion.

SPICES

Cinnamon is used in many tomato sauces, fillings, and stews. It is an important spice in many desserts—fried pastry sweets as well as cookies and the traditional baklava or the rest of the sweet pies.

Cloves are used pounded in sweets and breads, but they also give their wonderful aroma to meat cooked with quinces (page 180).

Cumin is used more in the north of Greece, the dominant spice in *Sutzoukakia* (Meat Rolls, page 165).

Aniseed. Ouzo, the most well-known Greek apéritif, is prepared from aniseed or star anise. Ground aniseed is the most common spice in traditional Greek breads.

Sesame Seeds. We sprinkle sesame seeds on breads and pies, and mix them with honey and spices to make *pasteli,* a chewy candy prepared for weddings—its many seeds symbolize fertility. Pounded sesame seeds become *tahini,* a paste used in the preparation of sauces and soups for the very strict Lenten days when even olive oil is prohibited. With tahini, a commercial confection we call *halva tou bakali* (grocer's halva) is prepared; to it chocolate, almonds, or peanuts are often added. People eat the *halva* on Lenten days, sprinkled with cinnamon and a little lemon juice to take the edge off its very sweet taste.

Saffron. In the beautiful Minoan frescoes of Santorini there are depictions of saffron being given to a princess, and the lovely crocus flowers gathered in baskets. Ancient Greeks used saffron for coloring, and also as a medicine and as a spice. Although produced in Crokos, a village in northern Greece, saffron is exported to Spain and the Middle East, and very rarely used in modern Greek cooking.

On some islands, people gather wild saffron for pilafs, while in Astypalaia it is used in the traditional Yellow Biscuits for Easter (page 208).

Mastic. The fragrant resin is gathered from the "mastic tree," as locals call the *Pistacia lentiscus* bush, which grows only on the southern part of the island of Chios. Mastic has been much appreciated since antiquity. Today it is used to flavor breads, sweets, drinks, and ice creams, and also made into a natural chewing gum. In fact, the Greek word for chewing gum is *masticha.*

Mahlep. The seed of a type of cherry tree (*Prunus mahaleb*), *mahlep* has a very distinguished sweet fragrance. It is pounded and used to flavor Greek festive breads.

WINES AND SPIRITS

In recent years, in addition to the expansion and great improvement in wines produced by traditional firms, there is a boom in interesting regional Greek wines produced by either local wine cooperatives or small independent producers. These people often don't expect to make money from their wines—they may already be successful business people in other fields—but they want the friendly competition of producing the best wine. They take great pride in their small productions, which are often enough to supply only one shop or restaurant in Athens or Thessalonica. Greeks also have a tradition of making their house wine in barrels, often kept in shaded gardens, balconies, or cellars.

GRAPE HARVEST, SANTORINI.

THE CULTIVATION OF THE VINE

Ancient Greeks produced their wines in large clay pots, very differently from the way we do it now. They seem to have liked strong aromatic wines, scented with thyme, mint, or cinnamon; they even poured seawater into the wine, believing that they could make it last longer. The modern Greek word for wine is *krassi*, which in ancient Greek meant "watered wine," because our ancestors hardly ever drank their very strong wines undiluted.

SPECIAL WINES

According to Economic Community (EC) regulations and Greek law, we have appellations of origin for wines, according to which the indigenous Greek varieties are matched to the areas where the best of their kind were traditionally produced. In addition, there are eight *vins de liqueurs*, which are also controlled by the state; they contain more alcohol than ordinary wines.

The sweet or muscat dessert wines are Samos (white), Muscat of Patras (white), Muscat of Rio (white), Muscat of Cephalonia (white), Muscat of Rhodes (white), Muscat of Lemnos (white), Mavrodaphne from Patras (red), and Mavrodaphne from Cephalonia (red). Many experts think that these dessert wines are of excellent quality, but they are practically unknown outside of Greece. Mavrodaphne is used in many sweet and savory recipes.

WINE REGIONS

The omnipresent hills and mountains of Greece divide the country into small regions, often completely cut off from each other. In each of these territories a unique microclimate exists, defined by mild winters, sunny but windy summers, and the sea or nearby mountains. Under these conditions a diversity of indigenous grape varieties—many of which existed in antiquity—give the regional wines a unique taste, aroma, and personality. They include Xinomavro, Debina, Savatiano, Agiorgitiko (St. Georges), Moschofilero, Limnio (mentioned by Aristotle), Athiri, Mondilavia, Kotsifali, and Liatiko, among others.

IOANNA KOUTSOUDAKIS' HOMEMADE SPIRITS: UNFLAVORED *TSIKOUDIA* AND GREEN WALNUT LIQUEUR (IN THE TALL BOTTLES), SPICY *TSIKOUDIA* AND ORANGE LIQUEUR (IN THE SMALL BOTTLES), PHOTOGRAPHED IN THE DOMA HOTEL, CHANIA, CRETE.

Although vineyards planted with Cabernet grapes are expanding throughout the country—a phenomenon repeated in most countries—Greece still keeps its old traditional grape varieties and so produces a world of very interesting, if not well-known, wines.

To name only a few of the diverse Greek wines, starting from the north, we have from Macedonia the robust dry red "brusco" wine of Naoussa, while from the relatively new vineyards of Chalkidiki we have the red and white Côtes de Meliton wines. From Epirus we have the light sparkling wines of Zitsa and the rich red Katoi.

Attica is the traditional producer of retsina, probably the most well-known Greek wine, and one that people either love or hate. Plutarch (first to second century) and Dioscorides (first century), among others, mention resinated wine. It seems that ancient Greeks threw pieces of pine bark into the wine, believing that they would preserve it from spoiling. This habit continued to the thirteenth century, when a bishop named Michael wrote that the wine served to him was bitter "due to the pieces of pine bark that were dipped in it." Another avid enemy of resinated wine was Lutprand, the bishop of Cremona who, having tasted it at some official Byzantine dinner, declared that it was "abominable."

But modern retsina, which was the only wine found in tavernas in and around Athens up until the early 1960s, is very different from this ancient form. It contains but a small amount of pine resin and is a fresh, tasty, fragrant wine still favored by many Greeks —and even more by tourists, although its consumption has fallen dramatically.

Attica also produces fine dry white wines, like Chateau Matsa. The Peloponnese produces the dark red, soft-tasting wine of Nemea, often called Hercules's blood, because of its color, while in Achaia, the region around Patras, excellent dry white and red wines are produced, together with the famous Mavrodaphne, which is the wine used by the Greek Orthodox Church for holy communion. This very special wine was called Glykopalaio (the Old Sweet) by the Byzantines.

From the Aegean islands of Samos, Lemnos, Rhodes and Santorini come diverse wines, mostly white, with the exception of the wine of Paros, which is a typical red. Robola from Cephalonia is the most well-known wine from the Ionian islands, along with one more version of Mavrodaphne. Crete produces distinguished wines, both red and white.

OUZO, MASTICHA, AND OTHER DISTILLED LIQUORS

Ouzo is the most popular Greek spirit. In many parts of the country similar, less fragrant, spirits are made: Distilling the *tsikouda*—which in Crete are the grape branches and the rest of the residues left from the wine pressings—produces *tsikoudia*, a clear unflavored spirit. It's more or less the same as the drink called *tsipouro* or *raki* in the north.

Ouzo, which is the product name of the drink that can be made only in Greece, according to EC regulations, is this distilled spirit flavored with anise and other aromatic grains. In the north, ouzo is dry; in the south, some sugar is added to make it sweeter. Many people believe that the best ouzo is made in Lesbos.

When *mastic*, the resin of the *mastic* bushes that grow in Chios, is also used to flavor the distilled spirit instead of anise, it produces a more aromatic drink called *Masticha*. It is used in baking, but also is drunk, mostly by women.

HOMEMADE LIQUEURS

Once, every family had homemade liqueurs to offer, together with coffee and a spoon sweet, to friends and neighbors who came for a visit or to wish "many happy returns" for some family member's name day.

For the first time in many years, I came across homemade liqueurs at the Doma Hotel in Chania, Crete. The owner, Ioanna Koutsoudaki, gave me several recipes and spoke enthusiastically about the very complicated walnut liqueur that she continues to make following her mother's instructions.

Portokali (Orange Liqueur) Oranges are peeled with a very sharp knife, so that only the outer layer of rind is cut off, and not the pith. There should be about two cups of peel. To these a cup of sugar is added and the peel is pounded with the sugar in a mortar. To the resulting mash, two cups of water and some cloves and a cinnamon stick are added, and it is transferred to a jar with a tight lid. After seven days the contents of the jar are briefly boiled (for about one to two minutes), then transferred to a larger jar that is filled with 1½ cups of distilled alcohol. After seven days, the liqueur is strained well, and served.

Following the same instruction, Lemoni (lemon), Mandarini (tangerine), Nerantzi (Seville orange), or Pergamonto (bergamot) liqueurs can be made.

Kerasso (Cherry Liqueur) The most common house liqueur is made from sour cherries. The fruit is mixed in a jar with two-thirds of their weight in sugar, covered with distilled alcohol, and left in the sun for four weeks. Then brandy is added, and the jar is again left in the sun for two weeks. The drink is then strained and kept in bottles. Often it is served with the addition of some Sour Cherry Preserves (page 234).

Tsikoudia Pikantiki (Spicy Tsikoudia) To the strong unflavored distilled spirit of Crete, Ioanna Koutsoudaki adds tangerine peels, cloves, cinnamon stick, and a little sugar. She leaves the bottle to macerate for one to two months, then strains it and serves the drink in very tiny tumblers.

GODS AND SAINTS
AT THE TABLE

Our customs and traditions, based on the Greek Orthodox religion, are very often a continuation of ancient Greek rites and pagan rituals. The official church festivals are closely related to the different agricultural or maritime tasks of the early Greeks; indeed, many Christian Saints assumed the role Olympian gods occupied in antiquity. For example, Saint Nicholas is the protector of sailors, as Poseidon was for our ancestors.

In the Greek Orthodox religion, fasting always precedes an important religious feast, and each festivity has its own foods, which are not necessarily the same in all parts of the country.

SPRING AND SUMMER FESTIVALS

The most colorful festivities take place from mid-February to the end of August. The significant holidays are Easter, the largest Greek festival and feast, and Assumption (August 15), the most important festival in the Greek islands. Greek Orthodox Easter is celebrated the first Sunday following the full moon after the spring equinox, and always following Passover.

Carnival Easter is preceded by a forty-day period of Lent. But before Lent come the merry days of carnival, which last for three weeks and four Sundays. Carnival, complete with disguises and mad parties, is not a religious festival but a collection of folk traditions that have their roots in the ancient celebrations for Dionysus, the god of wine.

The dances, communal rituals and performances, and large banquets were supposed to stimulate the earth and bring the plants to life after the winter. The church could not prohibit these festivities, so it incorporated them into its official calendar, and gave the

SPRING IN ASTYPALAIA.

time the name *apokreo* (the passing of meat). During the first week of carnival, every family slaughtered an animal (pigs in most places). During the second week, meat can be eaten even on Wednesday and Friday, which are days of abstinence during the rest of the year. The third week is called *tyrofagos* (cheese eating) and, as the word implies, cheeses and milk products are the main food. People make *Tyropita* (Fried Cheese Pies, page 72), *Galatomboureko* (Milk Pie, page 242), and *Ryzogalo* (Rice Pudding, page 241). Homemade pasta with lots of cheese is also a typical dish of this week; meat is not consumed.

During the joyous days of carnival, people also want to placate the dead, so that they, too, will take part in the universal effort to make the earth bear fruit again.

On *Psychosavata* (Saturday of the Souls), women go to the churches and cemeteries with plates of *Kolyva* (Boiled Sweetened Wheat, page 232) or *halva* (semolina flour, fried in olive oil with syrup), which are blessed by the priests and offered to friends and neighbors to commemorate deceased relatives.

In some parts of Greece, eggs are the last thing eaten on Sunday night before Lent. And eggs are also the first festive food eaten on the night of the Resurrection, after the forty days of abstinence.

The First Day of Lent

The first day of Lent is a public holiday in Greece. We call it Clean Monday (*Kathari Deftera*) because women clean their pots and pans to remove all traces of animal fat.

More a part of carnival than of Lent, Clean Monday is the last joyful day. Wine is not prohibited, and people make picnics of spinach pies without cheese, *Taramosalata* (Carp Roe Dip, page 56), *Rengosalata* (Smoked Herring Dip, page 57), olives, fresh garlic, and scallions. The special bread for this day, called *lagana,* is flat, its delicious crust sprinkled with sesame seeds. During traditional Clean Monday picnics, lots of wine is consumed and the day ends with dances. In some parts of Greece, a mock funeral for the carnival is staged during the afternoon, while in other places a pot containing pasta, meat, and cheese is buried, and people pretend to cry for all their favorite foods that they will miss during the following weeks.

The Forty Days of Lent

Lent means days of meditation, prayers, and church-going that prepare the devout for the Passion of Christ. No marriages, engagements, or any other family celebrations are permitted.

An exception is made for March 25, the feast of the Annunciation and also Greek Independence Day. On this day in 1821, the revolution against the Turks, which ended with the formation of the modern Greek state, began. On March 25, Greeks traditionally eat salt cod fritters with garlic sauce (page 89) and drink lots of wine.

Holy Week

Holy Week is a time of mourning and grieving. In some parts of Greece, during the first three days, people fast and drink only water. Traditionally all plays, movies, and other forms of entertainment cease; on television all comedies are replaced with religious dramas and church ceremonies.

On Good Wednesday, the village priests make rounds, passing from house to house to bless the eggs and flour that are to be used to prepare the Easter breads. In some parts of the country, this is the time to start the new sourdough, which will last throughout the year. Some people still believe that if the priest places the cross on a piece of dough made from flour and water, it will rise.

Good Thursday is the day all Easter preparations start. On that day, the sweet Easter breads called *Tsoureki* (page 196) are baked. Breads scented with *mastic, mahlep,* bay leaves, and cloves are prepared for each of the children in the family, with each loaf sometimes shaped as a doll. Godmothers are supposed to bake *tsoureki* for each godchild. Sweet Easter cookies are also baked on that day all over Greece; in Astypalaia they make traditional Yellow (Saffron) Biscuits (page 208). Good Thursday is also called "Red Thursday" because on that day Easter eggs are painted red. You won't find a single Greek house without red eggs on Easter.

The egg, which contains life and animal force, is a symbol of creation, according to ancient traditions. Painted red, they also link Jewish history with Christianity, since most Greek scholars believe that the red paint—which was also the ancient Greek color of mourning—commemorates the lambs' blood used to mark the doors of Jewish houses in Egypt at Passover,

KNEADING YELLOW (SAFFRON) BISCUITS, ASTYPALAIA.

as well as serving as a reminder of the blood Jesus Christ shed for all people.

The first Easter egg was believed to possess magical and healing powers, so it was kept next to the icons for the whole year. In some villages the shells of the first Easter egg were later buried in the field, at the place where the plowing started, to stimulate the grain, making it sprout and grow.

Good Friday is a day of mourning and a public holiday; absolutely no work is done on that day. Women and children gather flowers and bring them to the churches to decorate the wooden reliquary that will be paraded on the streets that night, followed by a candlelight parade held by the parishioners.

On Good Friday, people eat only vegetables and legumes boiled in water (*nerovrasta*) without olive oil; vinegar is always added to commemorate the vinegar that was given to Jesus on the cross.

Good Saturday is the day the men slaughter the Easter lamb or kid, which will be roasted the next day. The young lambs usually weigh no more than eighteen to twenty pounds. The women prepare the ceremonial late supper, which takes place after the midnight mass of the Resurrection. The head and some of the innards of the lamb are used to make the Easter soup,

Magiritsa (page 162), which is consumed after the midnight mass.

In some parts of Greece—especially the islands of the Dodecanese—the Easter lamb is stuffed with cracked wheat or rice, pine nuts, raisins, the innards, and lots of spices. It is wrapped in several layers of oiled paper and placed in the communal stone oven early Saturday afternoon. Left to roast slowly, the lamb will be ready by noon on Sunday.

Even people who don't go to church the rest of the year attend the Easter midnight mass, holding white candles with which they bring home the holy new light from the priest's candle. The ceremony takes place outside the church. As the bells toll to announce Christ's Resurrection, pandemonium starts: guns are fired, fireworks of all kinds are ignited, even pieces of dynamite are thrown; inevitably, there are some casualties. Although the police now forbid the use of dangerous fireworks, so far nobody has been able to stop the customary blasts.

Coming home right after the mass, each person chooses a red Easter egg and with it hits another person's egg to see whose egg will break. The Easter egg is the first festive food one consumes after the forty days of Lent, followed by the *Magiritsa*.

On Easter Sunday, very early in the morning, men start the fire with which they will roast the whole lamb on a spit. In backyards, gardens, or open spaces on the outskirts of the cities and in the country, the roasting of the Easter lamb or kid on the spit is a custom throughout Greece.

Originally spit-roasted lamb was the Easter dish of Roumeli, the region of mainland Greece around Athens. In Thessaly and in some parts of Macedonia, for example, the lamb's innards were cooked in tomato sauce with lots of spring onions, dill, and spinach or wild greens. On some islands of the Cyclades, lamb is stuffed with fennel, spring onions, and all sorts of wild greens; while on Andros, feta or kefalotyri, fresh mint, and fennel are used in the stuffing. The whole lamb is stuffed and then brushed with olive oil or butter and baked slowly in a stone oven.

The traditional Easter table also includes cheese pies, a large salad of finely chopped romaine lettuce with spring onions, and a milk pie as dessert.

The First of May The first of May, if it happens to come before Easter, is another exception to the gloomy days of Lent. May Day has been, for ancient as well as modern Greeks, a time of celebrations for Mother Nature, the flowers, and the first fruits.

On that day of hope for a fruitful summer, even city houses are decorated with crowns of flowers and branches of apricot and almond trees with their first fruits, very small and green. People also pray for more rain to water the parched earth before the dry and hot months of summer. If it happens to rain on May Day, village women collect some of the falling water to add to the vinegar that they make from the year's wine, believing that this water makes it stronger.

Saint George, the Holy Knight Saint George's Day (April 23), which usually falls in the middle of Holy Week, is customarily celebrated on Easter Monday. Because nearly half of Greek families celebrate one member's name day on Saint George's Day, there are more banquets, roasted meats, and sweets offered to the relatives and friends who come to visit.

Saint George is always depicted on horseback, killing a dragon with his spear. In popular myth, this dragon was believed to be a beast who guarded the water. In order to let it run, the dragon had to devour the king's daughter. The brave Saint George, by killing the fearful creature, liberated the beautiful princess and let everybody share the most precious of all elements, water.

Chamomile is traditionally gathered from the fields on Saint George's Day because it is thought to have maximum healing powers then. Flocks of sheep and goats are driven to the mountains, where there will be some green grass for them to graze on during the dry months of summer.

Saints Constantine and Helen Popular myth connects the festivities that commemorate Saint Constantine and his mother Saint Helen (May 21) with the last Byzantine emperor, Constantine Paleologos. There are big feasts in village churches, in which lambs, kids, or calves are slaughtered and cooked for the congregation. On the eve of that day in at least one village in eastern Macedonia, the very old custom of *anastenaria* takes place: people from some "chosen" families walk barefoot across a live charcoal fire without burning their feet. Holding special icons of Saint Constantine and Saint Helen that these families keep in their houses, and singing an old monotonous tune, men and women *anastenarides* dance around the fire and step into it when "the Saint calls them."

THE GOOD THURSDAY MASS, ASTYPALAIA.

Many scholars believe that this ritual has its roots in the pagan fire dances honoring Dionysus, the god of wine. Although it seems to have been incorporated into Christian religious practice, it doesn't have the approval of the official Greek church.

SUMMER FESTIVALS

There are relatively few big festivals in summer because village people are very busy in the fields, harvesting crops. Saint John's Day (June 24) coincides with the ancient rituals related to the summer solstice.

The prophet Elias (July 20) is considered the master of thunder and electric storms. According to popular myth, he goes up and down in the sky in his chariot chasing dragons and devils, and blasting them with thunder. For that reason all churches dedicated to him are on mountaintops.

On Saint Praskevi's Day (July 26), a bull is ceremonially sacrificed in Mitilini (Lesbos), and village men take part in a colorful horse race.

August is a month of plenty. Figs, grapes, and lots of other fruits are at their peak. In many parts of the country, plates of first fruits are taken to church to be blessed on the evening of the first of the month; the fruits are then divided among the parishioners. It is the first day of the fifteen-day period of abstinence before Assumption (August 15).

Assumption is, after Easter, one of the most popular festivities in the Greek islands. In Tinos and Paros, as well as in many islands of the Dodecanese and in some villages near Athens, people worship in special churches where some icons are believed to perform miracles.

FALL AND WINTER FESTIVALS

The different celebrations of this season are related to the care and worries about planting new crops. People are also concerned about the approaching winter, making all the necessary preparations for this especially difficult season for shepherds. This very busy time of the year is also marked by the opening of the new wines.

September is the first month of the agricultural calendar, and many people hang a little sack of wheat on their home shrine next to the icons, together with specimens of new produce: onions, walnuts, and cotton.

On September 14, the Day of the Cross, the pot in which fresh basil grows is taken to the church to be blessed. With sprigs of it the priest will sprinkle the congregation with holy water, and these same sprigs will later be divided among the village women, to be used in their new sourdough starter. They believe that only this blessed basil will give the starter the power to make bread rise. Basil, according to the popular myth, was the plant that grew next to the cross on which Jesus was crucified; thanks to this fragrant plant, Saint Helen was able to distinguish the holy cross among the many others.

October is the month of planting seeds. The weather is usually mild and sunny—Greeks call it the "small summer." Saint Demetrios's Day (October 26) is especially celebrated in Thessalonica. On that day the new wines are opened and the flocks come down to the plains, to their winter shelter. October 28 is the day of No (*ochi*), a national holiday. On that morning in 1940, the Greek government refused to let Mussolini's troops pass through the country, and Greece started its successful campaign against the Italian army in the Pindus Mountains. For six months the small Greek army managed to hold the aggressors at bay; only in April, after Hitler joined the attack, did the Germans defeat Greece.

November is considered the beginning of winter, and on November 14, Saint Philipo's day, the forty days of abstinence before Christmas begin.

Christmas and the New Year December is a month full of colorful celebrations. In this dark winter month, Greeks believe that *kalikantzari*—small, ugly creatures from the underworld—come to pester good men. These creatures adore sweets, and so houses are filled with them, hoping that the *kalikantzari* will eat them, satisfy themselves, and not harm the family. Saint Nicholas's Day (December 6) is when all sailors celebrate. A popular myth describes the saint—a bishop from Asia Minor—as a sailor whose clothes are always wet, with seawater dripping from his long white beard.

On some islands, *Kolyva* are taken to the churches to be blessed, and then kept in the boats, next to the icon of Saint Nicholas that is present in any Greek ship or boat. The blessed *Kolyva* are believed to possess the power to appease the sea, if some grains are thrown in when it is rough.

The day before Christmas, children pass by each house in the neighborhood, singing *kalanda,* songs that celebrate the much-anticipated day, beating a metal triangle. With their song, they announce Christ's birth and wish happiness and prosperity to the family. People give them money and sweets. *Melomakarouna* (Honey Cookies, page 221), festive breads, *Loukoumades* (Batter Fritters, page 217), and other fried pastry sweets are prepared. In Epirus, they fry *diples* (pieces of phyllo pastry) late at night, calling them *spargana* (swaddling cloths) of the baby Christ. With the same association, Cypriot women used to make the special biscuits they bake for all newly born.

After forty days of abstinence, the Christmas table is much anticipated. Pigs are ceremonially slaughtered for this day, much as they were by the Romans during Saturnalia (December 17–25). Pork is the basis for traditional Greek Christmas meals, cooked differently in each part of the country. In Macedonia, *Dolmades* (Stuffed Vine Leaves, page 138) are prepared with the household's pickled cabbage. In Thessaly, a baked sausage is made from the large intestine of the pig, with cracked wheat, pieces of pork and pork fat, leeks, and spices. In the islands, jellied pork is prepared (page 178). All these special dishes are served with the main course, which is roast pork.

Early in the morning of New Year's Eve, children singing a different kind of *kalanda* make the rounds, much as they do on Christmas Eve.

The New Year's table is similar to that of Christmas, with different sweets. But it also contains some symbolic foods: honey, almonds, walnuts, and pomegranates. On midnight, as the new year arrives, the traditional *vassilopita*, a sweet festive bread, is brought to the table. A coin has been baked in it, and when the bread is divided among the family and friends, the person who finds the coin is expected to start the year with blessings from heaven. Traditionally, pieces were cut not only for the different members of the family but also for the house, the animals, and so forth.

On New Year's Day, a pomegranate is broken in the entrance of each house, office, or shop, to bring fertility and good business, while a large *kremyda* (sea onion or sea squill), the same plant the ancient Greeks used in their purification ceremonies, is hung outside the door to bring good luck in the new year.

Epiphany (January 6), or Day of the Light (*Ton Foton*), is an important religious holiday. Until the fourth century, this day, on which Jesus was baptized, was the beginning of the new year. Priests bless the waters, and spectacular ceremonies take place in all seaside cities. A cross is thrown into the sea, and men jump in to catch it and bring it back. With holy water brought from the church, the houses are sprinkled, and the *kalikantzari*—the little creatures that pestered the people during the previous days—are driven back to the underworld. With the same holy water, the fields, vineyards, and flocks are blessed.

The next day (January 7) is *Ai Yianniou* (Saint John the Baptist's Day). January 8 is Saint Dominikis's Day, a female saint who is the protector of midwives. In some parts of northern Greece, there is a day of *gynekokratia* (women's rule). Women take over, doing what men traditionally do in the villages: they go to the coffee shop to have fun with their friends, leaving the household chores to their husbands. Many Greek scholars believe that these all-women celebrations have their roots in the ancient *Thesmophoria*, rituals dedicated to the fertility of the people and the earth. Obscene talk, characteristic of that day, is believed to provoke the birth of men and fruit.

Some of these traditional celebrations have lost their importance in the last few years, because they tend to be forgotten by the second-generation descendants of the villagers who moved to the big cities. There are also many traditional popular feasts that have become soulless tourist attractions, the ritual repeated just for the sake of foreign tourists. This, I think, is worse than forgetting the tradition altogether.

But in remote villages and islands, you can still find men and women who follow their ancestral customs with unbroken respect.

APPETIZERS, SALADS, AND EGG DISHES

Greeks frequently invite their friends and relatives to come for a leisurely *meze* (appetizer) party or for ouzo, the closest equivalent to an invitation for cocktails. At *meze* parties we offer a selection of dishes, from stuffed vine leaves to fried zucchini or eggplant, from small cheese pies to meatballs. Fried Whitebait (page 95), cured or dried mackerel (*lakerda* or *tsiros*), *Taramosalata* (Carp Roe Spread, page 56), and *Rengosalata* (Smoked Herring Spread, page 57) are also served as appetizers at home. Unlike the small portions served in tavernas and coffee shops, the *meze* offered at home at midday are plentiful—enough for each guest to have a full lunch. In fact, during those *meze* meals most people end up eating much more than they realize.

When you order ouzo with appetizers in a Greek taverna or coffee shop, you may be brought a small plate with two pieces of kefalotyri cheese and three olives, or some salted sardines with tomato and cucumber. If you are in Volos, you might get pickled wild pistachio shoots; in Crete, perhaps a plate of charcoal-grilled snails; and in the islands, pieces of grilled or pickled octopus.

It is very difficult to find two Greeks who will agree on the best *meze* to accompany ouzo or wine. Nikolas Manolakis, a friend from Astypalaia, described his favorite appetizer: the mollusk dye murex, which can still be found in abundance on the shores of the Dodecanese islands, blanched in seawater, then grilled on a charcoal fire. These shellfish are the source of a purple dye that was highly prized by the ancient Phoenicians, Greeks, and Romans.

Another friend, Georgios Podotas, who comes from Siphnos, an island in the Cyclades, thinks the best *meze* for ouzo is stewed capers with a lot of onions.

My favorite *meze* is a delicacy called *avgotaraho,* dried gray mullet roe, served thinly sliced on buttered bread. *Avgotaraho* is coated with wax to prevent it from drying out. It is very expensive and can be found only in a couple of stores in Athens and Thessalonica. As far as I know, it is not exported.

Despite the myriad possibilities, there is a general rule that strongly flavored cured fish and pickles are best suited for ouzo, while the more mild-tasting fried vegetables and cheeses go well with resinated or other kinds of wine.

Greeks very rarely drink without eating. In Athenaeus, we read that ancient Greeks despised people who drank "frog fashion, without eating anything." Athenaeus also describes the small plates of appetizers, each containing no more than one or two bites, that were offered to guests at ancient symposia. As one

frustrated guest put it, "While I am eating this, another is eating that, and while he is eating that, I have made away with this. What I want, good sir, is both the one and the other, but my wish is impossible. For I have neither five mouths nor five right hands."

This scene is repeated every day in ouzeries and tavernas that offer drinks with *meze*. The little plates are placed in the middle of the table for everyone to share. They empty so fast that you have to be alert if you want to try everything.

SALADS

In Greece, salads vary according to season and are served either with appetizers or with the main course.

In the winter Greeks enjoy a salad made of shredded raw cabbage seasoned with just lemon and olive oil. This salad is delicious when made with Greek cabbage—American and European cabbages are not as tender nor as tasty. Greeks at home very rarely eat tomato salads during winter, although there are now greenhouse tomatoes available year round. But the flavor of greenhouse tomatoes is nothing like that of ripe summer tomatoes, so we wait until summer to eat them.

In the spring Greeks eat romaine lettuce with dill, arugula, and spring onions. This salad usually accompanies the Easter spit-roasted lamb. During Lent, salads made of cooked vegetables, legumes, and greens (beets, zucchini, beans, wild greens) are often a main course, eaten with bread and olives.

After the first rains of fall and in the early spring Greeks enjoy our favorite wild greens salads. *Horta* (wild greens and weeds) are gathered from the hills and fields. On weekends, families go

CULTIVATED DANDELION GREENS.

on *horta*-gathering excursions in the country near the big cities. There, with a bag in one hand and a knife in the other, men, women, and children collect all kinds of wild greens. Our names for most of these plants are the same ones our ancestors used.

Many of these wild greens are believed to have special medicinal

properties. A few, like wild dandelion, are bitter tasting; others, like the rare, fleshy wild artichoke leaves, have strong flavors; and some, like sow-thistle (*zochos*), are gathered for their aroma. When they are boiled together, they produce a great salad, which can be dressed with lemon and olive oil. They can also be used to make *Hortopita* (Traditional Greens Pie, page 148), a standard dish in most parts of the country.

In Epirus, the mountainous northwestern region of Greece, wild greens collected in the fall are hung to dry in the cellar, so they will be readily available during the long winter months. Then when everything is covered by snow and no fresh greens can be found, they are soaked in water and used in traditional pies.

At greengrocers throughout Greece, one finds cultivated varieties of greens: two kinds of dandelion (sweet and bitter), a local variety of sorrel, as well as amaranth shoots (*vlita*). Boiled-greens salads are an indispensable part of our everyday diet.

In the open-air markets of Athens or Thessalonica, one can also find people selling wild greens—at exorbitant prices—for those who have neither the time nor the will to climb the hills and gather their own. But somehow, the greens taste better when you gather them yourself.

EGGS

In Greece, nearly every country household includes a few chickens, so fresh eggs are generally available. They are sometimes fried or boiled, but most often they are made into wonderful omelets with all kinds of vegetables.

When I was a child, my mother used to make a potato omelet that was my sister's and my favorite dinner: three or four beaten eggs were poured into a skillet full of freshly fried potatoes, to which crumbled feta cheese was also sometimes added. When the eggs started to thicken, the omelet was turned over, using a plate to ease the transition. We ate this omelet with feta cheese and salad. When I first went to Spain, I was astonished to find that this same omelet, with the addition of onions, is the traditional Catalan tortilla. Scrambled eggs with tomato sauce was another of my mother's specialties.

SNAILS

Athenaeus frequently mentions snails being eaten by the ancient Greeks at symposia. Snails were sometimes preferred to mussels and were called "dinner delayers," probably because they were eaten as appetizers. They are also mentioned—along with bulbs, crayfish, and eggs—as aphrodisiacs for men.

PICKLED OCTOPUS.

After the first rains of September, village people go out in the fields to gather snails. There was a time not long ago when snails played quite an important role in poor people's diet. In the ouzeries all over Crete, where snails are still very popular, the forks each have one of their tines bent inward, so customers can pick the snails out of the shells. Snails as prepared in the ouzeries are usually grilled in their shells over a charcoal fire, then served sprinkled with vinegar and chopped garlic.

I have been told that in Heraklion, on Crete, live garden snails, after having been washed well, are placed open side down in a skillet lined with a thick layer of salt. As they cook, the snails make squeaking noises. (This part of the recipe has prevented me from trying it.) When the noise stops, olive oil is poured over them, and after three to five minutes, ½ cup of vinegar and a branch of rosemary are added to the skillet. The heat is lowered, the snails are covered, and they are left to simmer for about five minutes, then served immediately.

In the smaller, arid islands of the Dodecanese, snails—most of them imported from Crete—are boiled in seawater and served with garlic and vinegar.

I have found recipes for snail pies; many snail stews, with zucchini, eggplant, potato, wild greens, and even with pearl onions; grilled or boiled snails; moussaka with snails; and even snail brochettes.

Greece exports snails to the rest of Europe, especially France. Ironically, you can find packages of frozen, stuffed snails imported from France, which are probably prepared with Greek snails, in large Athenian supermarkets.

Eggplant Caviar

MELINTZANOSALATA

A classic, simple, and delicious Greek spread, *Melintzanosalata* can also be used as a sauce for steamed potatoes and other vegetables. Alas, the version tourists taste in the tavernas is a mixture of mayonnaise with a little eggplant mixed in—it has very little to do with the real thing.

I'm not exaggerating by saying that every Greek cook has his or her own version of *melintzanosalata*. The best is found in the small ouzeries in northern Greece. It often contains nothing more than eggplant, a little oil, and some vinegar. In Sotiri's ouzo bar in Thessalonica, the eggplant skin is scorched over a charcoal fire, then the flesh is carefully removed with a spoon and made into the *melintzanosalata*, which is then returned to the boatlike eggplant skin and served.

You can make *Melintzanosalata* in a food processor, but I prefer the coarse texture it has when made with a food mill. Prepare it several hours or a day in advance and keep it in the refrigerator. It tastes better the day after it is made.

3 medium eggplants (about 2 pounds total)

1 green bell pepper, roasted and peeled (see page 52)

½ cup olive oil

3–4 tablespoons red wine vinegar

2 cloves garlic, crushed

⅓–½ teaspoon minced fresh chili pepper, or freshly ground black pepper to taste

½ cup chopped fresh flat-leaf parsley (optional)

Sea salt

MAKES ABOUT 2 CUPS

Pierce the eggplants twice near the stem with a fork. There are 3 possible ways to give the eggplant the smoky flavor this recipe requires: If you have a charcoal grill, cook the eggplants over the coals until the flesh is tender. If you have an electric stove, place 3 layers of aluminum foil on a burner set at medium heat. Place the eggplants on the foil and let them cook, turning them frequently, until the skin is crisp all over and the flesh is tender, 25 to 30 minutes. If you have a gas stove, hold each eggplant with a barbecue fork over the flame until the skin is crisp, then bake at 400° F. until the flesh is tender, 20 to 30 minutes.

Peel the eggplants while still hot and discard most of the seeds. Chop the flesh, or pass it through the coarse disk of a food mill. Chop the pepper finely and mix with the eggplant.

In a medium bowl beat the eggplant and pepper with a wooden spoon, adding the oil and vinegar a little at a time. Add the garlic, chili pepper, and parsley while continuing to beat. Season with salt. Taste, and add more vinegar if needed.

Note: If you want to serve *Melintzanosalata* as a sauce with steamed vegetables and potatoes, add 1 more garlic clove and 1 cup Greek-style yogurt just before serving.

Cucumber with Feta Cheese and Mint

ANGURI ME FETA KE DIOSMO

When I was a child, cucumber never entered our house because my father considered it to be unhealthy. I remember its fresh aroma on hot summer evenings, when everyone had dinner outdoors.

This salad is very easy to make and is a perfect side dish for grilled lamb or any broiled meat.

1 large cucumber, half-peeled
   in lengthwise strips to give
   striped appearance
1 cup crumbled feta cheese
½ cup chopped fresh mint leaves
6 tablespoons olive oil
3 tablespoons lemon juice
Sea salt and freshly ground pepper

SERVES 4

Wash and dry the cucumber and cut it into very thin crosswise slices. Place the slices in a salad bowl, sprinkling with the feta cheese and mint.

In a small bowl whisk the oil and lemon juice with the salt and pepper to make *ladolemono* (a vinaigrette made with lemon juice). Pour over the salad and toss thoroughly. Serve immediately.

Grilled Bell Peppers

PIPERIES PSITES

Many Spaniards believe that grilled peppers are a strong aphrodisiac. If they are right, then the Greeks from the northern part of the country, where this dish is eaten all the time, should feel very sexy indeed.

Peppers, like tomatoes, were brought to Greece after the discovery of the Americas. They have become an indispensable part of Greek cooking, especially in northern regions.

The large, fleshy red peppers of Florina are famous. Long, with a pointed end, they are much sweeter and more flavorful than the red bell peppers found in the United States. Fresh red peppers from Florina have a very short season in late August, but they can be bought year-round, pickled in glass jars. They are delicious broiled, as described here, but because red peppers are sweeter than green, you might want to add more vinegar to the sauce.

Fresh, summer green peppers are also very tasty, although they have a slightly different flavor. You can broil a lot of both green and red peppers and store them in the refrigerator covered with the sauce, in airtight jars, to use whenever you like.

Serve this dish as an appetizer or as an accompaniment to grilled meat or fish.

2 pounds large green or red bell
    peppers
⅓ cup olive oil
5–6 tablespoons red wine vinegar
1 clove garlic, minced
½ teaspoon dry mustard
½ teaspoon minced fresh chili pepper
Sea salt

SERVES 4

Preheat the boiler and place the peppers on the rack about 5 inches away from the source of heat. Broil peppers until the skins blister, turning them carefully so they cook on all sides. When the skins are blackened and cracked, 2 to 3 minutes on each side, transfer to a big bowl and cover with plastic wrap. Let them sit for about 10 minutes. The skins will detach completely, and the peppers will be very easy to peel. Peel the peppers, discard the stems and seeds, and cut the flesh lengthwise into 2 or 3 sections. Collect the juices.

Mix the oil and vinegar in a small glass jar. Add the pepper juices, garlic, mustard, chili pepper, and salt and mix well.

While the peppers are still warm, arrange them in a deep dish and pour the dressing over them. Partially cover the dish and let it cool, then cover and refrigerate until 1 or 2 hours before you are ready to serve. Serve at room temperature.

Garlic Sauce

SKORDALIA

Skordalia is ubiquitous to Greek cooking—you find it served as a spread, with *meze* for ouzo or wine, to accompany fried or boiled fish, and even served with meat dishes. Ancient Greeks had a sauce called *skorodalmi* that contained garlic, salt, and vinegar, similar to the *skordostumbi* one finds in Northern Greece today. *Skordalia* is even used to cook vegetables, meat, or fish. In some parts of Greece, especially in the Peloponnese, *skordalia* is prepared using just potatoes and no bread, and is frequently called *aliada,* a reference to the Italian *agliata,* which was described by Bartolomeo Scappi in *Dell' Arte Cucinare,* published in 1570. (*Agliata* was made with walnuts, almonds, and bread soaked in meat sauce, with plenty of garlic cloves, all pounded in a mortar.) This medieval garlic sauce, which contained no olive oil, was also served with eggplant. In Greece, you can find *skordalia* prepared with almonds instead of walnuts. In Turkey and the Middle East, a very similar sauce is called *tarator.*

The traditional *Skordalia* uses seven cloves or even a whole head of garlic. If you want a less potent sauce, use five cloves or fewer. And you can make it in a food processor or prepare it in the traditional way in a wooden or stone mortar. It's a good idea to cut the cloves lengthwise and discard the inner green bud before crushing the garlic in the mortar or food processor. This will make the *Skordalia* more digestible.

3 thick slices of whole wheat bread,
    crusts removed, soaked in water
½ cup mashed potatoes
5–7 cloves garlic
½ cup chopped walnuts
1 cup olive oil
⅓–½ cup lemon juice
Sea salt to taste

Squeeze the bread to remove excess water. In a mortar or food processor, process the bread, potatoes, garlic, and walnuts until the mixture becomes a smooth paste. Continuing to beat, very slowly pour in the oil as if you were making mayonnaise. Add ⅓ cup lemon juice and taste. If necessary, season with salt and more lemon juice.

MAKES ABOUT 3 CUPS

Parsley Spread

MAIDANOSALATA

This is a very tasty and easy spread, with a lovely bright green color, which I tasted at a friend's house in Athens. She had learned the recipe from Carmella, a lady from the island of Syros, who used to prepare *Maidanosalata* in a wooden mortar. She didn't use egg yolk, but my friend added it to her spread when she started making it in the blender.

Serve it with raw vegetables, fresh country bread, or bite-size rusks as an appetizer.

1 thick (1-inch) slice Country Bread
    (page 194) or whole wheat bread,
    crusts removed, soaked in water
1 medium onion, quartered
2–3 cloves garlic
⅓–½ teaspoon minced fresh
    chili pepper
1 pound flat-leaf parsley,
    stems trimmed
1 egg yolk (optional)
3 tablespoons lemon juice
⅓ cup olive oil
1–2 teaspoons balsamic vinegar
Sea salt
Small black olives, for garnish

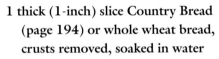

MAKES 2 CUPS

Squeeze the soaked bread to remove excess water. Discard any hard parts, and place half the bread in a food processor with the onion, garlic, chili pepper, and half the parsley. Process until everything is reduced to a paste. Add the remaining parsley and bread to the blender along with the egg yolk, half the lemon juice, and half the olive oil. Blend again, slowly adding more olive oil, 1 teaspoon vinegar, and some salt. Taste and adjust the seasoning by adding more salt, pepper, and lemon juice or vinegar. The spread should be very flavorful.

Pour the spread into a bowl and garnish with olives.

Carp Roe Spread

TARAMOSALATA

Taramosalata is eaten in every Greek household during Lent. Served with olives, bread, and boiled wild greens or a lettuce salad, it is more than just an appetizer; it is the central part of a substantial meatless meal. *Taramosalata* is also a wonderful sauce for boiled, steamed, or baked potatoes.

Although the pink *tarama,* or carp roe, makes a more attractive spread, the pale-colored type tastes the best.

3 slices whole wheat bread (about
    1 inch thick), crusts removed,
    soaked in milk or water, and
    squeezed dry (about 1½ cups)
½ cup (about 3½ ounces) *tarama*
    (carp roe)
5 scallions (white part plus 1 inch of
    green), or 1 medium onion
7 sprigs flat-leaf parsley
2 tablespoons capers, well rinsed
    (optional)
Juice of 2 lemons (4–5 tablespoons)
¾ cup olive oil
2 tablespoons water

MAKES 2½ CUPS

In a food processor combine the bread, *tarama,* scallions, 3 sprigs of parsley, capers, and lemon juice. Slowly add the olive oil and water.

Finely chop 3 sprigs of parsley. Place the *tarama* mixture in a bowl and stir in the parsley. Taste and add more lemon juice if needed. Cover and refrigerate for 2 to 3 hours or overnight, and serve garnished with the remaining sprig of parsley.

Note: The taste of this spread, which is usually eaten with fresh bread or crackers, is quite sharp. If you plan to serve it with vegetables, you may want to make it milder by adding more soaked bread.

Smoked Herring Spread

RENGOSALATA

When I was a child my mother used to make *Rengosalata* instead of *Taramosalata* on Clean Monday, the Greek Orthodox first day of Lent. We lived at the time in Patissia, an area then on the outskirts of Athens with very few houses in the midst of large gardens.

Friends and relatives used to come to our house to celebrate this glorious, early spring holiday. Each year we flew our kites in the fields and had a traditional picnic in our garden. My mother's *Rengosalata* was always the most popular dish and many people asked for the recipe. Smoked Herring Spread, like Eggplant Caviar (page 50), tastes better the day after it is made.

According to Greek Orthodox rules, the only fish products that can be eaten during Lent are fish eggs and mollusks. So Greeks make this herring spread using just the roes of the smoked herring. Smoked herring roe is nearly impossible to find in the United States, but the dip can be made very successfully using herring fillets.

As with *Taramosalata,* if you plan to serve this with vegetables, you may want to make it milder, in this case by adding more potato.

½ cup chopped smoked herring fillet; or a combination of roe, milt, and fillet

3–4 scallions (white part plus 1 inch of green)

3 teaspoons red wine or sherry vinegar

1–2 medium potatoes, boiled and peeled

3 tablespoon lemon juice

¾ cup olive oil

Fresh dill, for garnish

In a food processor puree the herring fillets with the scallions and vinegar.

In a mixing bowl, mash 1 potato and add the roe puree and half of the lemon juice. While stirring with a wooden spoon, add the oil a little at a time. Taste and add more lemon juice if you want.

Cover and refrigerate for at least 2 to 3 hours, preferably overnight. Serve garnished with dill sprigs.

Note: You can substitute ½ cup boned salted sardines or anchovies for the herring to make *sardelosalata* (sardine spread).

MAKES 2 CUPS

Smoked Trout in Dill and Scallion Marinade

PESTROFA KAPNISTI ME ANITHO

A dill-flavored *ladolemono* (a vinaigrette made with lemon juice) is usually served with cured or dried fish, especially with *tsiros* (sun-dried mackerel) and *lakerda* (smoked mackerel slices preserved in olive oil). I add chopped scallions and a little mustard to my *ladolemono* and serve it with smoked trout fillets. My friends love it, and it has become one of my trademark appetizers.

The lakes and rivers of northern and central Greece produce a lot of farmed trout. Most of it is smoked and exported to EC countries, since Athenians are not used to eating freshwater fish. In fact, in the central fish market of Athens, fresh trout is usually the cheapest fish one can buy.

In northern Greece, however, trout is eaten much more frequently. It is usually fried in olive oil and served with lemon quarters and fresh parsley.

4 smoked trout fillets
½ cup chopped scallions
½ cup chopped fresh dill
⅓ cup olive oil
3–4 tablespoons lemon juice
½ teaspoon Dijon mustard

SERVES 4

Place 2 trout fillets in a deep dish and sprinkle with half the scallions and half the dill. Place the other 2 fillets on top, and sprinkle with the rest of the dill and scallions.

Mix the oil and lemon juice in a glass jar and add the mustard. Pour the sauce over the trout fillets, which should be half-covered by it. Cover the plate with plastic wrap and refrigerate for 2 to 3 hours, or overnight.

Serve at room temperature with thin slices of toasted Country Bread (page 194).

SMOKED TROUT IN DILL
AND SCALLION MARINADE,
BY LAKE IOANNINA.

Lima Bean and Beet Salad with Smoked Herring

OSPRIA KE PANTZARIA SALATA

During Lent, salads with boiled lima beans or with beets and potatoes are a very common lunch or dinner dish. On Wednesdays and Fridays, some devout Greeks abstain even from olive oil, eating salads dressed with only salt and vinegar.

The combination of beans, beets, and potatoes—with or without smoked herring—can be found in many parts of the Peloponnese. In Mani there is even a potato salad with orange slices (a quite exotic combination, not much to my taste) because oranges are cultivated there.

When making this dish, keep the cut beets separate until the last moment to avoid turning the other vegetables red.

3½ ounces smoked herring fillet

1 cup milk

3 large boiled potatoes, peeled

3–4 cooked medium beets

2 large carrots, peeled and cooked

1½ cups cooked dried lima beans

3–4 scallions (white part plus 1 inch of green), thinly sliced

⅓–½ cup olive oil

3–4 tablespoons red wine vinegar

1 teaspoon Dijon mustard

¼–½ teaspoon fresh chili pepper or freshly ground black pepper to taste

Sea salt

⅓ cup chopped fresh flat-leaf parsley

SERVES 4–6

Cut the herring fillet into small strips, place in a bowl, and pour the milk over them. Leave for about 30 minutes, stirring occasionally. This will cut some of the very sharp and salty taste.

Cut the potatoes and beets into 1-inch cubes and slice the carrots. Mix the potatoes, lima beans, carrots, scallions, and herring in a large bowl.

Mix the olive oil and vinegar and add the mustard and chili pepper. Add very little salt, as the herring will still be quite salty. Pour this dressing over the salad, toss, and arrange the beets on top. Sprinkle with the chopped parsley. Serve warm or at room temperature.

Eggplant and Zucchini Fried in Batter

MELINTZANES KE KOLOKITHIA TIGANITA

Crunchy and delicious, fried eggplant and zucchini are the most popular appetizers in Greek tavernas. When served with *Skordalia* (Garlic Sauce), they become the foremost *meze* for ouzo or resinated wine.

These are especially good when tomato juice is used in the batter because the slight acidity of the tomato complements the sweetness of the vegetables.

Unfortunately, this is a last-minute dish, not suitable for cooks who like to be free when their guests arrive. Batter-fried vegetables shouldn't be left to cool but, rather, eaten as they come out of the frying pan.

1½ pounds large eggplants
1½ pounds large zucchini
Sea salt

BATTER

2 cups fresh or canned tomato juice
1½ cup all-purpose flour
1 tablespoon baking powder
Freshly ground black pepper
½ cup very finely chopped scallions
    (optional)

Olive and sunflower oil, for
    deep-frying
Skordalia (page 54) or 2 cups Greek
    yogurt

SERVES 8–10

Slice the eggplants crosswise to obtain ⅓-inch-thick round slices, salt well on both sides, and leave in a colander to drain for at least 30 minutes. Slice the zucchini into ⅓-inch-thick disks, salt them, and let them drain in a separate colander.

Prepare the batter. In a medium bowl pour the tomato juice over the flour and baking powder and stir well. Add the pepper and scallions and set aside, covered, for 30 to 40 minutes.

Thirty minutes before serving, heat the oil to 375° F. in a deep skillet.

Dry the vegetable slices with paper towels. Dip each into the batter and fry until golden brown on both sides, about 1 to 2 minutes on each side. Place on paper towels to drain for a few seconds, then serve immediately, accompanied by *Skordalia* or Greek yogurt.

Note: You can also dredge the eggplant and zucchini slices in plain flour, shake off the excess, and fry them.

Freshly Salted Sardines

SARDELES PASTES

The best sardines are caught in the Gulf of Kalloni on the island of Mytilini (Lesbos). The sardines are preserved with coarse salt collected from the rocks as soon as the fish are taken out of the sea in the early morning, then they are eaten that evening as *meze* with ouzo, another local specialty.

These sardines can also be found in wooden barrels at the markets of Athens. Greeks call them *sardeles vareliou* (sardines from the barrel) to distinguish them from canned sardines, which are usually imported from Portugal. As the sardines age in the barrels they lose their fresh fishy taste, but they are still delicious. I chop them and add them to my version of *Horiatiki* (Country Tomato Salad, page 82) or make a spread with them (page 57).

2 pounds small sardines, about
   16–20 fish

Coarse sea salt

15–20 fresh or frozen vine leaves
   (see page 138)

Olive oil

Lemon juice or vinegar

3 large tomatoes, sliced in eighths
   almost to stem end

SERVES 8–10

Cut off the heads and gut the fish. Open them with a sharp knife and take out the backbones. Sprinkle with coarse salt, close the fillets, and place next to one another in a basket lined with vine leaves.

Sprinkle with more salt, arrange some vine leaves on top of the first row of sardines, and continue making alternate rows of sardines, salt, and vine leaves until all the fish have been used. Cover with vine leaves, and place the basket over a bowl to drain. Leave the sardines in the refrigerator for at least 12 hours before serving. (They will keep for about 1 week in the refrigerator.)

To serve, pour some olive oil and lemon or vinegar over the sardines and eat with fresh bread and *domata garifalo* (carnation tomatoes). Additional coarse salt is sprinkled over the tomato pieces as they are cut off to be eaten.

Feta Spread

HTIPITI

I learned about this spread only fairly recently, when I tried several variations of it in Thessalonica and other parts of Macedonia. *Htipiti* means "beaten" in Greek, and it probably refers to the process of making the spread in a mortar, which is not always the way it is made today.

Htipiti should not be confused with *kopanisti,* a crumbled matured cheese spread found in the Greek islands. *Kopanisti* is made by grating the local cheeses and leaving them in clay or glass jars for two to three months, until they mature and acquire a pungent flavor similar to that of strong blue cheese.

In Nevin Halici's *Turkish Cookbook* I found a dish similar to this, which, as she explains, comes from the Turkish part of Thrace. In her recipe curd cheese is used, while in the Greek version we use crumbled feta cheese.

You may find many different versions of this spread in the tavernas of northern Greece, but this is the one I like best. Serve *Htipiti* with fresh or toasted Country Bread (page 194).

⅓ cup olive oil
½–1 fresh chili pepper, minced;
   or ⅓–½ teaspoon dried red
   pepper flakes
1 clove garlic, minced (optional)
1½ cups crumbled soft feta cheese
1–2 grilled red peppers or canned
   Florina peppers (see page 52)

In a skillet heat the olive oil over medium heat and sauté the chili pepper for ½–1 minute—use more or less hot pepper, according to your taste. Add the garlic and remove pan from the heat. Let cool for about 3 minutes.

In a blender or food processor, puree the feta with the roasted peppers, then add the chili pepper mixture. Serve immediately or refrigerate for up to 7 days.

SERVES 8–10

Fried Peppers

PIPERIES TIGANITES

Throughout Macedonia, the most common appetizer is fried small light green peppers. Although they are usually prepared the day before serving and then sprinkled with a little vinegar and served cold, they taste better warm, straight from the skillet.

Olive oil, for frying
6–8 Italian frying peppers
Red wine vinegar
Sea salt and freshly ground pepper

Pour the oil into a skillet to a depth of about ⅓ inch and heat over medium heat. Fry the peppers on both sides until soft, 3 to 4 minutes. Remove with a slotted spoon, transfer to a plate, and sprinkle with vinegar. Season with salt and pepper and serve immediately.

SERVES 3–4

Tomato Patties

DOMATOKEFTEDES

Vegetable patties are an impecunious cook's interpretation of meatballs, a Greek favorite. During the years when meat was extremely expensive and there were plenty of vegetables grown in the garden, vegetable patties became a fixture of Greek life. They are a perfect dish to serve during Lent because no cheese or eggs are used.

Parsley patties are found in Thrace, and chick-pea, onion, zucchini, and potato patties are found all over Greece. There are even wild greens patties, prepared using the different kinds of *horta* people gather from the hills and mountains.

The basic recipe is the same: Chop, grate, or mash the vegetables or greens, and mix them with flour, herbs, and spices to make a thick batter. Then drop spoonfuls of the batter in olive oil and fry until golden.

In the case of potato patties, a different procedure is followed, making them similar to potato croquettes. Only a very small amount of flour is used, and cheese is always added to the mixture, which is then shaped into small balls that are flattened before frying.

SANTORINI

My mother used to make stuffed potato croquettes, putting a small amount of spiced ground meat inside the potato mixture.

The best tomato patties can be found on the islands of the Aegean. Those from the island of Santorini are thought to be the very best, mainly because the local tomatoes are so good. Because it seldom rains there, the tomatoes have a firm and very tasty flesh that can be chopped without turning into mush. The special taste of Santorini tomato patties cannot be recreated, not even in Athens.

People in the islands will tell you that *Domatokeftedes* can also be eaten cold, but although they are tasty, they lose their crunchiness as they cool off. Tomato patties are served as an appetizer, but can also accompany grilled meat and fish. When served with Eggplant and Zucchini Fried in Batter (page 61) and Garlic Sauce (page 54), they make a delicious light summer lunch.

As I was trying to come up with a tasty alternative to Santorini tomatoes, I combined ordinary tomatoes with some sun-dried tomatoes and the result was quite good.

2–2½ cups finely peeled, cubed, and drained fresh tomatoes (about 3–4 tomatoes)
1 cup finely chopped sun-dried tomatoes
1 cup finely chopped fresh flat-leaf parsley
¾ cup finely chopped scallions
½ cup finely chopped fresh mint leaves
1 tablespoon dried oregano
1–1½ cups all-purpose flour
1 tablespoon baking powder
Sea salt and freshly ground pepper
Olive oil, for frying
¾ cup finely chopped onions
1 clove garlic, minced

SERVES 8

Mix the fresh and sun-dried tomatoes with the parsley, scallions, mint, and oregano. Add 1 cup flour and the baking powder and stir well, until you have a thick batter. Add a little more flour if necessary and season with salt and pepper.

In a skillet heat enough olive oil to come halfway up the sides of the patties, about ⅔ inch. Briefly sauté the onions and garlic, drain them, reserving the oil, and add to the batter. Stir well.

Pass the oil through a fine sieve or cheesecloth and pour back into the skillet. Place it over high heat and fry tablespoonfuls of the tomato mixture until golden brown on both sides, about 3 to 4 minutes. Transfer to a plate lined with paper towels to drain excess oil and serve hot.

Note: Taste the first patty, and if needed, add more salt and pepper to the mixture.

You can also deep-fry the tomato patties. Greeks have not traditionally deep-fried patties or potatoes, but they have started to use the technique since special electric deep-fryers have become available. Tomato patties take on a better shape when they are deep-fried.

Overleaf: TOMATO PATTIES WITH JARS OF DELICIOUS TINY CRETAN OLIVES, CHANIA, CRETE.

Potato and Carp Roe Patties

TARAMOKEFTEDES ME PATATA

A typical *meze* served during Lent, these patties can also be served as an entree. There are many different kinds of *taramokeftedes*, some using soaked bread as a thickener instead of potato. There are even *taramokeftedes* made with wild greens (*horta*).

Olive oil, for deep-frying
1 cup finely chopped scallions
1½–2 cups freshly mashed potatoes
2 tablespoons *tarama* (carp roe)
½ cup finely chopped fresh dill
1 tablespoon chopped fresh mint
Flour, for dredging

SERVES 8–10

In a skillet, heat 2 tablespoons olive oil and sauté the scallions until transparent. Remove with a slotted spoon.

In a bowl, mix the mashed potatoes with the scallions, *tarama*, dill, and mint. Stir well and set the mixture aside for 1 to 2 hours or overnight.

Thirty minutes before serving, heat the oil to 350° F. Shape teaspoonfuls of the mixture into balls, roll in the flour, and deep-fry until golden, about 3 minutes. Place on paper towels to drain excess oil. Serve hot.

Note: As *tarama* is sometimes very salty, you may want to use less of it and add more mashed potato to the mixture. You can also substitute spinach or wild greens, blanched, mashed, and well-drained, for the mashed potato. In that case, add 1 cup dry bread crumbs, and 2 tablespoons flour and a pinch of baking powder.

All vegetable patties take on a better shape and are more presentable if you add 1 to 2 eggs (or just egg whites) to the mixture before frying.

Fresh Cheese with Garlic and Dill

TIRI ME SKORDO KE ANITHO

I first tasted this cheese at a friend's house eight years ago. I now make it all the time. I doubt it is an old recipe, but I love it so much that I felt I had to include it in this chapter.

3 cups thick Greek yogurt, or
    2 cups plain yogurt and 1 cup
    heavy cream
1–2 cloves garlic, minced
1 teaspoon sea salt
1 teaspoon ground white pepper
1 cup chopped fresh dill

SERVES 8–10

Combine the yogurt, cream if using, garlic, salt, pepper, and dill in a bowl and mix well. Line another bowl with cheesecloth or a linen kitchen towel, and pour the yogurt mixture into it. Gather the ends of the cloth together, tie them with string or garden wire, and hang bag to drain over a bowl for 10 to 12 hours.

Unwrap the cloth and remove the cheese. Serve immediately with fresh Country Bread (page 194). The cheese will keep in the refrigerator for 5 to 6 days.

GARLIC AND PEARL ONIONS
IN THE CENTRAL MARKET OF ATHENS.

Fried Cheese Pies

TIGANITES TIROPITES

These delicious pies are made on the islands of Chios and Lesbos, near the coast of Asia Minor. They are the traditional dish cooked during the last week of Carnival, just before Lent.

Serve *Tyropites* as an appetizer or as a main dish, accompanied by a green salad. I prefer to serve them warm, but they can also be eaten cold.

2 cups all-purpose flour

½ teaspoon sea salt

1 egg

3 tablespoons olive oil

½ cup warm water, or more

FILLING

4 eggs

⅔ cup grated kefalotyri or
   pecorino cheese

⅔ cup crumbled hard feta cheese

½ cup chopped fresh mint or
   1 teaspoon dried

Olive and sunflower oil,
   for deep frying

MAKES 12 PIES

In a large bowl, mix the flour with the salt. Make a well in the center and break the egg into it. Add the olive oil and ⅓ cup water. Mix the ingredients and start kneading, adding a little more water if you need to, to make a smooth dough. Set aside for about 30 minutes, covered.

Mix the eggs, cheeses, and mint in a large bowl.

Divide the dough into 12 pieces, each about the size of a golf ball. On a floured board, roll out each piece with a rolling pin and stretch with your hands. Don't worry if they are not perfect circles. Place 1 tablespoon of the filling in the center of each disk, spreading it over half the dough, leaving a ⅔-inch border. Brush the edges of the disks with water and press the two sides together with your fingers or with a fork to seal them.

Heat the oil in a deep skillet until 325–350°F., and deep-fry the cheese pies on both sides until golden and puffed, 2 to 3 minutes on each side. Transfer to paper towels to drain excess oil, and serve while still warm.

Note: You can make triangular cheese pieces using commercial phyllo and this filling. Double the amount of filling and use one 1-pound package of commercial phyllo. Preheat the oven to 350°F. Keep the phyllo well covered as you work, to prevent it from drying out. Cut each phyllo sheet into thirds, making three long strips. Take one strip, brush with olive oil, and place 1 teaspoon of filling on the end nearest you. Fold over diagonally, so the right corner meets the left side. Continue folding to make a triangular-shaped pie. Brush again with olive oil and place in an oiled pan. Continue until you have used all the filling. Bake for 25 minutes, until golden. Serve hot.

Fried Snails with Peppers

SALIGARIA SAVORI ME PIPERIES

This recipe is a variation of Fried Fish in Vinegar Sauce (page 88) and comes from Heraklion, Crete. For a more formal dish, serve it with rice, or simply with fresh Country Bread (page 194), which is delicious when dipped in the sauce. This recipe can only be made with live snails—don't bother with it if you can only find the canned version.

2 pounds live snails (Starve them in a covered basket outside for a week, and the last 1–2 days feed them a little flour.)

Olive oil, for frying

Flour, for dusting

4 green bell peppers, cut in 6 pieces lengthwise

3 medium potatoes, thinly sliced

2 medium onions, sliced

3–4 cloves garlic, chopped

½–1 fresh red chili pepper, chopped; or ⅓–½ teaspoon dried red pepper flakes

1 sprig fresh rosemary, or 1 teaspoon dried

Sea salt

½ cup red wine vinegar

½ cup red wine

Wash the snails thoroughly. Bring a large pot of water to a boil, add snails, and blanch for 15 to 20 minutes, skimming surface frequently. Drain and rinse with running water. Extract the snails from their shells with a pin or small fork and discard the shells. Cut off and discard the intestines.

In a deep, heavy skillet, heat ½ to ¾ cup olive oil over high heat. Dredge the snails in flour, then fry on both sides until golden and tender, about 3 to 4 minutes. Remove the snails from the skillet and set aside. Sauté the peppers and potatoes in the same pan until tender, about 15 minutes. Drain.

Pass the sautéing oil through a fine sieve or cheesecloth, wipe the skillet with paper towels, and pour the strained oil back into the skillet. Heat it over high heat, then sauté the onion for 5 minutes or until transparent.

Add the garlic and chili pepper to the skillet. Return the snails, peppers, and potatoes as well, and add the rosemary and salt. Pour the vinegar and wine over all and simmer for about 5 to 8 minutes, or until heated through. Serve hot.

SERVES 4–6

Charcoal-Grilled Octopus

KTAPODI STA KARVOUNA

On summer evenings, the aroma of grilled octopus fills the air from all the Greek seaside tavernas. Even small coffee houses that serve just coffee, sweets, and drinks place small grills outside their door, so that they can grill octopus and serve small pieces as *meze* for ouzo.

Octopus can also be boiled in water until tender, then placed in a sterile glass jar filled with vinegar and flavored with herbs and spices. When served with olive oil and oregano, this pickled octopus can be a very tasty *meze*.

In the morning, people pound the octopuses on the rocks by the sea, then hang them on lines to dry in the sun before grilling them.

¼ cup olive oil

2 tablespoons red wine vinegar

1–2 teaspoons dried oregano

1 medium octopus, 1–1½ pounds, fresh or frozen, cleaned

SERVES 6–8

Prepare charcoal fire. Mix the oil, vinegar, and oregano in a small bowl.

Wash and dry the octopus and place it on the grill about 4 inches above the coals. Brush with the marinade. Grill for about 15 minutes on each side. When the octopus is tender—when it can be pierced with a fork—remove from the grill, place on a plate, cut into small pieces, and pour the marinade over it.

Serve immediately as an appetizer, accompanied by ouzo or wine.

Right: CHARCOAL-GRILLED OCTOPUS; DRYING OCTOPUSES, HYDRA

Pickled Wild Hyacinth Bulbs

VOLVI

This is one of the most typical of Lenten appetizers, known to Greeks since ancient times. Athenaeus writes that pickled bulbs served with lentil soup are "like ambrosia." In early spring, the freshly dug bulbs are sold in the open-air markets for people to make their own pickles. The slightly bitter bulbs are served as a *meze* with ouzo, or they can accompany lentil soup or any boiled green salad.

2–3 tablespoons coarse sea salt

2 pounds untreated wild hyacinth bulbs, peeled

2–3 cups good-quality white wine vinegar

6 cloves garlic, halved

1 teaspoon coriander seeds

3 bay leaves

½–1 whole fresh chili pepper

MAKES ABOUT 1 QUART

Bring a large pot of water to a boil and add the salt. Blanch the bulbs for 5 to 7 minutes. Drain and place in a large bowl, covered with cold water. Leave in the water overnight, changing the water at least 3 times.

In a nonreactive pan, bring the vinegar to a boil and add the garlic, coriander seeds, and bay leaves. Remove from the heat. Drain the bulbs, and pack them tightly in a sterilized quart jar. Add the chili pepper and pour the hot vinegar over all to fill jar. Stir or spin jar to eliminate air bubbles. Seal and let cure for at least 10 days before serving.

PICKLED WILD HYACINTH BULBS, ON FILOPAPPOU HILL, ATHENS.

Beets and Pickled Hyacinth Bulbs with Garlic Sauce

VOLVI, KOKINOGOULIA
KE SKORDALIA

Beets have been a favorite winter vegetable in Greece since antiquity, and we find them mentioned several times in Athenaeus. Ancient Greeks considered them a delicacy, and ate them with salted fish and other greens to accompany the wine before the meal during important symposia. Nowadays, beets served with garlic sauce is a very common Lenten dish. Since in Greece we buy the beets raw together with their leaves, this dish is a combination of sweet roots and greens, magnificently complemented with a piquant garlic sauce.

If we add slightly bitter hyacinth bulbs and augment the beet greens with some different greens, the dish becomes even more interesting. This salad is an ideal accompaniment to Fried Salt Cod (page 89), but can be served with any kind of fried or salted fish.

The garlic sauce with almonds and potato, which is called *aliada*, was given to me by Vali Manouilides, an excellent cook whose family comes from Istanbul.

2 pounds mixed greens (amaranth, beet greens, dandelions, spinach, sorrel)

1 pound cooked beets, sliced

1 cup Pickled Wild Hyacinth Bulbs (see page 76)

GARLIC SAUCE

2 thick slices white bread, crusts removed

1 cup mashed potatoes

1 cup shelled almonds, blanched

1 teaspoon sea salt

5–8 cloves garlic

⅓–½ cup balsamic vinegar

1 cup olive oil

Wash and trim the greens. Discard all leaves that are not fresh. Bring a large pot of salted water to a boil. Add the greens, and after the water comes to a boil again, cook for 5 to 8 minutes. Drain greens and arrange on a plate. Top with sliced beets and pickled hyacinth bulbs or pearl onions.

Soak the bread slices in water to cover. When soft, squeeze dry between your hands; you should have 1 cup of bread pulp. Put the bread, potatoes, almonds, salt, and garlic in a blender and process until the mixture is a paste. Add the vinegar and oil, and blend again for 2 seconds, until well mixed.

Spoon the sauce over the vegetables and serve.

SERVES 4

Wild Asparagus Omelet

OMELETA ME AGRIOSPARANGIA

Wild asparagus is a rare springtime delicacy that is particularly popular in Crete. This asparagus is a long, thin form called *Asparagus acutifolius,* different from the wild asparagus found in the New World, *Asparagus officinalis,* which is the domestic variety gone wild. Greeks eat wild asparagus boiled, stewed with a lot of onions, and in omelets. Because it is somewhat bitter, it tastes delicious in omelets. If you can't get it, use young, bitter dandelion shoots instead.

1½–2 pounds asparagus, wild
   if possible
5 eggs
Olive oil, for sautéing
Sea salt and freshly ground pepper

SERVES 3–4

Wash the asparagus and trim it, keeping only the very tender tops. Blanch it by dropping it into a large pot of boiling water and cook for 3 to 5 minutes. Drain in a colander.

Beat the eggs lightly. Heat the olive oil in a heavy skillet over medium heat and pour in the eggs. Add the asparagus, and season with salt and pepper. Stir with a fork for a few seconds, or until the omelet begins to thicken. Continue cooking for about 1 minute, or until the omelet is almost firm and starts to brown on the bottom. Carefully slide the omelet onto a plate, invert the skillet over it, and turn over. Cook for a few seconds on the other side.

Transfer to a serving dish and serve immediately.

Raw Artichoke Salad

AGINARES SALATA

This unusual salad can be found only in Crete in the early spring, on the first days of Lent. It is served with the Lenten fish spreads—*Taramosalata* (page 56) and *Rengosalata* (page 57)—as an appetizer.

Only very young, tender artichokes should be used for this dish. If you try it once, you will certainly want to make it again.

3 lemons
5–6 small artichokes, about 2 inches
    in diameter

DRESSING

2 tablespoons lemon juice
5 tablespoons olive oil
1 teaspoon prepared mustard
1 clove garlic, minced

½ cup chopped fresh dill
Sea salt and freshly ground pepper

SERVES 4–6

Pour about 1 quart of water into a bowl and add the juice of 2 lemons. Remove the hard outer leaves of each artichoke with a sharp knife and keep snapping off leaves until you are left with a soft cone formed by the inner leaves and the heart.

Cut the remaining lemon in half and rub the cut surfaces of the artichokes to prevent discoloration. Trim the green tops of the cones and, with a teaspoon, reach in and remove the choke. Quarter each artichoke and cut each piece in half; rub with lemon again, and place on a plate.

When you have prepared all the artichokes, put the lemon juice, olive oil, mustard, and minced garlic into a glass jar with a lid. Close the jar and shake well.

Pour the dressing over the artichokes, sprinkle with the dill, season with salt and pepper, toss well, and serve immediately.

PURPLE ARTICHOKES IN
AN ATHENS STREET MARKET.

Artichoke and Fresh Fava Bean Omelet

OMELETA ME AGINARES
KE KOUKIA

The traditional omelets from the island of Andros are famous throughout Greece. They include *froutalia,* a flat omelet filled with thinly sliced fried potatoes and slices of country sausage or homemade smoked pork, and many vegetable omelets— including my favorite, which contains artichokes and fresh fava beans.

3 small artichokes, trimmed (see
    page 80)
1 cup fresh or frozen green fava beans
    or flageolets
Olive oil, for frying
1 medium onion, sliced
1–2 cloves garlic, minced
4 eggs
1½ cups sliced spicy sausage
    (optional)
Sea salt and freshly ground pepper
Chopped fresh parsley

SERVES 2–3

Halve the artichokes and slice each half into 4 segments. Wipe dry with paper towels.

Blanch the fava beans for 5 minutes in boiling salted water, then plunge into cold water. Drain and reserve.

In a heavy skillet, heat the oil over medium heat and sauté the artichokes, onion, and fava beans. When the vegetables are tender, about 15 minutes, add the minced garlic and sauté briefly.

With a slotted spoon, remove the vegetables from the skillet, leaving as much of the oil in the skillet as possible. Pass the oil through a fine sieve, wipe the skillet with paper towels, and pour the oil back into the skillet.

Beat the eggs lightly. Heat the oil over low heat and pour the eggs into the skillet. Add the sautéed vegetables and sausage slices, and season with salt and pepper. Stir the egg mixture with a fork for a few seconds, until the omelet begins to thicken. Continue cooking for about 1 minute, or until the omelet is almost firm and starts to brown on the bottom. Carefully slide the omelet onto a plate, invert the skillet over it, and turn over. Sauté the omelet for a few seconds on the second side.

Transfer to a serving dish, sprinkle with chopped parsley, and serve immediately.

Country Tomato Salad

DOMATOSALATA HORIATIKI

The salad tourists find in all Greek tavernas by the name *horiatiki* (country or village salad, known in the United States as Greek salad), is a combination of tomatoes with various other things—from salted sardines to olives—of which only onion slices and feta are a must. From then on, every cook can improvise.

Capers are my addition to *Horiatiki*. I find that the home-cured capers I get every year from the island of Paros are a perfect addition to sweet, ripe summer tomatoes. From then on, I use whatever I can find in the house: cucumbers, bell pepper rings, salted sardines, hard-cooked eggs, Kalamata olives, and, of course, onion rings and feta. Purslane, the weed known and loved by ancient as well as modern Greeks, is another green in my tomato salad. I always sprinkle the salad with oregano and pour quite a lot of olive oil over it. Fresh country bread dipped in the dressing and eaten with good-quality feta cheese is a taste I dream of all winter. But, of course, the tomatoes have to be of the right quality for this salad to be good. I find that tomatoes kept in the refrigerator lose whatever taste they had.

This salad, eaten just with bread, can be a light lunch or appetizer or can accompany fish or meat.

3 large ripe tomatoes
2 tablespoons drained capers
1 medium onion, sliced into thin rings
½ green bell pepper, cut into rings
2 salted sardines, rinsed in running
    water, dried with paper towels,
    and cut into ⅓-inch pieces
6–10 Kalamata olives
½ cup chopped purslane (optional)
1 cup diced feta cheese
Oregano
Sea salt and freshly ground pepper
Olive oil
1 hard-cooked egg, quartered
    (optional)

Cut the tomatoes in half and discard the cores. Slice the tomatoes, place in a bowl, and add the capers, onion and pepper rings, sardine pieces, olives, purslane, and feta. Sprinkle with oregano, salt, and pepper, and pour olive oil over it.

Toss the salad at the last minute, and don't worry about the resulting mess. Place the egg quarters on top (if using) and serve with fresh Country Bread (page 194).

SERVES 4–6

COUNTRY TOMATO SALAD (center), CUCUMBER WITH FETA CHEESE AND MINT (page 51), RAW ARTICHOKE SALAD (page 80) AND A SIMPLE ROMAINE AND ARUGULA SALAD, ASTYPALAIA.

Steamed Amaranth Salad

VLITA SALATA

Nearly all of our wild greens were known to the ancient Greeks. Some of them—amaranth among them—have been cultivated since ancient times. In fact, amaranth shoots were frequently mentioned by many classical Greek writers as an edible green—together with cabbage and lettuce—while the plant's grains were used in sauces. Amaranth leaves with olive oil, made into a pulp and rubbed on the head, was recommended by Hippocrates as a remedy for a headache!

One day I turned on my television set and, to my great surprise, I fell on a documentary series called "Beyond 2000." It was a report on ancient foodstuffs that are being rediscovered in the United States. And they were raving about amaranth! The commentator spoke about the bush cultivated by the Incas and the Aztecs, who ate "the spinach-like leaves" and also the seeds. These seeds are now being reintroduced as an important grain, because they have been found to contain double the amount of protein in corn. The Aztecs used to fry the seeds until they popped, just like popcorn.

The Greeks have never ceased to eat this wonderful green, which grows wild in many parts of the United States. Serve amaranth with fried or grilled fish or with any kind of grilled meat.

2 pounds amaranth shoots
2 tablespoons lemon juice
4 tablespoons olive oil
1 teaspoon prepared mustard
1 clove garlic, minced (optional)
Sea salt and freshly ground pepper

Wash the amaranth, and steam or blanch until tender but not mushy, about 10 minutes. Drain and place in a bowl.

In a small jar, mix the lemon juice, olive oil, mustard, and garlic. Season with salt and pepper, mix thoroughly, and pour over the greens.

SERVES 4

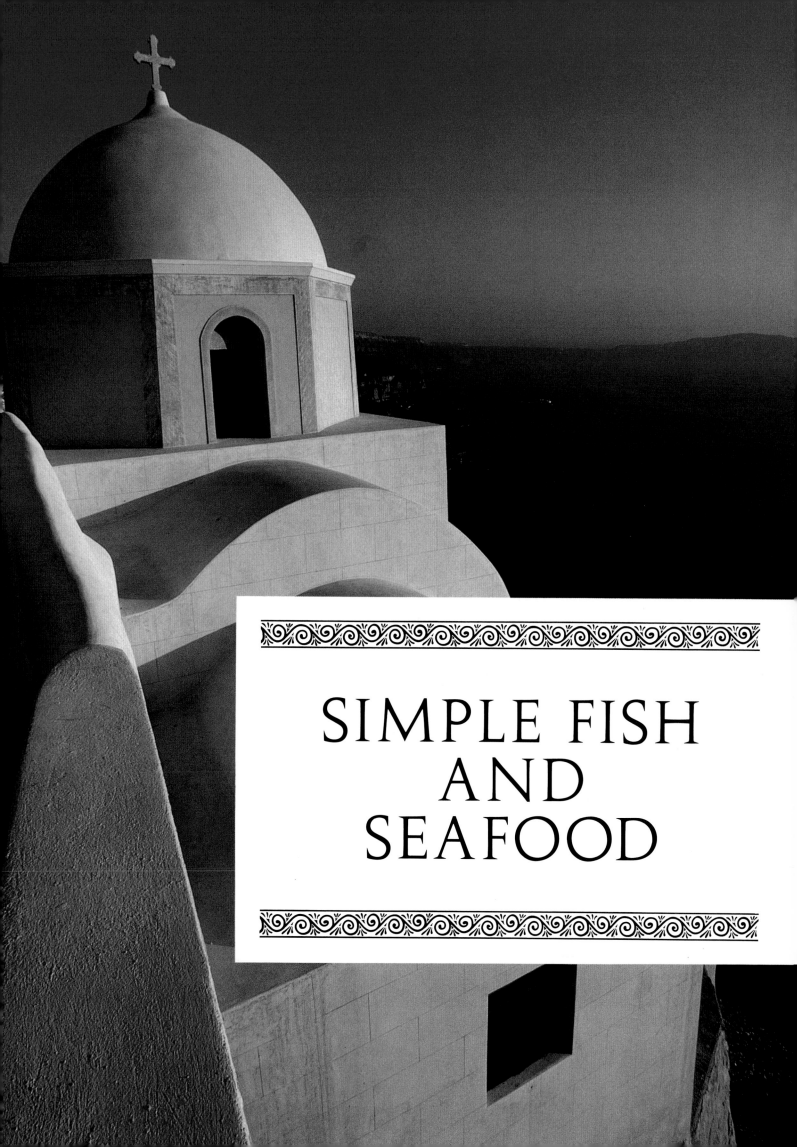

SIMPLE FISH
AND
SEAFOOD

"First I took some shrimps; I fried them all to a turn. A huge dogfish is put in my hands; I baked the middle slices, but the rest of the stuff I boiled, after making mulberry sauce. Here I fetch two very large pieces of gray fish cut near the head, in a big casserole; in it I have added sparingly some herbs, caraway seed, salt, water, and oil. After that I bought a very fine sea bass. It shall be served boiled in an oily pickle with herbs, after I have served the meats roasted on spits. Some fine red mullets I purchased, and some lovely wrasses. These I immediately tossed upon the coals, and to an oily pickle I added some marjoram. Besides these I bought some cuttlefish and squids. A boiled squid stuffed with chopped meat is nice, and so are the tentacles of cuttlefish when roasted tender. To these I fitted a fresh sauce of many vegetables, and after them came some boiled dishes, for which I made a mayonnaise to give them flavor. To top this I bought a very fat conger eel. I smothered it in a fresher pickle. Some gobies, and some rockfish of course; I snipped off their heads and smeared their bodies in a batter of flour, just a little, and sent them on the same journey as the shrimps. Then a widowed bonito a very fine creature, I soaked just enough with oil, wrapped it in swaddling-bands of fig leaves, sprinkled it with marjoram [or oregano], and hid it like a firebrand in a heap of hot ashes. . . ."

This could be the description of the day's menu recited by the owner of a contemporary island fish taverna. But in fact it is the cook's monologue from a play called *Locked Up,* by Sotades, written between 404 and 340 B.C.

After so many centuries, little has changed in the way Greeks cook fish. We may no longer wrap fish in fig leaves, but we wrap it in vine leaves and we dip some fish in batter before frying. And we

THE BEACH AT KALLONI, LESBOS.

also stuff squid and cuttlefish, if not with meat, then with rice, herbs, and spices. We don't use caraway seeds in fish dishes today, although we use cumin to flavor meat or vegetable dishes.

Fish was a very important source of protein for Greeks until very recently. Unfortunately, during the last few years—as Greece has become more Westernized—we tend to eat less fish and a lot more meat. Meat consumption rose 155 percent between 1961 and 1985, while the consumption of fish fell 7 percent during the same period.

It is interesting to note that the modern Greek names for the various local fish are almost the same as those used by the ancient Greeks. And by reading Athenaeus, we see that our ancestors had exactly the same feelings toward fishmongers as do modern Greeks, considering them to be profiteers who ask exorbitant prices for the fish they sell to their poor customers.

While the French like to cover their fish and seafood with complicated sauces, Greek cuisine calls for minimal additions. Cooked over a charcoal fire, this is the best way to enjoy a nice bream, a bass, a red snapper, an octopus, or some shrimps, just basted with lemon and olive oil and scented with oregano.

Fish soup is another traditional dish found in many different variations. Called *kakavia* on many islands, takes its name from an ancient Greek pot (*kakavi*) in which the fish was boiled. Sometimes the fish is cooked in seawater.

According to a common Greek proverb "the best fish is the fresh fish," and by fresh we mean no more than half-a-day old. It is not uncommon for vacationers to wait, together with the taverna owners, at the docks for fishing boats to return in the morning; they all choose on the spot the fish they would like for lunch or dinner that day. The just-caught fish from the Aegean have an exquisite flavor that is impossible to find anywhere else in the world.

Sometimes imported Mediterranean fish can be found in American fishmarkets, but I've included the closest equivalents that are more generally available. Note also that Mediterranean fish are quite different from the ones in the colder waters of the North Atlantic or the Pacific ocean. And our view of various fish is sometimes very different from people elsewhere. For example, fresh trout is one of the cheapest fish you will find in Athens's central market, because Greeks don't think much of it.

One fish that Greek gourmets love is *skaros,* a kind of parrotfish that in early summer is common in the southeastern Aegean. About 15 inches long with thick scales, *skaros* is the only fish we grill or bake without gutting or scaling. Only the bitter gall is removed; when cooked, the skin can be easily removed, while the intestines are mashed and mixed with olive oil and lemon to produce a delicious sauce.

Fried Fish in Vinegar Sauce

PSARI SAVORI

Apicius, the well-known Roman gourmet cook, advises people who want to preserve fried fish to sprinkle it generously with hot vinegar. Like most of the recipes Apicius recorded in his writings, it is probable that this idea originated in ancient Greece.

This method of cooking fish and sometimes snails is called *savori* in modern Greek, which uses the Italian word. It is one of the rare contemporary Greek recipes that includes rosemary, an herb that has been used since antiquity for its preserving qualities.

My mother made *savori* sauce to serve with fried fish left over from lunch, so that we could eat them for dinner or the next day.

Olive oil, for frying
1 pound goat fish, mackerel, small
    seabass, or sea bream (about ⅓–½
    pound each) cleaned, with heads
    left on
Flour, for dredging
2 medium onions, sliced
½–1 minced fresh chili pepper, or
    ⅓–½ teaspoon dried red pepper
    flakes
3–4 cloves garlic, chopped
1 sprig fresh rosemary, or 1 teaspoon
    dried leaves
2 bay leaves
½ cup red wine
½ cup red wine vinegar
Sea salt to taste

In a skillet, heat about 1 inch of olive oil over high heat. Dredge the fish in the flour, shake to lose excess flour, and fry on both sides until golden. (The time will depend on the size of fish.) Be careful not to overcook. Place fish on paper towels to drain.

Pass the cooking oil through a fine sieve or cheesecloth, wipe the skillet with paper towels, and pour the clean oil back in. Heat over medium heat and sauté the onion for 3 minutes or until translucent.

Add the chili pepper and the garlic to the skillet. Return the fish to the skillet, and add the rosemary and bay leaves. Pour the wine and vinegar over and simmer for about 5 minutes. Season with salt. Serve fish with the sauce, warm or cold.

SERVES 2–3

Fried Salt Cod with Garlic Sauce

BACALIAROS SKORDALIA

This is one of the most popular Greek fish dishes, usually made with salt cod. It's the typical dish prepared on March 25, a double holiday: the Annunciation of Virgin Mary and Greek Independence Day, marking the beginning of the great revolution of 1821 against Turkish domination.

Bacaliaros Skordalia is frequently served with boiled red beets.

2 pounds salt cod
1½ cups all-purpose flour
1 cup skim milk
¼ teaspoon baking soda
¼ cup ouzo (optional)
½ cup finely shredded fresh mint
   leaves
Olive oil, for frying
1 recipe *Skordalia* (page 54)

SERVES 4–5

Cut the salt cod into 4 or 5 pieces, and soak in water overnight. The next day, remove the skin and bones and taste the cod. If it is still too salty, soak again in warm water for several hours.

Thirty minutes before serving, drain the water and cut the cod into bite-size pieces. Mix the flour, milk, and baking soda to make a batter. Add the ouzo and mint.

Heat the oil in a frying pan until almost smoking. Dip each piece of cod in the batter and fry the cod pieces until they are golden brown, about 3 to 4 minutes.

Transfer fish to a plate lined with paper towels. Serve immediately, accompanied with *Skordalia*.

Note: Ouzo, the typical Greek drink similar to the French Ricard, adds an interesting aroma to the fried cod, but you can omit it or substitute dry white wine.

Mussels or Shrimp in White Wine

MIDIA OR GARIDES SAGANAKI

Mussels are eaten regularly in Thessalonica, Kavalla, and all over northern Greece. They are sold shucked, in small airtight plastic bags filled with seawater. The packaging and expiration date—no more than two days later—are stamped on the packet.

As in Athens, we rarely find mussels in the fishmarkets, so each time I travel to the north I always eat a lot of the local specialties: mussels dipped in batter and fried, cooked with rice, or this way in white wine, which I enjoy enormously.

At home, I usually cook imported frozen mussels or make this dish with shrimp. If you are not particularly fond of feta cheese, omit it and add more lemon juice. This recipe also makes a good appetizer, served in smaller portions.

¼ cup olive oil

5–6 scallions, coarsely chopped

1 pound shucked mussels, or
    2 pounds mussels in shell, briefly
    steamed and taken out of their
    shells; or 2 pounds shrimp, briefly
    steamed and peeled, leaving tail on

1 cup dry white wine

1 teaspoon dry mustard

½–1 teaspoon minced fresh chili
    pepper, or ⅓–⅔ teaspoon dried
    red pepper flakes

1½ cups chopped fresh flat-leaf
    parsley

½ cup water or fish stock

2–3 tablespoons lemon juice

¾ cup crumbled feta cheese

Sea salt to taste

SERVES 2–3

In a deep, heavy skillet, heat the olive oil and sauté the scallions for 2 minutes. Add the mussels or shrimps, and cook for 1 minute. Pour in the wine, and when it starts to boil, add the mustard, chili pepper, half the parsley, and the water or stock. Cook for about 3 minutes, then add the lemon juice, feta cheese, and the rest of the parsley. Do not stir, but shake the pan to distribute the ingredients evenly.

Remove from the heat, taste, and add salt if needed (usually feta cheese is quite salty). Let cool to just warm, and serve. It can also be refrigerated for 2 to 3 days. Serve at room temperature.

Fish Soup

KAKAVIA OR PSAROSOUPA

This is the way fish soup is made in the islands, and it goes without saying that the taste depends entirely on the freshness of the fish, as well as the quality of potatoes and the ripeness of tomatoes. At home, my mother used to make a fish and vegetable soup by boiling leeks, zucchini, carrots, and fennel bulbs before adding the fish to the stock. The cooked fish was removed from the stock and boned, and the cooked vegetables were passed through a food mill. The vegetable-enriched broth was served with the pieces of boned fish on the side.

This simple version of fish soup is sometimes thickened with *avgolemono*, egg-lemon sauce (page 158), at the end, which makes it richer and alters its taste a little.

5 cups water

4 large potatoes, each cut in
    4 lengthwise pieces

4 medium onions, halved

3 medium tomatoes, halved

¾ cup olive oil

3–4 pounds rockfish, sculpin,
    searobin, or sea bass, cleaned, with
    heads left on

Sea salt and freshly ground pepper

Juice of 2 large or 3 small lemons

SERVES 6

Put the water in a large saucepan and add the potatoes and onions. Bring to a boil and cook for 15 minutes, then add the tomatoes. After 10 minutes, add the oil and fish, and season generously with salt and pepper. Continue cooking for 15 minutes, then add the lemon juice. Cook until the flesh comes away from the bones of the fish.

Remove the potatoes, tomatoes, and onions with a skimmer and set on a plate. Strain the soup and reserve the broth and solids. Bone the fish and reserve meat.

Serve the broth in individual bowls. On a separate plate, serve the fish and vegetables.

THE CENTRAL FISH MARKET IN ATHENS.
Overleaf: FISH SOUP, HYDRA.

Barbecued Fish

PSARI PSITO STA KARVOUNA

Panagiotis Patiniotis, the owner of a small hotel and tavern in the village of Maltezana on Astypalaia, grills fish better than anyone else I know—in Greece or elsewhere. Panagiotis loves to grill fish, and he looks happy only when he stands by his old and rusted outdoor grill, turning his hinged fish grills over and over again, basting the fish and occasionally spraying the burning charcoal with water to reduce the heat.

It is difficult enough to grill one- or two-pound fish and to keep the fish moist and lightly scented with the wild oregano Panagiotis uses in the oil and lemon basting sauce. But he manages to grill eight- and nine-pound fish in this way, without letting them dry out at all. His trick is to turn the fish every couple of minutes, never letting one or the other side get overcooked.

Lemon juice
Red or gray mullet, goatfish, red
    snapper, sea bream (porgy),
    striped bass, or any other kind of
    white fish, preferably no smaller
    than 1 pound each, cleaned and
    left whole (about ¾ to 1 pound
    for each portion)
Sea salt

OIL AND LEMON BASTING SAUCE

2 parts olive oil
1 part lemon juice
Oregano
Sea salt and freshly ground pepper

One hour before cooking, pour lemon juice over the fish and turn them so they are moistened all over. Salt generously and set in a cool place or in the refrigerator.

Make the basting sauce by whisking the oil and lemon juice in a bowl. Add the oregano, salt, and pepper.

Prepare the charcoal fire. When ready, place the fish in a well-oiled hinged grill, baste them well with the sauce, and grill about 1 to 2 inches from the heat. The cooking time depends on the thickness of the fish, and you must be very careful not to let them overcook. As a rule, fish need 10 minutes of cooking for every inch of thickness.

While cooking, turn the hinged grill several times and baste the fish, so that they cook on both sides simultaneously.

When the fish are done, transfer them very carefully to a plate, pour a little of the basting sauce over, and serve immediately with the remaining basting sauce on the side.

Fried Whitebait

MARIDES TIGHANITES

Fried Whitebait—*marides* or *atherina* (as the smaller fish are called in Greek)—is a much-loved delicacy, enjoyed whenever one can find these tiny fish in the fishmarket. They are usually placed in the middle of the table, often served as an appetizer before the main fish course in island or seashore tavernas. The small fish are picked up and eaten with the fingers—bones and all. But they can also be served as a main course, accompanied with Steamed Amaranth Salad (page 84) or Country Tomato Salad (page 82).

1 pound whitebait
Olive and sunflower oil, for frying
Flour, for dredging
2 cloves garlic, minced
½ cup chopped flat-leaf parsley
1 lemon, quartered
Juice of 1 lemon

SERVES 2–3

Wash and drain the fish well. If very small—as they should be—no other cleaning is needed.

Pour the oil into a skillet to a depth of about ⅔ inch, and heat over high heat. Dredge the fish in flour, and stick every group of three together by their tails. Transfer to skillet with the help of a flat ladle or spatula. Fry in batches for 1 to 2 minutes on each side, or until golden and crisp. Place on paper towels to drain, keeping warm.

Transfer fish to a heated plate, and sprinkle each layer of fish with chopped garlic and parsley. Decorate with lemon quarters. Squeeze fresh lemon juice over the fish at the last minute and serve immediately.

Red Mullet on a Bed of Dill

BARBOUNIA PSITA
STON ANITHO

The recipe for this simple and delicious dish was given to me by a lady from Patras, a town on the western coast of the Peloponnese. Red mullet is a delicious Mediterranean goatfish, not related to the American gray mullet. Red mullet is sometimes available in American fishmarkets that specialize in Mediterranean fish. A good western hemisphere substitute, if you can find it, is Caribbean red goatfish.

4–5 red mullet, red goatfish, or red
    snapper, about 2 pounds, cleaned
    but with heads left on
Juice of 2 lemons
Sea salt
1 medium eggplant
3 green bell peppers
½ cup olive oil
3 cloves garlic, crushed
Bunch of fresh dill, about 15 branches
Freshly ground pepper to taste

SERVES 4–5

Wash the fish and drain in a colander for about 10 minutes. Transfer the fish to a plate. Whisk the juice of 1 lemon with a teaspoon of salt, and pour over the fish. Let the fish marinate in the refrigerator, turning at least once, for at least 1 to 2 hours.

Preheat the oven to 375° F.

Wash and dry the eggplant and peppers. Pierce the eggplant a couple of times with a fork and bake for 45 minutes. Broil the peppers, moving the rack as close to the source of heat as you can. Turn the peppers on all sides, and when the skin is black and blistered, put the peppers between sheets of a newspaper and set aside for 30 minutes. Remove the skin from the eggplant and peppers, and cut the flesh into small pieces.

Mix the remaining lemon juice, oil, and garlic and season with salt and pepper. Pour over the eggplant and peppers, toss well, and set aside.

Thirty minutes before serving, line a broiler pan with the dill, put the fish on top, brush sides with olive oil, and broil for 7 to 9 minutes on each side, brushing with oil when you turn fish.

Serve immediately, accompanied by the vegetables.

Squid or Cuttlefish Baked with Pasta

**KALAMARAKIA OR SOUPIES
ME MAKARONAKI**

A traditional Lenten dish, this squid or cuttlefish entree is usually cooked during Holy Week, but also during the week before the Annunciation of the Virgin Mary on August 15.

Unlike the Italians, Greeks hardly ever use squid or cuttlefish ink in cooking.

2 pounds medium squid or cuttlefish

1 cup olive oil

1½ cups chopped onions

3–4 cloves garlic, minced

2 cups dry red or white wine

**4 cups tomato puree, fresh or good-
    quality canned (see page 32)**

**1–2 fresh chili peppers, minced, or
    ⅓–½ teaspoon dried red pepper
    flakes**

1 cinnamon stick (optional)

4 cups fish or chicken stock

Sea salt and freshly ground pepper

1 pound ditali or elbow macaroni

1 cup chopped fresh dill

SERVES 6

To clean the squid or cuttlefish, pull to separate the body from the tentacles and head. The ink sac and the intestines will come out; cut off and discard them. Turn down the tentacles to uncover the mouth in the center. Cut it off and discard it. Take out the soft bone from the squid's pouch or the cuttlebone from the cuttlefish. Wash the pouch thoroughly, turning inside out.

Cut the pouch in ½- or 1-inch slices or rings, and the tentacles into 2 or 3 pieces each.

In a deep skillet, heat half of the olive oil over medium heat and sauté the onions until translucent, about 3 minutes. Add the squid and garlic, and sauté, turning with a wooden spoon, for 3 to 4 minutes.

Preheat the oven to 350° F.

Pour the wine into the skillet and simmer for 2 to 3 minutes. Add 2 cups of tomato puree, the chili peppers, cinnamon stick if using, and the remaining olive oil and cook for 20 to 30 minutes, or until the squid starts to soften.

Add the rest of the tomato puree together with the stock and some salt and pepper. When the mixture starts to boil, transfer to a deep earthenware pot. Add the pasta and mix well with a wooden spoon. Transfer to oven and bake for 25 to 35 minutes, or until the pasta and squid are tender. Stir 2 or 3 times during the cooking, adding a little more water or tomato puree if needed to keep mixture moist. Taste and add more salt or pepper if needed.

Sprinkle with dill and serve immediately.

Squid or Cuttlefish with Dill and Green Olives

**KALAMARAKIA ME ANITHO
KE PRASSINES ELIES**

This is a recipe from Crete, made with either fennel or dill. I prefer the taste of dill, which is added at the end of cooking so its aroma is not lost.

Originally the recipe called for fruity—but very salty—Greek cracked olives, which were added to the pan without being pitted, but I use pitted green olives here for convenience.

Serve with rice or steamed potatoes.

3 medium onions, coarsely chopped
1 pound fresh or frozen medium
    squid or cuttlefish, cleaned and cut
    into ½-inch rings
½ cup olive oil
3 cloves garlic, minced
1½ cups dry white wine
½–1 fresh chili pepper, minced,
    or ¼–½ teaspoon dried red
    pepper flakes
Pinch of sugar
1½ cups pitted green olives
1 cup chopped fresh dill
1½ teaspoons cornstarch dissolved in
    3–4 tablespoons lemon juice
Sea salt (optional)

In a heavy, nonreactive saucepan over medium heat, sauté the onions and squid in the olive oil until the onions are translucent, about 3 minutes. Add 2 cloves of garlic, and after 1 minute pour in the wine, then add the chili pepper and sugar. Reduce the heat to very low, add about 1 cup of water, and simmer for about 1 hour, or until the squid are tender and most of the sauce is absorbed.

Meanwhile, blanch the olives in boiling water to rid them of most of the salt, and drain.

Add the dill, remaining clove of garlic, and the olives to the pan. After 5 minutes, pour in the cornstarch–lemon juice mixture, stir, and cook for 1 to 2 minutes. Taste and add more lemon, some salt, or some more hot pepper.

Serve warm or cold.

SERVES 3–4

Bream Baked in Wine Sauce

FAGRI KRASSATO

Good-quality fresh fish is better when baked in a wine sauce, rather than in the tomato sauce we tend to overuse in Greece.

Fish cooked in this way can also be eaten cold, and that is one of the reasons I often serve it for summer lunches or dinners, when the last thing you want is to be trapped in front of a hot oven while your guests sip their icy drinks. Serve this accompanied by small steamed potatoes and Steamed Amaranth Salad (page 84).

2½- to 3-lb sea bream or bass, cleaned, with head left on
1½ cups dry white wine
Juice of 1 lemon
½ cup olive oil
1 tablespoon dried oregano
½–1 teaspoon minced fresh chili pepper, or ⅓–½ teaspoon dried red pepper flakes
Sea salt
3 medium onions, thinly sliced
1 cup chopped fresh flat-leaf parsley

SERVES 5–6

Rinse the fish and dry with paper towels.

Mix the wine, lemon juice, olive oil, oregano, some chili pepper, and salt to taste. Rub the fish with the marinade outside and in the cavity. Place the fish in a glass or clay baking dish just large enough to hold fish, stuff cavity with onion slices, remaining chili, salt, and some parsley, and pour the marinade over. Cover and set aside in the refrigerator for 2 to 3 hours. Take the fish out of the refrigerator at least 30 minutes before baking.

Preheat the oven to 350° F.

Spoon some marinade over the fish and bake uncovered, basting many times while it bakes. The fish is done after 30 to 35 minutes, or when it starts to flake easily. Remove from the oven and baste once more, then cover with aluminum foil.

Uncover after 5 minutes, sprinkle with the rest of the parsley, and serve.

METSOVO VINEYARDS.

Mackerel Wrapped in Vine Leaves

SKOUMBRI SE KLIMATOFILA

Even if you are familiar with the taste of vine leaves, you cannot imagine how good they are with mackerel, making this somewhat oily fish taste fresher and lighter. This recipe comes from Mytilini (Lesbos), where vine leaves are also used to separate layers of salted sardines.

This dish needs a lot of olive oil to cook, but you don't have to eat it all. Serve the cooked fish with a slotted spoon, skim the cooking liquid, and pour only the defatted sauce over the fish. Serve with steamed potatoes.

12–15 small mackerel (about 2 pounds total), cleaned and heads removed
Sea salt
2 medium onions, finely chopped
1 teaspoon dried oregano
Freshly ground black pepper
30 fresh or frozen vine leaves (see page 138)
Juice of 1 lemon
½ cup olive oil

SERVES 6

Rinse the mackerel and pat dry. Salt the stomach cavities and set aside for 15 minutes.

Mix onions and oregano, and season with salt and pepper.

Preheat the oven to 375° F.

Stuff each mackerel with the onion mixture, wrap in 1 or 2 vine leaves, and place in an oiled glass or clay baking dish. Mix the lemon juice and olive oil, and pour over the fish. Place dish in the oven and bake for about 30 minutes, adding a little water if necessary.

Serve hot or cold.

Crayfish in Garlic and Walnut Sauce

KARAVIDES SKORDALIA

I came across this delicious dish completely by chance.

We visited the Green Coast Restaurant, on the lake of Ioannina in northwestern Greece, looking for a suitable spot to photograph the Smoked Trout in Dill and Scallion Marinade (page 59).

We found our spot, and as we were preparing our shots, Mrs. Parthena Koloka, the owner, offered to cook us this specialty of hers. I had never heard of a dish like the one she described, but I quickly recognized the garlic and walnut sauce, which was similar to the one for Chicken in White Garlic Sauce (page 173).

The crayfish, picked from a nearby stream, were another surprise. The ones I had tasted many years ago in Florina, near the former Yugoslav border, were very different, and didn't turn so bright red when cooked.

After boiling and shelling the crayfish, Mrs. Koloka sautéed them in olive oil and then prepared the sauce. In my version I have omitted the sautéing, which made the dish heavy. Serve this with fresh Country Bread (page 194) and boiled wild greens.

About 40 crayfish
2 medium onions, quartered
2–3 stalks celery
1 cup dry white wine
Sea salt and freshly ground pepper

SAUCE

4–5 cloves garlic
Sea salt
2 tablespoons balsamic vinegar
2 tablespoons olive oil
1–1½ cups ground walnuts

SERVES 3-4

Wash the crayfish, place them in a pot, and cover with water. Add the onions, celery, wine, salt, and pepper. Bring to a boil and then boil for 8 to 10 minutes, or until crayfish are red. Remove with a skimmer and set aside to cool. Peel the meat from the tails, keeping some crayfish whole for decoration. Cover and set aside.

Crush the shells in a mortar and add them to the stock; they will give taste and a nice color. Boil until the liquid is reduced to about 3 cups. Strain the stock using a fine mesh sieve and discard the shells and solids.

Pound the garlic cloves in a mortar with some salt to obtain a paste. Add the vinegar and stir well.

In a large saucepan, heat the oil over medium heat and add the walnuts and the garlic paste. Cook briefly, then pour in the reduced stock. Cook, stirring with a wooden spoon, until the sauce thickens.

Place the crayfish tails in a deep dish, decorate with the whole crayfish, and pour the sauce over all. Serve immediately.

Fish Steaks in Tomato Sauce with Currants

FETES PSARIOU ME DOMATA
KE STAFIDES

This recipe from Kalamata, in the Peloponnese, originally called for salt cod, the cheapest fish and the only one available all over the country, even in places far from the sea. Soaked in water overnight, salt cod is used in a number of Greek dishes. But now that there is electricity in nearly all Greek villages—bringing with it refrigerators and frozen fish—all kinds of fish steaks or fillets are used for this dish.

The currants sweeten the tomato sauce, making it more interesting in taste and texture than the tomato sauce sweetened with sugar, which Greeks usually use.

4–6 small fish steaks such as
    swordfish or tuna
Olive oil, for frying
Flour, for dredging

SAUCE

⅓ cup olive oil
2 medium onions, thinly sliced
2–3 cloves garlic, minced
½–1 teaspoon minced fresh chili
    pepper, or ⅓–½ teaspoon dried
    red pepper flakes
⅓ cup dry red wine
1½ cups fresh or good-quality canned
    tomato puree (see page 32)
1 cup dried currants
Sea salt, to taste
4–6 thin slices fresh tomato
⅓ cup chopped fresh flat-leaf parsley

SERVES 4–6

Rinse the fish steaks and dry. Heat the olive oil over high heat in a skillet. Dip the fish in the flour and shake it to remove any excess. Brown the fish on both sides, just to seal their juices. They don't have to be cooked through, as they will continue to cook in the sauce. Transfer to paper towels.

Preheat the oven to 375° F.

In a heavy skillet, heat the olive oil and sauté the onions until translucent. Add the garlic and chili pepper, and pour the wine over them. Bring to a boil, let the sauce simmer for 1 minute, then add the tomato puree. Cook over high heat until the sauce thickens slightly. Add the currants and remove from the heat. Season with salt.

Arrange the fish steaks in a glass or clay baking dish and place a tomato slice on each. Pour the sauce over and bake for 20 to 30 minutes, or until fish flakes.

Sprinkle with the parsley and serve warm or at room temperature.

MONASTERIES BUILT LIKE EAGLE'S NESTS
ON TOP OF STEEP ROCKS, METEORA.

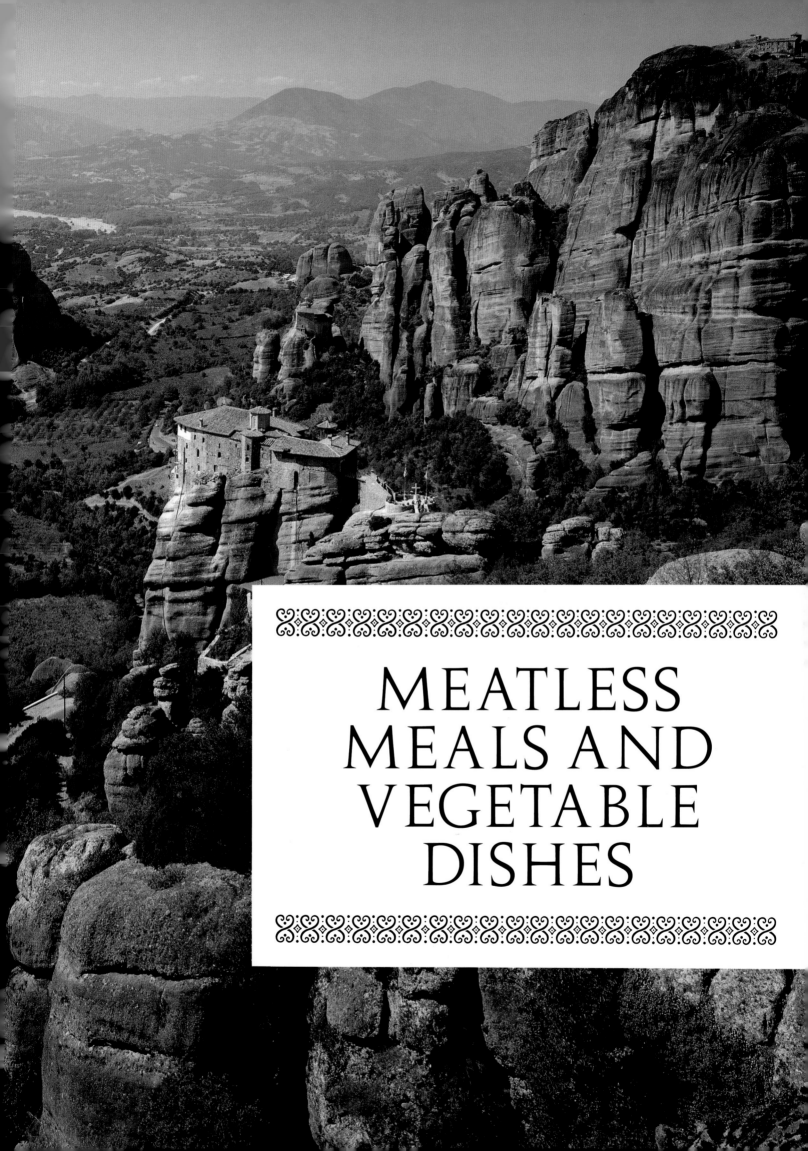

MEATLESS
MEALS AND
VEGETABLE
DISHES

I think the most interesting part of Greek cuisine is the many different ways we cook vegetables, legumes, and grains. Many Greek vegetarian recipes are so well balanced that the dishes seem to be conceived by modern nutritionists, but in fact the roots of these combinations lie far back in our history and folk traditions.

Greeks were not vegetarians by choice, although abstinence from meat was a doctrine of the philosopher Pythagoras of Samos, in the 6th century B.C. Later, the Greek Orthodox Church laid down strict dietary rules, prohibiting all foods derived from animals for forty days before Christmas and Easter, fifteen days before the Assumption of the Virgin Mary (August 15), and on many other occasions. Also, good Christians were not supposed to eat any food that came from animals on Wednesdays and Fridays.

With prosperity, Greeks have forgotten their old habits and tend to eat meat every day. But until thirty years ago, meat was expensive; it was considered a festive dish to be enjoyed on Sundays and maybe once more during the week. The rest of the time we made do with vegetables, legumes, and grains of all kinds.

Bean soup was considered the archetypal Greek dish, and many jokes were made about it. Ironically, now that every knowledgeable country considers our humble *Fassolada* (Lima Bean Soup, page 128) an ideal health food, we have almost forgotten it. It's getting more and more difficult to find the large lima beans called *gigantes* in supermarkets, because very few people still cook them.

Traditionally, the creative village cook worked miracles using the same seasonal garden vegetables every day. Stuffing them, frying them, making patties or pies with them, or using them in stews, salads, and soups, cooks have always made vegetables the principal ingredient in our traditional cuisine. Even when combined with meat or poultry, vegetables often play a leading role. You will still hear some people ask a waiter: "Just the potatoes and hold the meat" when ordering roast leg of lamb with potatoes, or "Just the greens" when ordering lamb and greens with white sauce. More often, they will say *"sketo apo youvetsi"* ("Just the pasta") when ordering *giouvetsi,* or roasted lamb with orzo.

LEGUMES

Most of the legumes we eat today were eaten in ancient Greece. Chick-peas were roasted and eaten as *tragemata,* or snacks, much as we eat our *stragalia* (roasted chick-peas) today. Just as Americans buy popcorn at the movies, Greeks buy a small paper bag full of *stragalia* or *passatempo* (salted roasted pumpkin seeds). Athenaeus liked lentils and mentioned them many times in his writings: "In the winter season, a bulb [wild hyacinth] and lentil soup is like ambrosia in the chilly cold." We still enjoy lentil soup on cold winter days.

PUMPKIN, ASTYPALAIA.

There are numerous passages in Athenaeus' *Deipnosophistai* that refer to what the translators call beans, but the Greek text specifies fava beans, about which much was written in antiquity because they sometimes cause severe reactions in people who are allergic. We also read about a legume called *calavance.* Its Greek name, *fasili,* came to mean "bean" in modern Greek, but the beans we now call *fasili* came to Greece much later from the New World.

Beans, fava beans, and—more rarely—chick-peas are also eaten fresh in season. When young, they are eaten in the pod. Fresh fava beans are shelled, peeled, and eaten raw in the spring as a snack to accompany ouzo, but they are also cooked in their pod with artichokes and carrots (page 120).

Dried legumes are a staple food for many Greeks. In remote villages, goat or sheep farmers trade their cheeses to the local grocery store in exchange for a sack of beans or lentils, the foundation of their winter diet.

RICE

Although rice is mentioned by Theophrastus (ca. 370–285 B.C.) and other Greek writers as a grain from India, it was not eaten regularly in Greece until the Byzantine Empire, and in the small, poor, and more remote villages it remained uncommon. Rice became a more highly prized delicacy when the Ottoman Turks conquered Greece, for the Turks loved their pilafs. Greeks still tell the story of the Ottomans' believing that paradise is a place where the mountains are piles of pilaf.

The memoirs of French and English adventurers who traveled through the country during the eighteenth century include descriptions of ceremonial meals they were offered. In many of these accounts, one pilaf came after the other, cooked in chicken or lamb stock, with or without meat. Greeks did not habitually prepare three-course meals; they just offered a series of similar dishes to honored guests, and rice always accompanied meat and poultry on these festive occasions.

Modern Greeks adore rice, which is made into a variety of pilafs, with vegetables or meat, but also plays an important role in most Greek stuffings. We also make desserts with it.

STUFFED OR WRAPPED VEGETABLES

Stuffed vegetables play an important role in the cooking of all Mediterranean countries. These dishes must have originated in ancient times as inexpensive variations on elaborately stuffed lamb, kid, and veal dishes served at symposia, the dinner parties of the rich in those ancient times.

Because most people grew vegetables and grains were also available, it was not difficult to create a combination that gave a new image and meaning to humble cabbages, vine leaves, and zucchini. Athenaeus speaks about "appetizers served in vine leaves" in *The Deipnosophistai* (written around A.D. 193), in which he quotes several writers and poets of classical Greece and Rome about the eating habits of their contemporaries and the different foods. Unfortunately we don't find any stuffed vegetable recipes in the book of Apicius, the well-known Roman gourmet. He probably thought them good only for the poor and underprivileged, who could not afford to travel from Rome to Libya to savor some shrimp, as he did.

In the Byzantine era, we see mentioned for the first time a dish consisting of rice and minced meat wrapped in cabbage leaves. It is none other than the very popular *dolmades* (which means "stuffed" in Turkish), a dish prepared all over Greece in many variations: mixtures wrapped in vine leaves, rolled in chopped parsley, in the flowers of zucchini, in diverse spinachlike wild greens, in dried apricots, and so forth.

Another big category of stuffed vegetables is generally called *gemista* ("stuffed"), and describes various vegetables such as tomatoes, peppers, zucchini, eggplant, and onions that have to be emptied of their flesh before being stuffed with minced meat, rice or cracked wheat, and all kinds of spices and herbs.

As I mentioned before, all stuffings come in two variations: with and without meat. Both are very tasty, but I prefer the stuffings without meat, known as *sarakostiana*. These can be prepared in advance and left in the refrigerator for one or two days, so the different flavors mix to perfection. Then they are eaten cold, with egg-lemon sauce or just plain yogurt.

MEATLESS PIES

In my father's house, when he was a child, every time an unexpected guest arrived, his mother "layed" a pie, as the Greek expression goes, using two or more pieces of phyllo that she prepared effortlessly. She stuffed it with anything she had in the house: cheese with eggs was the most common version, but wild greens, spinach, zucchini, eggplant, or any other vegetables—even pickled cabbage or salt cod or rice—was used to fill a pie. Leftovers, especially meat or poultry, are frequently used for pie fillings. The most famous Greek pies are coiled with home-made phyllo and filled with wild greens. These are made in Metsovo where the local women roll the pies with spectacular skill.

One of the most famous and delicious pies in Greece is the one prepared by Mrs. Kiki in her small taverna in the picturesque village square of Monodendri in Epirus. Kiki's pie is no more than a wrinkled piece of fairly thick phyllo, sprinkled with goat cheese and egg, and baked—or fried and baked—to a crisp perfection. She refuses to give her recipe, so you will have to rely on my version (see page 146).

Braised Okra with Tomato Sauce

BAMIES LADERES

Braised Okra is a very popular summer dish. On the islands and in the villages all over Greece you will find pans of okra in the sun, on rooftops, or on balconies, especially on Wednesdays and Fridays, the days when no meat is eaten.

This dish is somewhat time consuming to prepare, although less so than green beans. Frozen okra can be used very successfully.

Serve with fresh Country Bread (page 194) and feta cheese.

2 pounds fresh or frozen okra
Sea salt
½ cup red wine vinegar
½–¾ cup olive oil
3–4 medium onions, chopped
1½ cups chopped fresh flat-leaf parsley
½–1 teaspoon chopped fresh chili pepper, or ⅓–½ teaspoon dried red pepper flakes
3 cups finely chopped fresh or good-quality canned tomatoes

SERVES 4–6

Trim the okra close to the stem, dip the cut surface in salt, sprinkle with vinegar, and toss well. Let the okra stand for about 30 minutes in the sun or at room temperature, until it gives off a gummy juice. Rinse well and drain.

Heat the olive oil in a large, shallow, nonreactive pan with a cover and sauté the onions over medium heat until translucent, about 3 minutes. Add the okra, parsley, and chili pepper. Season with salt and add the tomatoes. Reduce the heat to low, cover, and simmer for 30 to 45 minutes, or until the okra is tender but not mushy. Do not stir, but shake the pan occasionally to prevent sticking. Check the amount of liquid in the pan regularly and add a little water if needed.

Serve hot or cold.

Baked Squash with Garlic and Walnut Sauce

KOLOKITHA STO FOURNO
ME SKORDO KE KARIDIA

Big winter squashes appear in Greek markets in late September. As they are very large, they are usually sold in pieces. People from different regions use squashes to make wildly different dishes, such as squash cooked in syrup and studded with almonds, savory squash pie with leeks and cheese, sweet squash pie with cinnamon and sugar, and baked squash with garlic sauce. This last dish, which comes from Macedonia, is one of my favorites. Serve it as a main course with bread and a gruyère-type cheese, or as an accompaniment to grilled meat, chicken, or sausages.

1½ pounds winter squash, such
    as butternut

GARLIC AND WALNUT SAUCE

5–6 large cloves garlic
5 tablespoons balsamic vinegar
⅓ cup dry white wine
1 thick slice of bread, soaked in water
    and squeezed dry
1 teaspoon minced fresh chili pepper,
    or freshly ground black pepper
1 cup finely ground walnuts
⅓ cup olive oil
Sea salt
½ cup coarsely chopped walnuts

SERVES 4-6

Cut the squash into small sections, discard the seeds, and cut the flesh from the skin using a very sharp knife. Cut the flesh into very thin slices.

Preheat the oven to 375° F.

Oil a glass or earthenware baking dish and arrange half the squash slices in 1 layer, one slice overlapping another by about one-third to one-half.

Prepare the sauce. In a mortar or food processor, pound the garlic, vinegar, wine, bread, chili pepper, and finely ground walnuts until smooth. Add half the olive oil, little by little. Taste and season with salt, more vinegar, and more pepper, if needed. This thick sauce should have a very strong flavor.

Spoon half of the sauce over the first layer of squash slices, and make another layer using the remaining slices. Spoon the rest of the sauce over the squash and the rest of the olive oil on top.

Bake for 20 to 30 minutes, or until the squash is soft but not mushy. Sprinkle with the coarsely chopped walnuts about 10 minutes before the squash is done.

Serve warm or at room temperature.

Potato and Olive Stew with Tomato Sauce

PATATES YAHNI ME ELIES

Potatoes were introduced to Greece in the early nineteenth century by Ioannis Kapodistrias, our first governor, after the revolution that freed Greece from Turkish domination. There is an amusing story about their introduction that is a good indication of the Greek character.

At that time, the nation's capital was at Nauplia, in the Peloponnese. The enlightened governor wanted to give potatoes to the people, thinking that they would be an ideal food for the starving nation, but nobody wanted to try them. So, one day he stacked some potatoes by the Nauplia harbor and placed an armed soldier to guard them, proclaiming that whoever stole even one was going to be executed. By the next day all the potatoes had disappeared. (In fact, the impoverished people of the Peloponnese were grateful for any food after the overthrow of Turkish rule, so this story has no historical validity.)

The recipe for this delicious potato stew comes from the island of Zante in the Ionian Sea. Serve with feta cheese.

½–¾ cup olive oil

2 pounds new potatoes, peeled and quartered

3 large onions, thickly sliced

5–6 cloves garlic, sliced

½–1 teaspoon minced fresh chili pepper, or ⅓–½ teaspoon dried red pepper flakes

½ cup dry white wine

1 teaspoon dried oregano

2 cups chopped fresh or good-quality canned tomatoes

1 cup small black olives, rinsed and pitted

Sea salt

½ cup chopped fresh flat-leaf parsley

SERVES 2–3

In a large, heavy, and deep nonreactive skillet, heat the olive oil over high heat and sauté the potatoes until they turn a golden brown on all sides, about 5 minutes. They don't need to cook through because they will continue cooking in the sauce.

Preheat the oven to 375° F.

Remove the potatoes from the skillet and add the onions. Sauté until transparent, about 3 minutes, then add the garlic and chili pepper. After a few seconds, pour in the wine and add the oregano, tomatoes, and olives. Cook for 1 minute, then remove from the heat.

Place the potatoes in a clay or glass ovenproof pan that can hold them in 1 layer. Pour the sauce over them, and bake uncovered for 30 to 45 minutes—adding a little water if needed—or until the potatoes are tender. Taste after 15 minutes and add more salt if needed—the olives are quite salty—or more chili pepper. Sprinkle with the parsley and serve while still hot.

THREE LENTEN DISHES, PHOTOGRAPHED IN METEORA: LEEK RICE (page 135), POTATO AND OLIVE STEW WITH TOMATO SAUCE, GREEN BEAN AND OKRA STEW WITH CRACKED WHEAT (page 117).

Braised Green Beans and Potatoes with Tomato Sauce

FASSOLAKIA LADERA

Stuffed tomatoes and peppers and *Fassolakia Ladera* are the principal Greek summer dishes. We buy fresh, tender green beans from the street markets and all members of the family help string and prepare them for cooking.

In most Greek kitchens a good vegetable knife is considered an unnecessary luxury, so preparing the beans is not easy—it is very hard to string green beans with an unsuitable knife. Nevertheless, many cooks make these beans at least once a week because everybody loves them.

Some cooks add zucchini to the pot to extend the dish with a vegetable that is much easier to prepare. You can also serve the green beans as an accompaniment to lamb, chicken, or veal in tomato sauce. Runner beans are best for this dish, but you can also use thin, young green beans. Needless to say, fresh beans taste much better and are usually more tender than frozen ones.

Serve this dish with fresh Country Bread (page 194) and feta cheese.

2 pounds fresh or frozen whole runner or young green beans

½–¾ cup olive oil

3–4 medium onions, chopped

1½ cups chopped fresh flat-leaf parsley

½–1 teaspoon chopped fresh chili pepper, or ⅓–½ teaspoon dried red pepper flakes

3–4 medium potatoes, peeled and cut into 1-inch cubes

Sea salt

3 cups finely chopped fresh or good-quality canned tomatoes

SERVES 4–6

Using a very sharp knife, trim the strings from both sides of the beans, then slice each bean in half lengthwise. You can also use a string-bean slicer.

Heat half the olive oil over medium heat in a large, shallow, nonreactive pan with a cover and sauté the onions until translucent, about 3 minutes. Add the beans, parsley, and chili pepper, and mix well. Arrange the potatoes on top of the beans in one layer, season with salt, and pour the tomatoes and the rest of the olive oil over them.

Reduce the heat to low, cover, and simmer for 30 to 45 minutes, or until the potatoes are cooked and most of the juices have been absorbed. Do not stir, but occasionally shake the pan a little to prevent sticking. Check the amount of liquid regularly and add a little water if needed. Remove the pan from the heat and let the beans cool for 15 minutes before serving.

Note: The beans can be eaten hot or cold, and are equally tasty the next day, but the potatoes should be eaten when they are still warm.

Green Bean and Okra Stew with Trahana or Bulgur

FASSOLAKIA KE BAMIES ME PLIGURI

Sometimes grains are added to simple vegetable dishes to make them more nourishing. Bulgur, or cracked wheat, takes on a delicious flavor when you cook it with green beans and okra.

This dish was described to me by a distant relative who comes from Thessaly. She told me that she has never cooked it herself—she considers it to be a dish fit only for poor persons—but she remembers it from her childhood.

Serve with fresh Country Bread (page 194) and feta cheese.

⅔ pound green beans

⅔ pound fresh okra

½–¾ cup olive oil

3–4 medium onions, chopped

1½ cups chopped fresh flat-leaf parsley

½–1 teaspoon chopped fresh chili pepper, or ⅓–½ teaspoon dried red pepper flakes

Sea salt

3 cups finely chopped fresh or good-quality canned tomatoes

1½ cups Sour or Sweet *Trahana* (page 206) or bulgur

1 cup warm water

SERVES 4–6

Using a sharp knife, trim the strings from both sides of the beans, then slice each bean in half lengthwise. You can also use a string-bean slicer.

Trim the okra close to the stem, dip the cut surface in salt, sprinkle with vinegar, and toss well. Let the okra stand for about 30 minutes in the sun or at room temperature, until it gives off a gummy juice. Rinse well and drain.

Heat the olive oil in a large, shallow, nonreactive pan with a cover and sauté the onions over medium heat until translucent, about 3 minutes. Add the beans, okra, parsley, and chili pepper. Season with salt and add the tomatoes.

Reduce the heat to low, cover, and simmer for 30 to 45 minutes, or until the beans and okra are tender but not mushy.

About 15 minutes before the end of the cooking, add the *trahana* or bulgur and the warm water. Don't stir the food, but shake the pan a little to avoid sticking. Simmer for another 10 to 15 minutes, checking constantly to see if more water is needed. The vegetables should be quite moist when cooked.

Taste and adjust the seasoning. Remove from the heat and set aside, covered, for 5 minutes, until the bulgur has absorbed the liquid.

Baked Mixed Vegetables

BRIAM

During our summer holidays, we used to prepare this classic dish early in the morning. We would leave it with the village baker on our way to the beach, then pick it up baked on the way home. The top was always a little burned, but that did not spoil the taste.

Don't be appalled by the amount of olive oil in the recipe. The vegetables need it to cook, otherwise they will be dry and tasteless. You don't need to eat it all—you can leave most of it in the pan by serving the vegetables with a slotted spoon.

Serve with fresh Country Bread (page 194) and feta cheese.

1 pound eggplant, cut in ⅓-inch slices
1 pound zucchini, cut in ⅓-inch slices
Sea salt
1 cup olive oil
4 medium onions, chopped
½–1 chili pepper, minced, or about
　½ teaspoon freshly ground pepper
4 cloves garlic, minced
1 pound medium potatoes, cut in
　⅓-inch slices
½ pound green bell peppers, diced
1 teaspoon dried oregano
3 cups fresh or good-quality canned
　tomato puree (see page 32)

SERVES 4–6

Sprinkle the eggplant and zucchini slices with salt and place in a colander. Let drain for 30 minutes, then rinse and drain on paper towels.

Preheat the oven to 400° F.

In a skillet, heat ⅓ cup olive oil over medium heat and sauté the onions until soft, about 5 minutes. Add the chili pepper and garlic, mix well, and remove from the heat.

Oil an earthenware baking dish. Arrange alternating slices of potato, eggplant, and zucchini in rows, letting each slice overlap the previous one by two-thirds. Scatter the bell pepper between the rows of the vegetables and sprinkle with the oregano. Pour the tomato puree over the vegetables, season with salt, and top with the rest of the olive oil.

Bake, uncovered, for about 1½ hours, or until the vegetables are tender and most of the liquid has evaporated, checking from time to time to see if more water is needed.

Serve warm or cold.

Artichoke, Carrot, and Fresh Fava Bean Stew

AGINARES KE KOUKIA LADERA

A typical spring dish, this can be prepared only during the brief period when fresh, tender fava beans and artichokes are plentiful. Carrots, with their sweet taste, are added to all Greek artichoke dishes.

If you can't find fresh fava beans, you can always make this dish without them and enjoy the delicious, lemony flavor of the artichokes and carrots.

1 whole lemon and the juice of
   2 lemons
6–7 artichokes, about 2½–3 inches
   in diameter
1 pound fresh young fava beans in
   their pods (optional)
½ cup olive oil
2 medium onions, chopped
5–6 scallions, chopped
3 medium carrots, peeled and cut
   into thick slices
5–6 dill sprigs, chopped
Freshly ground pepper or minced
   fresh chili pepper to taste
Sea salt

SERVES 4

Pour about 4 cups of water into a bowl and add the lemon juice. Remove the hard outer leaves of the artichokes with a sharp knife and keep snapping off leaves at the base until you are left with a soft cone formed by the inner leaves and the heart. Cut the lemon in half and rub the cut surfaces of the artichokes to prevent discoloration. Trim the green tops of the cones, and with a teaspoon, remove the chokes. Halve the artichokes, rubbing the cut surfaces with a lemon half, and place in the lemon water.

With a sharp knife, string the pods of the fava beans.

In a large sauté pan, heat the olive oil over medium heat and sauté the onions and scallions until transparent, about 3 minutes. Drain the artichokes, reserving the lemon water, and add to the pan, followed by the carrots and fava beans. Pour in about 2 cups of the lemon water. Season with the pepper and salt, bring to a boil, reduce the heat, and simmer for about 10 minutes. Add the fava beans and continue cooking for 10 minutes more.

Add the dill and cook for another 10 to 15 minutes, adding more water if necessary, until all the vegetables are tender. Taste and correct the seasoning, then serve hot, cold, or at room temperature.

CAPER PLANTS, SANTORINI.

Mashed Yellow Split Peas with Tomato-Braised Capers

FAVA ME KAPARI

This variation of *fava* is found only on the island of Santorini. There and on Siphnos—another Cycladic island—fresh capers, just picked from the bushes, are frequently used in summer cooking. The capers are also preserved by drying them in the sun, not by pickling them as is done in the rest of Greece.

These fresh or dried capers are combined with tomatoes to make a very tasty sauce that flavors the bland *fava*. Serve with fresh Country Bread (page 194) and feta cheese or cured fish such as mackerel or Salted Sardines (page 62).

½ pound yellow split peas
1 tablespoon salt
1 teaspoon dried oregano

SAUCE

½ cup fresh, dried, or pickled capers
   (see Note)
⅓ cup olive oil
2–3 medium onions, chopped
2 cups fresh or good-quality canned
   tomato puree (see page 32)
½ teaspoon minced fresh chili pepper,
   or dried red pepper flakes
1 tablespoon sugar (if pickled capers
   are used)
1 cinnamon stick (optional)

SERVES 4

Rinse the peas and put them in a heavy pot with cold water to cover. Add the salt and bring to a boil. Skim, reduce the heat, add oregano, and simmer for 30 to 45 minutes, or until the peas absorb most of the water and turn into a smooth paste. (*Note:* Don't leave *fava* to cook unattended. These peas have the tendency to stick to the bottom of the pan and burn. So stir frequently and add more water if needed.) Remove from the heat and let cool for about 15 minutes. The mixture thickens, and can even be cut into shapes.

If you are using fresh capers, soak them in cold water for at least 30 minutes, then blanch briefly in boiling water. Rinse again with cold water and drain. Dried capers also need to be soaked for 30 minutes; pickled and soaked capers should be rinsed well and blanched briefly to rid them of their salty taste.

In a deep skillet, heat the oil over medium heat and sauté the onion until tender, about 5 minutes. Add the tomato puree, capers, chili pepper, sugar, and cinnamon stick. Lower the heat and simmer until the sauce thickens and the capers are tender, about 10 to 15 minutes. Remove the cinnamon stick, taste, and season with salt, if necessary.

Serve the *fava* in a bowl and the caper sauce alongside. Place 2 or 3 spoonfuls of *fava* and 1 spoonful of sauce on each plate and serve.

Note: If you are using pickled capers, soak them in water overnight.

Mashed Yellow Pea Soup

FAVA SOUPA

This very easy and delicious soup was served frequently when I was a child, but I hated it. I was always punished because I refused to eat it. Now I love it and make it all the time. I serve it with fresh Country Bread (page 194) and feta cheese or with Salted Sardines (page 62) or any other kind of cured fish.

½ pound yellow split peas
6 cups water
1 tablespoon salt
1 teaspoon dried oregano
⅓–⅔ cup olive oil
2–3 cloves garlic, finely chopped
½–1 fresh chili pepper, minced; or
⅓ teaspoon dried red pepper flakes
1 cup dry white wine or water
Sea salt

SERVES 4

Rinse the peas and put them in a heavy pot with the water. Add the salt and bring to a boil. Skim, add oregano, then reduce the heat and simmer for 30 to 45 minutes, or until peas absorb most of the water and turn into a smooth paste. (*Note:* Don't leave *fava* to cook unattended. The peas have a tendency to stick to the bottom of the pan and burn. So stir frequently and add more water if needed.)

Transfer the *fava* paste to a bowl, wipe the pot dry with paper towels, and warm the olive oil in it. Sauté the garlic briefly, add the chili pepper, and pour in the wine if using or water. Add the fava and another 2 to 3 cups of water to obtain a creamy but pourable soup. Simmer for 10 to 15 minutes; taste and season with salt and pepper. Serve warm.

FRESHLY PEELED YELLOW SPLIT PEAS,
THE SPECIALTY OF SANTORINI.

Mashed Yellow Split Peas

FAVA

We know from ancient Greek texts that our forebears ate a lot of legumes. Because the legumes were tough and needed to be boiled for endless hours, the ancient Greeks used to grind them first and then boil them in water, making a kind of puree. They seasoned the mixture with *garos*, the famous fermented fish sauce called *garum* by the Romans, which flavored almost every food they consumed.

Today, Greeks have better-quality legumes. But we are still attached to our *fava*, flavored now with a lot of herbs. Although in Turkey and other Mediterranean countries *fava* is made from fava beans, in Greece only the peeled yellow split peas are used. In fact, only they are called "*fava*" in Greek.

The best yellow split peas were grown on Santorini, before the island became so full of tourists. Now very few are grown there, but the inscription "Santorinis fava," which signifies high quality, can still be found on big sacks of yellow split peas in the central market of Athens.

Boiling the split peas requires a lot of attention because, if the water evaporates, they stick and burn easily. The Greeks have a saying: "It tastes as bad as burned *fava*." There is no alternative but to throw everything away and start again.

Fava is usually eaten cold, either as a main course or as an appetizer, accompanied by *lakerda* (cured mackerel) in oil and lemon sauce or sardines.

½ pound yellow split peas
1 tablespoon sea salt
1⅔ teaspoons dried oregano, plus
    more for serving
⅓–½ cup olive oil
1 teaspoon mustard
Juice of 1 lemon
3 scallions (white part plus 2 inches
    of green), chopped
Sea salt and freshly ground black
    pepper to taste
½ cup chopped arugula (optional)
½ cup chopped fresh dill
3 tablespoons capers, for garnish

Rinse the peas and put them in a pot with cold water to cover. Add the salt and bring to a boil, then reduce the heat, add the oregano, and simmer for 30 to 45 minutes, or until peas have absorbed most of the water and turned into a smooth paste. (*Note:* Never leave *fava* to cook unattended. It has a tendency to stick to the bottom of the pan and burn. Stir frequently and add more water if needed.)

Remove pot from the heat and let peas cool for about 15 minutes. The fava will thicken and can even be cut with a knife when completely cold.

Just before serving, add the oil, mustard, lemon juice, and scallions, and mix with a fork. Taste and season with salt and pepper. Sprinkle with arugula and fresh dill and top with capers and additional oregano.

SERVES 4

Lentil Soup

FAKI

Athenaeus mentions *faki* frequently—it seems that it was the ancient Greeks' favorite winter soup. They considered lentils to be especially nourishing, so the painter Agatharchus depicted Orestes eating lentils when he was recovering from illness. But the ancients must have used an abundance of spices in their lentil soups—they had a proverb stating, "A wise man does everything wisely and in lentil soup, uses spices in moderation."

In one of the recipes of Apicius, the Roman author of the earliest extant cookbook, a lot of coriander, mint, oregano, fennel seeds, wine, honey, vinegar, leeks, and vegetable juices are used to flavor the Roman version of lentil soup.

In this version of the classic dish, bay leaves and garlic give fragrance, while tomato and vinegar provide the acidity needed to set off the sweetness of the lentils.

Serve as a main course with cured fish—*lakerda*, sardines, or smoked herring—or better yet with Smoked Herring Spread (*Rengosalata*, page 57) and fresh Country Bread (page 194).

2 cups large green lentils

1½ quarts water

3 bay leaves

½ cup olive oil

3–4 medium onions, chopped

3–4 cloves garlic, finely chopped

½–1 fresh chili pepper, minced

3 cups fresh or good-quality canned tomato puree (see page 32)

2 tablespoons tomato paste

1 tablespoon dry mustard

Sea salt

⅓ cup red wine vinegar, or more

½ cup chopped fresh dill

Rinse the lentils and place in a large pot with the water and the bay leaves. Bring to a boil, strain, and discard the water. Add more water and bring to a boil again, then reduce the heat, and simmer for 20 to 30 minutes.

In a skillet, heat the olive oil over medium heat and sauté the onions until soft, about 3 minutes. Add the garlic and chili pepper, and transfer the sautéed vegetables and cooking oil to the pot with the lentils. Add the tomato puree and paste and the mustard, stir well, and continue simmering for another 30 minutes, or until lentils are tender, adding a little more water if necessary.

Season with salt and vinegar, and remove the bay leaves. Taste and add more salt and vinegar if needed.

Serve hot, sprinkling each soup plate with fresh dill.

SERVES 6–8

Baked Chick-peas

REVITHIA STO FOURNO

On the island of Siphnos they still make special clay casseroles for this dish, which were left to cook slowly overnight in the communal village oven.

1 pound dried chick-peas, soaked in
    water overnight
2 tablespoons dried oregano
1 cup olive oil
3 medium onions, sliced
1 fresh chili pepper, finely chopped
4 cloves garlic, minced
Sea salt

SERVES 6

Drain the chick-peas and place in a pot, cover with cold water, and bring to a boil. Skim surface and reduce the heat, then sprinkle with 1 tablespoon of oregano and simmer for 1 hour. Strain the chick-peas, reserving the liquid.

Preheat the oven to 300° F.

Heat the olive oil in a skillet over medium heat and sauté the onions and chili pepper until soft, about 5 minutes. Remove from the heat and add the garlic, remaining oregano, and chick-peas. Mix well, season with salt, and transfer to an earthenware or glass oven-proof casserole with a cover. Add about 2 cups of the reserved liquid, mix well, cover, and bake for 1 to 1½ hours, or until the chick-peas are tender. Add a little more liquid during cooking, if needed.

PEELING SOAKED CHICK-PEAS.
Left: BAKED CHICK-PEAS AND MASHED YELLOW PEA SOUP, ASTYPALAIA.

Lima Bean Soup

FASSOLADA

As I mentioned in the introduction to this chapter, *Fassolada* was considered the Greek national dish some years ago and many jokes were made about it. But now it's getting more and more difficult to find good-quality beans to produce the thick soup I remember from my childhood. It seems as though people got fed up with it and no longer cook it, and so no effort is being made to grow good beans. Fortunately, I have friends in Kastoria—where good-quality beans are still cultivated—and they send me my year's supply.

Many Greeks, including my mother, believe that adding dry mustard to legume dishes eliminates their unpleasant side effects.

1½ cups dried lima beans, soaked in
    water overnight
2½ quarts water
½ cup olive oil
3 medium onions, coarsely chopped
2 medium carrots, peeled and sliced
2–3 stalks celery with leaves,
    coarsely chopped
2 green bell peppers, diced
1 fresh chili pepper, minced
Sea salt
3 tablespoons tomato paste
1 tablespoon dry mustard
Juice of ½ lemon, or more

SERVES 4–6

Drain the beans and place in a large pot. Add the water and bring to a boil. Drain and discard the water. Pour cold water over the beans and bring to a boil again, then reduce the heat and simmer for 30 minutes.

In a skillet, heat the oil over medium heat and sauté the onions, carrots, celery, bell peppers, and chili pepper until the onions are translucent, about 3 minutes. Pour the sautéed vegetables with the cooking oil into the pot with the beans. Season with salt and add the tomato paste and mustard, stirring well to dissolve them. Continue simmering the beans for 30 minutes more, or until beans are tender.

Ladle out 1½ cups of the soup mixture and pass it through the fine disk of a food mill or puree in a blender or food processor. Return puree to the pot and add the lemon juice. Taste and add more lemon juice and salt if needed. Serve hot.

Note: Fassolada can be kept 2 to 3 days in the refrigerator and reheated just before serving.

PEELING LARGE
LIMA BEANS, METSOVO.

Large Lima Beans in Garlic Sauce

GIGANTES SKORDATI

Gigantes, which means "extremely large" in Greek, is what the Greeks call the very large lima beans used for this dish, a typical main course all over Greece during Lent and an appetizer year-round. These beans are usually baked in a spicy tomato sauce, but I prefer this simpler version, which is more common in northern Greece. The beans, scented with the garlic and dill, have a lovely sweet taste that they lose when tomatoes are added to the sauce.

1 pound large lima beans, soaked in
    water overnight
2 tablespoons dried oregano
⅔–1 cup olive oil
2 medium onions, sliced
½–1 teaspoon finely chopped fresh
    chili pepper, or ⅓–½ teaspoon
    dried red pepper flakes
6 cloves garlic, coarsely chopped
1 cup dry white wine
1½ cups chopped fresh dill
1 tablespoon dry mustard
Sea salt

SERVES 6

Drain the beans and place in a pot, cover with cold water, and bring to a boil. Skim surface, then reduce the heat, sprinkle with 1 tablespoon of oregano, and simmer for about 1 hour, or until the beans start to become tender. Drain the beans, reserving the liquid.

Preheat the oven to 300° F.

Heat the olive oil in a skillet over medium heat and sauté the onions and chili pepper until soft, about 5 minutes. Remove from the heat and add the garlic, the rest of the oregano, the wine, 1 cup of dill, mustard, and the beans. Mix well, season with salt, and transfer to an earthenware or glass ovenproof casserole with cover. Add about 1½ cups of the reserved cooking liquid, mix well, cover the casserole, and bake for about 1 hour, or until the beans are soft and most of the liquid has evaporated. Add a little more liquid during cooking, if needed.

Sprinkle with the rest of the chopped dill and serve warm.

Small Olive Pies

ELIOPITES

These very tasty individual pies, which originated in Cyprus, are somewhere between olive bread and a more traditional Greek pie. Despite the universal use of olive oil, olives themselves are not used very much in Greek cooking. This recipe is my adaptation of the traditional dish. You can make the pies smaller, using half as much dough, or divide the pastry in half and make a whole round or square pie.

PASTRY

1 package (1 tablespoon) active
    dry yeast
2 cups warm water
½ teaspoon sugar
5 cups all-purpose flour
1 teaspoon sea salt
¼ cup lemon juice
½ cup olive oil

FILLING

⅓ cup olive oil
2 medium onions, chopped
2 leeks (white part plus 2 inches of
    the green), chopped
1½ cups black Amphissa olives, pitted
    and halved
¼ cup pine nuts (optional)
⅔ cup chopped fresh parsley
⅓ cup chopped fresh mint

Olive oil, for brushing

MAKES 14 PIES

Dilute the yeast with 1 cup warm water and add the sugar. Let stand for 5 minutes, until it starts to froth.

In a large bowl, sift the flour and add the salt. Make a well in the center and pour in the yeast mixture, lemon juice, olive oil, and remaining water. Mix with a wooden spoon. Turn out onto a floured surface and knead well to obtain a soft, shiny, elastic dough. Add a little more flour or water if needed. Form dough into a ball, cover it, and let stand in a warm place as you prepare the filling.

In a skillet, heat the olive oil over medium heat and sauté the onions and leeks until soft and translucent, about 3 minutes. Add the olives, pine nuts, parsley, and mint, and remove from the heat.

Divide the dough into 14 pieces, and form each piece into a disk about the size of a saucer. To fill the pies, put 2 tablespoons of filling on each disk, brush the edges with a little water, and fold in half to make half-circles. Press the borders with your fingers to seal them and transfer to an oiled pan.

Brush pies with a little olive oil. Place in a 145° F. oven for 20 minutes, then turn up the heat to 375° F. and bake for about 45 minutes, or until golden brown. Place on a rack to cool and serve warm or cold.

Note: Instead of brushing with olive oil, you can brush the pies with water and sprinkle with sesame seeds.

SMALL OLIVE PIES
IN AN OLIVE GROVE, KANTZA.

Vegetarian Moussaka

MOUSSAKAS NISTISIMOS

My mother and her family called this dish *Pseudo-moussaka,* and I presumed that it was a name used by all Greeks. But once in Heraklion, Crete, I mentioned it in a conversation and everybody laughed. They thought I had created a fancy name for a nameless dish, usually referred to as Baked Eggplant with Tomato Sauce.

If you omit the cheese, this is one more Lenten version of a popular dish (see also page 184).

2–3 medium eggplants
Sea salt
3 large green bell peppers
⅓ cup olive oil
1 very large or 2 small potatoes,
   thinly sliced

TOMATO SAUCE

2 large onions, coarsely chopped
   (about 2 cups)
1 large green bell pepper, diced
1½ teaspoons minced fresh chili
   pepper, or to taste
½ cup dry red wine
5 large tomatoes, peeled and diced
   (about 2½ cups)
4 large garlic cloves, minced
Grated nutmeg
Ground cinnamon (optional)
½ cup dark raisins
1 tablespoon sea salt, or to taste

1 cup feta cheese, crumbled
½ cup ground walnuts
2 ripe tomatoes, peeled and sliced
½ cup bread crumbs
Sea salt and freshly ground pepper

Cut off the stems from the eggplants and peel in strips, leaving roughly half the skin on the eggplants. Cut across into ⅓-inch slices. Salt well on both sides, and leave in a colander for at least 30 minutes to drain and rid of bitterness.

Cut the peppers in halves or in thirds lengthwise to obtain flat pieces. Discard the stems and seeds, and place under the broiler, skin side up. Roast for about 10 minutes, or until the skins blister and turn black. Remove from the oven, place in a bowl, and cover with a plastic wrap or aluminum foil. Let stand for 10 to 15 minutes, then peel.

Rinse the eggplant slices under running water and pat dry with paper towels. Brush both sides with olive oil, and broil, turning once, for 10 to 15 minutes, or until both sides are golden.

Heat the remaining oil in a nonreactive frying pan over high heat and fry the potatoes for 3 to 4 minutes, until just soft. Remove with a ladle and arrange in a layer on the bottom of a clay or glass baking dish (about 15½ × 10½ inches). It doesn't matter if some gaps are left between slices.

In the oil in which you have fried the potatoes, sauté the onions, bell pepper, and chili pepper until the onions are translucent, about 3 minutes. Add the wine and cook for about 2 minutes. Add the tomatoes and simmer for about 10 minutes. Add the garlic, nutmeg, a little cinnamon, and the raisins. Simmer for another 10 minutes, or until the sauce starts to thicken. Taste and add more salt and chili pepper if needed. The sauce should be quite strongly flavored.

Preheat the oven to 375° F.

SERVES 10

Arrange the eggplant slices on top of the potatoes. Spoon half the tomato sauce over them. Sprinkle with the feta cheese and walnuts. Cover with the broiled peppers, spoon the rest of the tomato sauce over the peppers, and spread evenly. Top with the tomato slices, sprinkle with the bread crumbs, and season with a little salt and freshly ground pepper.

Place on the bottom rack of the oven and bake for 1 hour. Check after 45 minutes and if the top has browned, cover loosely with aluminum foil for the rest of the cooking time.

Let cool completely on a rack before serving.

Rice with Chick-peas and Currants

PILAFI ME REVITHIA KE STAFIDES

A traditional dish of chick-peas and rice with currants is still served at weddings in Konya (Iconium), a once-Greek city in Asia Minor. My friend Vali Manouilidi, who grew up in Istanbul, told me that rice with chick-peas was the traditional New Year's dish in her home. The recipe calls for the chick-peas and the rice to be cooked separately and drained. Currants are added and a lot of browned butter is poured over the dish just before serving.

In Thessaly, in central Greece, there is a fantastic rice and chick-pea pilaf that I find much more interesting. So the recipe that follows is my combination of both these dishes.

1 cup chick-peas, soaked in water
    overnight
½ cup olive oil
2 medium onions, chopped
1 cup long-grain rice
½ cup dry white wine
Juice of 1 lemon, or more
½–1 teaspoon minced fresh chili
    pepper, or ⅓–½ teaspoon dried
    red pepper flakes
½ cup dried currants (optional)
Sea salt
½ cup grated kefalotyri or pecorino
    cheese (optional)

SERVES 4–6

Drain the chick-peas and place in a large pot. Cover with water and cook over low heat for 45 minutes to 1 hour, or until they are tender but not mushy. Drain them, reserving the liquid. You should have about 2 cups. If necessary, add a little warm water.

In a heavy skillet, heat the olive oil over medium heat and sauté the onions until translucent, about 3 minutes. Add the rice and sauté for 30 seconds. Add the wine and cook over high heat for 1 minute.

Add the chick-peas and their cooking liquid, lemon juice, chili pepper, and currants. Season with salt and simmer for 15 minutes, adding a little water if needed. Taste and adjust the seasoning, adding more salt, chili pepper, or lemon juice.

Serve immediately, sprinkled with cheese.

Spinach Rice
SPANAKORIZO

Leek Rice
PRASSORIZO

Cabbage Rice
PRASSORIZO

Vegetables and greens combined with rice is a very common theme in everyday Greek cooking. Because cabbage, leeks, spinach, and other wild or cultivated greens are readily available, they can be combined with rice to make easy and inexpensive lunches or dinners. You will even find these dishes in village restaurants, especially on Wednesdays and Fridays, the days Greeks are supposed to abstain from meat according to Orthodox tradition.

½ cup olive oil

2 medium onions, coarsely chopped

½ teaspoon minced fresh chili pepper,
    or ⅓–½ teaspoon dried red
    pepper flakes

1½ cups long-grain rice

2½–3 cups water or chicken stock

2½ cups fresh spinach, wilted and
    chopped; or sliced leeks, sautéed in
    2 tablespoons olive oil; or cabbage,
    briefly blanched and chopped

Sea salt

½ cup chopped fresh dill (optional)

1 cup thick yogurt, sheep's milk
    if possible (optional, see Mail-
    Order Sources)

SERVES 4–5

In a deep, heavy skillet, heat the oil over medium heat and sauté the onions until translucent, about 3 minutes. Add the chili pepper and the rice. Stir for a few seconds to coat with oil.

In the meantime, heat the water or stock with the vegetable of your choice in a separate saucepan. When it starts to boil, pour it over the rice and reduce the heat. Season with salt, mix well with a wooden spoon, and cover. Simmer for 15 to 20 minutes, or until the rice is cooked but still moist. Serve immediately, sprinkled with chopped dill and with a dollop of yogurt on each plate.

Note: Instead of using one green in this recipe, you can use a combination of spinach and leeks or cabbage and leeks.

Eggplants Stuffed with Onions and Tomatoes

MELINTZANES PAPOUTSAKIA

Eggplant cooked in this way is sometimes called *Imam bayildi* (the Imam fainted), presumably from the delight this dish gave him. But don't be fooled by the Turkish name. I have eaten a nearly identical dish in Sicily, which has never been under Turkish domination. This recipe may have originated in Persia.

In the version often encountered in Greek restaurants, a meat stuffing is used and bechamel sauce or mashed potatoes cover the eggplant. Serve with fresh Country Bread (page 194) and feta cheese.

4 small eggplants
Sea salt
Olive oil, for frying
½ cup olive oil
4 large onions, sliced lengthwise
3 cloves garlic, minced
½–1 teaspoon minced fresh chili peppers, or ⅓–½ teaspoon dried red pepper flakes
1–2 green bell peppers, cut into strips
1½ cups chopped fresh tomatoes or imported canned
1 cup chopped fresh flat-leaf parsley
1½ cups grated kefalotyri or pecorino cheese
8 tomato slices
½–1 cup bread crumbs

SERVES 4

Cut the stems from the eggplants and slice them in half lengthwise. Salt thoroughly and let drain in a colander for at least 30 minutes. Rinse and wipe dry with paper towels.

Heat some olive oil in a skillet over medium heat and sauté the eggplant on all sides until golden brown. It doesn't need to be cooked through because it will be baked later. Let it drain in the colander again.

Preheat the oven to 375° F.

In a heavy skillet, warm ¼ cup olive oil over medium heat and sauté the onions until soft, about 5 minutes. Add the garlic, chili pepper, and bell peppers. Sauté briefly, then add the tomatoes. Cook over high heat until most of the liquid has evaporated. Add the parsley, remove from the heat, and let cool slightly.

Oil an earthenware or clay ovenproof pan and arrange the eggplants in it cut side up. With a teaspoon remove about 2 tablespoons of their pulp, to make room for the stuffing.

Chop the eggplant pulp and add to the onion mixture.

Stir in the grated cheese with a wooden spoon and taste. Add salt and adjust the seasoning.

Spoon the stuffing into the eggplants and place 1 tomato slice over each one. Sprinkle with the bread crumbs and pour the remaining oil evenly over all the eggplants. Bake for 35 to 40 minutes, or until eggplant is tender.

Serve warm or cold.

EGGPLANT STUFFED WITH
ONIONS AND TOMATOES AND
TOMATOES AND PEPPERS STUFFED WITH
TRAHANA (page 142), MARATHON.

Stuffed Vine Leaves with Fava Beans

DOLMADES WITH KOUKIA

The fresh and distinctive taste of vine leaves was appreciated from the ancient times, as Athenaeus writes.

In early May, all over Greece but especially in the islands of the Dodecanese where this dish is made year-round, the women go to the vineyards to collect their year's supply of fresh and tender vine leaves. While the leaves are still fresh, they wrap bunches of fifty or so in aluminum foil and put them in the freezer. Or they put as many as they can squeeze in big glass jars—called leaf jars in some places— and store them in the refrigerator without brine. It is surprising how well this method preserves them for many months. However, once the jar is opened and some leaves taken out, the rest of them should go immediately into the freezer.

Of course one can buy vine leaves preserved in brine. Unfortunately their taste is altered; furthermore, as they are usually tough, they have to be boiled in water for 10 to 15 minutes before they can be used, and so their distinctive flavor almost disappears. If you like the taste of fresh vine leaves, I strongly advise buying fresh vine leaves in early summer and freezing them in bunches. Two pounds of vine leaves, stored in five packets, should last the entire year.

Garden-picked tender leaves or fresh frozen ones need no boiling, and *dolmades* made with them always taste infinitely better. My favorite version contains fava beans. I serve them with thick Greek yogurt as a first course or appetizer.

½ cup dried fava beans, soaked in
    water overnight
1 teaspoon dried oregano
1 cup olive oil
1½ cups finely chopped scallions
1 cup finely chopped fresh dill
½ cup chopped fresh mint
¾ cup short-grain rice
½ cup pine nuts
½–1 teaspoon minced dried chili
    pepper, or ⅓–½ teaspoon dried
    red pepper flakes, or freshly
    ground pepper
Sea salt to taste
1½ cups hot water
Juice of 3 lemons
1 pound fresh, frozen, or brine-
    packed vine leaves (about 50–70)

MAKES 50-60

Drain the beans, transfer to a pan, cover with water, and bring to the boil, adding the oregano. Simmer for 20 to 30 minutes, or until tender. Drain and let cool. Skin them, pressing each bean between your forefinger and thumb so that the inside comes out and you are left with the skin in your hand. Discard the skins. Puree the fava beans in a food processor.

In a heavy skillet, warm 3 tablespoons olive oil over medium heat and sauté the scallions, dill, and mint for 3 minutes, stirring with a wooden spoon. Add the rice, pine nuts, chili pepper, and salt and stir well. Pour ½ cup hot water and the juice of 1 lemon into the pan. Simmer for 3 to 5 minutes, then remove from the heat and add the mashed beans. Stir well, taste, and adjust the seasoning.

Carefully separate the vine leaves. Place each leaf on a wooden board shiny side down, with its stem toward you. Put a teaspoon of the stuffing near the bottom of the leaf, fold the bottom and 2 sides to cover the filling, and roll tightly toward the tip of the leaf.

Line a heavy stainless-steel pan with 2 layers of the small or torn vine leaves that cannot be stuffed. Place each rolled *dolma* seam side down, and press tightly together. When all the stuffing is finished, top the pan with the remaining oil, remaining lemon juice, 1 teaspoon salt, and enough hot water to just cover the *dolmades*. Place an inverted plate on top, so the *dolmades* won't unroll while cooking. Place a weight on top of the plate.

Cook at very low heat for about 45 minutes to 1 hour, or until the rice and the leaves are tender and the juice absorbed. Let the *dolmades* cool in the pan.

When completely cool, transfer to a bowl or plate, cover, and place overnight in the refrigerator. Serve cold. They will keep for up to 10 days.

Variation: In the spring, one can find the most delicious small artichokes in Crete. To stuff vine leaves with these artichokes, wash and peel 3 pounds of artichokes, keeping only the hearts. Cut the hearts in half lengthwise and let them stand in a bowl of water acidulated with the juice of 2 lemons. Chop 2 of the artichokes into small pieces and add to the stuffing. Roll the *dolmades* as in the master recipe, then alternate layers of artichokes and *dolmades* in the pan, starting with artichokes. Cook as directed.

Zucchini Blossoms Stuffed with Bulgur

LOULOUDIA KOLOKITHIAS
GEMISTA ME PLIGURI

Zucchini blossoms are a delicious summer specialty. They are very delicate and do not keep well, so I advise you to cook them the day you get them.

1 cup olive oil
1 cup chopped onion
1 cup chopped scallions
3 cloves garlic, minced
1 cup grated zucchini (1–2 zucchini)
1 cup bulgur (cracked wheat)
⅔ cup raisins (optional)
½–1 teaspoon finely chopped fresh chili pepper, or ⅓–½ teaspoon dried red pepper flakes
1½ cups water
½ cup pine nuts (optional)
3 tablespoons chopped fresh mint
½–⅔ cup chopped fresh dill
Sea salt and freshly ground pepper
20–25 zucchini blossoms
3 cups strained plain yogurt

SERVES 6–8

Preheat the oven to 375° F.

In a deep skillet, heat half the oil over medium heat and sauté the onion, scallions, and garlic until soft, about 5 minutes. Add the zucchini, bulgur, raisins, chili pepper, and 1 cup water. Reduce the heat and simmer for 10 minutes. Add a little more water if all is absorbed. Turn off the heat and add the pine nuts, mint, and dill to the stuffing. Season with salt, stir, and taste. Add more salt and pepper if needed.

Using a spoon, carefully stuff each blossom. Fold the top over and place on their sides, very closely together, in an earthenware casserole. Pour in the remaining olive oil and ½ cup water. Cover the dish and place in the oven. Bake for about 1 hour, checking periodically to see if a little more water is needed, until most of the liquid has been absorbed.

Serve hot or cold, accompanied by yogurt.

Tomatoes and Peppers Stuffed with Trahana

GEMISTA ME TRAHANA

When Greeks make stuffed vegetables, they very rarely prepare just one kind. By mixing together stuffed tomatoes, peppers, or eggplants, we create a more interesting dish. When serving, we can ask our guests which vegetable they prefer, or if the vegetables are large, we can serve half of each.

Rice has replaced cracked wheat as the main ingredient in most stuffings today, but one of my favorite stuffed vegetable dishes is an unusual recipe from Crete that contains sour *trahana,* a homemade pasta consisting of cracked wheat mixed with sour milk and left to dry. I found a similar recipe on Skyros, an island of the northern Aegean.

ROADSIDE MARKET IN EPIRUS.

5–6 large ripe tomatoes
4–5 green bell peppers

STUFFING

½ cup olive oil
1½ cups chopped onions
1 cup finely diced green bell pepper
½–1 teaspoon dried red pepper flakes
1¼ cups Sour *Trahana* (page 206)
1 cup skim milk
1 cup raisins
1 cup chopped fresh flat-leaf parsley
3 tablespoons chopped fresh mint
1 cup crumbled feta cheese
Sea salt to taste

1 medium potato, peeled and cut in
    1-inch cubes
½ cup olive oil
½ cup bread crumbs
Sea salt

SERVES 6–8

Preheat the oven to 350° F.
Wash and dry the tomatoes and place them stem side down on a plate. With a very sharp knife, cut the top off each tomato without detaching it completely. Using a spoon, remove the pulp very carefully. Take out as much pulp as possible without damaging the skin. (If you leave a thick layer, the tomatoes will release liquid during the cooking, thus changing the consistency of the stuffing.) Chop the tomato pulp into small pieces and drain, then set aside.

Wash, dry, and cut the tops off the peppers, reserving the tops as covers after stuffing. Remove the seeds from the peppers.

In a large skillet, heat the oil over medium heat and sauté the onions until soft, about 5 minutes. Add the chopped pepper and the red pepper flakes. Add the reserved tomato pulp and the *trahana*, milk, and raisins. Stir well and simmer for 3 to 4 minutes. Remove from the heat and add the parsley, mint, and feta cheese. Stir, taste, and adjust the seasoning.

To finish, arrange the vegetables in an ovenproof dish and stuff them, leaving a little room for the stuffing to expand. Cover the tops of the tomatoes and the peppers. Arrange the diced potato in the gaps between the stuffed tomatoes and peppers. Brush all the vegetables with oil and sprinkle with the bread crumbs and a little salt. Pour the rest of the olive oil in the pan. Bake for about 1 hour. Let cool for at least 15 minutes before serving.

Note: Substitute bulgur for *trahana*, if desired, increasing to 1½ to 2 cups the amount of feta cheese.

If you like, substitute 2 small eggplants for 2 tomatoes and 1 or 2 peppers. After washing and drying them, cut them in half lengthwise, remove most of their flesh with a spoon, and add to the stuffing. Salt the eggplants. Leave them for 20 to 30 minutes to drain in a colander. Dry with paper towels, heat some olive oil in a skillet, and fry briefly in high heat on all sides. Place in the colander to drain some of the oil they absorbed. Arrange the eggplants in the ovenproof dish with the rest of the vegetables and stuff them. Cover the stuffing with tomato slices, brush with oil, and sprinkle with bread crumbs.

Zucchini Pie

KOLOKITHOPITA

This is my mother's recipe, a dish she makes frequently as a first course when she has people for dinner or lunch. It can be reheated and is just as good the next day.

As in spinach pie, the cheese plays an important role. I use semidry goat cheese from Metsovo, but it is not available in the United States. You can use a combination of feta, cottage cheese, pecorino, blue cheese, and Parmesan, which works quite well as a substitute, or you can use dried mizithra (see Note). You can also experiment with any combination of sharp and soft cheeses, and adjust the seasonings accordingly.

2 pounds zucchini
Sea salt
½ cup olive oil
3 medium onions, chopped
2 eggs, lightly beaten
½ cup crumbled feta cheese
½ cup whole-milk cottage cheese
¼ cup crumbled blue cheese
¼ cup grated pecorino cheese
½ cup grated Parmesan cheese
½ cup chopped fresh mint leaves
3–4 tablespoons semolina or Sweet
    Trahana (page 207)
1 small fresh chili pepper, minced; or
    ground black pepper to taste
4 sheets homemade (page 205) or
    16 sheets thick commercial phyllo
    (see page 192)
Oil, for brushing

SERVES 6–8

Trim and coarsely grate the zucchini. Salt it and set aside in a colander to drain for 30 minutes.

Preheat the oven to 375° F.

Heat the oil in a skillet over medium heat and sauté the onions until translucent, about 3 minutes. Remove with a slotted spoon, leaving as much oil in the pan as possible, then sauté the zucchini until most of the liquid has cooked away, 10 to 15 minutes. Remove skillet from the heat and let the zucchini cool a little before stirring in the eggs, onions, cheeses, mint, semolina, and chili pepper. Taste and add salt and more pepper if needed.

Oil a 16-inch round baking dish. If using homemade phyllo, lay the first sheet of phyllo dough loosely on it, then brush with oil. Lay the second sheet on top of the first, then spread the zucchini mixture evenly over it, smoothing with a spoon. Cover with the third and the fourth sheets of dough, brushing each with oil. Trim the dough, leaving only 1½ inches hanging over the edge of the pan. Brush the edges of all the sheets with water and roll up together inward. Press with a fork to seal. If you are using commercial phyllo, layer 8 sheets for the bottom and 8 for the top, brushing each with a little olive oil. Finish as described above.

Bake for 40 to 45 minutes, or until top is lightly browned. Let cool for 15 minutes before serving.

Note: You can substitute pumpkin or winter squash for zucchini. If you want, omit all other cheeses and use 1½ cups mizithra (see page 30).

Crustless Zucchini Pie

MAMALIGA

Some people call this dish a lazy cook's pie. It is really more a tart than a pie, a traditional dish in many parts of Greece that can be prepared quickly, when there is no time to make phyllo. The recipe was given to me by my friend Soula Rigou. Her mother and grandmother used to make it in their native village near Atalante in central mainland Greece.

Mamaliga can be eaten warm or cold. It can even be frozen and reheated for about 30 minutes before serving.

2 pounds zucchini, coarsely grated
3 medium onions, finely minced
1 cup all-purpose flour
1 cup Sweet *Trahana* (page 207),
    bulgur, or short-grain rice
½ cup minced fresh mint
1 cup milk
3 cups shredded cheeses (feta and
    Parmesan, or whole-milk cottage
    cheese and blue, or any other
    combination of sweet and
    sharp cheeses)
4 eggs, lightly beaten
Sea salt
1 small fresh chili pepper, minced, or
    freshly ground pepper to taste
⅓ cup olive oil

SERVES 6

Preheat the oven to 375° F.
In a large bowl, mix the zucchini, onions, flour, *trahana*, mint, milk, cheeses, and eggs. Add the salt and chili pepper to taste, keeping in mind that the cheeses can be very salty. Pour half of the oil into a deep earthenware baking dish 10 to 12 inches in diameter and brush oil on all its sides. Pour the zucchini mixture into the dish and top with the rest of the oil. Bake in the oven for 1–1½ hours, or until it is set and golden brown on top. Let it cool on a rack for 10 to 15 minutes before serving.

Note: You can substitute ½ pound of peeled, seeded, and diced fresh tomatoes for the same amount of zucchini.

A GARDEN IN SANTORINI.

Kiki's or Lazy Woman's Pie

PITA TIS KIKIS OR TIS TEMBELAS

In contrast to the Crustless Zucchini Pie (page 145), this contains hardly any filling. Mrs. Kiki, who owns the restaurant on the central square of Monodendri—one of the very picturesque villages that make up Zagoria in Epirus—made this pie famous. Visitors always stop at her place and savor her excellent pie, the recipe for which she stubbornly refuses to give out. From various cooks I collected different versions of this pie using commercial phyllo. None achieved the fantastic crunchiness of Kiki's pie, but making a small portion of your own phyllo is more trouble than it's worth.

So I have developed my own version of Kiki's pie. Although Kiki uses butter for her pie, I use olive oil and it comes out beautifully.

½ cup all-purpose flour
½ cup fine semolina
½ teaspoon salt
2 tablespoons olive oil
½ cup warm water
Olive oil or butter to brush the pastry

FILLING

1 cup crumbled feta cheese
1 egg
3 tablespoons milk

SERVES 2–3

Follow the instructions on page 210 to make the dough. Let rest for at least 30 minutes.

Preheat the oven to 400° F.

Divide the dough in half. Working with one piece at at time on a floured board, roll the dough as thin as you can, then flour your hands and stretch carefully to a 12 × 17-inch sheet. Don't worry if there are some holes. Keep it covered to prevent drying while you roll out the second sheet.

Generously brush a 9 × 13-inch flameproof baking pan with olive oil or butter, then lay in the first phyllo sheet, wrinkling it to fit the pan. Brush it with olive oil or butter. Scatter half the feta on the sheet. Beat the egg with the milk in a bowl, and pour half the mixture into the pan. Layer the second phyllo sheet on top, brushing it well with oil.

Place the pan over medium heat and fry the pie, moving the pan back and forth so that all of the bottom is golden brown. It should take about 5 minutes, depending on the kind of pan you use. A heavy cast-iron one works best.

Remove the pan from the heat and sprinkle the rest of the feta cheese on top. Pour on the rest of the egg mixture, then transfer to the oven. Bake for 15 to 20 minutes, or until golden brown and crisp on top. Serve very hot.

Yogurt Pie with Vine Leaves

YAOURTOPITA TIS DRAMAS

This very unusual pie is wrapped not in any kind of pastry but in vine leaves. The dish is made only in the region of Drama, in Macedonia, and is sometimes called *asmapita* (*asma* meaning "tall vine" in Turkish).

I had heard some vague descriptions of a kind of omelet made with yogurt that is wrapped in vine leaves and fried in a skillet. Somehow it didn't seem right. Throughout Macedonia I asked about the dish, but nobody had ever heard of it. But in Drama, seven women who were sitting with me exchanging recipes all answered—almost with the same words—and told me the correct ingredients. They could not agree on the amount of yogurt and cornmeal, but they insisted that it was best without eggs.

I was extremely lucky when I cooked it at home. The result of my first try was a very fresh-tasting pie, and I made only small adjustments for the final recipe.

1¼ pounds thick Greek sheep's milk yogurt (see Mail-Order Sources)
⅔ cup cornmeal
⅔ cup finely chopped scallions
⅔ cup chopped fresh dill
⅔ cup chopped fresh mint
½ teaspoon freshly ground white pepper, or to taste
Sea salt
25–30 vine leaves, fresh or frozen (see page 138)
¼ cup olive oil

Preheat the oven to 375° F.

In a bowl, mix the yogurt with the cornmeal. Add the scallions, herbs, pepper, and salt, and stir well.

Oil an oval 12 × 9-inch glass or clay ovenproof dish and line the bottom and sides with half the leaves. Brush with oil and pour in the yogurt mixture. Top with the rest of the leaves and brush with the remaining oil. Cover loosely with aluminum foil and bake for about 45 minutes, or until set and a knife inserted in the center comes out clean.

Let the pie cool for 10 to 15 minutes before cutting to serve. It can also be eaten at room temperature the next day.

Note: You can also make individual pies in ramekins.

SERVES 6–8 AS A FIRST COURSE
OR APPETIZER

Traditional Greens Pie

HORTOPITA

Every Greek cook has a version of this classic pie. In the villages, very little spinach is used. Instead, a combination of different wild greens, gathered from the hills and fields, are used for the filling. Village people never buy the greens, which are not sold in stores; everyone gathers his or her own.

As the women in Metsovo told me, for the perfect *Hortopita* you need seven different kinds of wild greens, some sweet, some bitter, some sour, some with a light fragrance, and each complementing the other. Wild sorrel, dandelion, and mustard greens are available in the United States, but *kafkalithra* (*Scantis pecten veneris*) and sow thistle (*zochos* in Greek, *Sonchus nymani* or *Urospermum picioides* in Latin) are some local Greek greens considered very good for the pie.

The success of this pie depends on the greens you choose. Sorrel and spinach need some bitter or spicy greens, such as dandelion, watercress, mustard greens, or even arugula to give the pie extra bite. Spinach with leeks and dill, augmented by some greens with a more pungent taste, makes a very nice *Hortopita*.

1 pound fresh spinach
1 pound mixed greens (sorrel, dandelions, mustard greens, watercress)
½ cup olive oil
2 medium leeks, finely chopped (white part with 2 inches of the green)
1 cup chopped scallions
1–1½ teaspoons minced fresh chili pepper, or ⅓–½ teaspoon dried red pepper flakes
1½ cups crumbled feta cheese
1½ cups shredded kefalotyri, Parmesan, or pecorino cheese
2 eggs, lightly beaten (optional)
1 cup chopped fresh dill
1 cup chopped fennel or finely sliced fennel bulb

Wash the spinach and other greens thoroughly, drain, and coarsely chop. Heat about 1 cup of water in a heavy skillet and add half the spinach and greens. Cover and cook for 5 to 10 minutes, or until the greens are wilted and tender. Add the rest of the greens, stir, and cover. When all are soft, transfer to a colander and let drain. Press with your fingers to extract most of the liquid, then chop the greens.

Preheat the oven to 375° F.

Pour half the olive oil into the skillet and sauté the leeks and scallions over medium heat until soft and transparent, about 5 minutes. Add the remaining oil and sauté the greens and chili pepper for 3 minutes. Let cool for 5 minutes and add the cheeses, eggs, dill, fennel, and raisins. Mix well with a wooden spoon and season with salt, taking into consideration the saltiness of the cheese.

Brush a 15-inch round baking dish with oil. If using homemade phyllo, lay the first sheet of dough loosely in pan. Brush with oil and lay the second sheet over the first. Spread the spinach mixture evenly, pressing with a spoon. Cover with the third and the fourth sheets of

1 cup raisins

Sea salt

Olive oil, for brushing

**4 sheets homemade phyllo
(page 205) or 16 sheets thick
commercial phyllo (see page 192)**

SERVES 6–8

phyllo, after brushing each with oil. Trim the edges of the phyllo, leaving only 1½ inches hanging over the edge of the pan. Brush the hanging top and bottom sheets of phyllo with water and roll inward. Press with a fork to seal them.

If using commercial phyllo, layer 8 sheets on the bottom and 8 on the top of the pie, brushing each layer with a little olive oil.

Bake for 40 to 45 minutes, or until golden brown. Let cool for 15 minutes before serving. Spinach pie can be served warm or cold.

Note: This spinach pie can also be rolled like a strudel. See the description of the method in the recipe for Rolled Eggplant Pie with Walnuts (page 150).

ROLLING PHYLLO PASTRY
AND PREPARING THE TRADITIONAL
GREENS PIE OF METSOVO,
WHICH IS ROLLED INTO A COIL.

Rolled Eggplant Pie with Walnuts

MELINTZANOPITA

Of all the vegetables we use in pies, eggplants are the tastiest. But in modern Greek cooking, eggplant pie seems to be forgotten. The recipe that follows is my own, inspired by two different recipes: a *Melintzanopita* from Thessaly that is flavored with ground cumin and contains sweet *trahana*, or rice and 3 or 4 eggs; and an eggplant pie from Kozane, which contains no eggs or *trahana* but has coarsely ground walnuts.

The rolling of the pie with commercial phyllo, as described here, attains the same effect as the rolled pies of Metsovo prepared with homemade phyllo.

Sea salt
3 medium eggplants, cut into
 thick slices
4 medium leeks (white part plus
 1 inch from the green part),
 thinly sliced
Olive oil, for frying and brushing
1½ cups grated graviera or
 cheddar cheese
1 cup grated kefalotyri or
 pecorino cheese
1½ cups coarsely chopped walnuts
1–1½ teaspoons ground cumin
Freshly ground black pepper
24 sheets thick commercial phyllo
 pastry (see page 192)

SERVES 8–10

Salt both sides of the eggplant slices generously and let drain in a colander for at least 1 hour.

In the meantime, sauté the leeks in 2 tablespoons olive oil over medium heat, and set aside.

Rinse the eggplant slices and dry with paper towels. In a heavy skillet, sauté until golden brown on both sides. Be careful not to use too much oil because eggplants have a tendency to absorb it. Let them cool in a colander so the excess oil can drain off. When cold, chop coarsely and mix with the leeks, cheeses, walnuts, and cumin. Season with salt and pepper and stir well.

Preheat the oven to 375° F. Fold 2 sheets of phyllo in the middle, brush the top with olive oil, and place 4 or 5 tablespoons of the eggplant mixture on it. Spread the mixture evenly on the dough, leaving 2 inches all around free from filling. Fold the left and right sides of the sheet over to cover part of the stuffing, brush with oil, and start to roll as you would a strudel, brushing the dough with oil. You will obtain a 9-inch-long cigarlike pie. Fold 2 more sheets of dough in half, brush the top with oil, place the already rolled eggplant pie in the middle, turn the 2 sides inward, and roll the pie, brushing with oil.

Repeat with the rest of the phyllo and stuffing until you have 6 strudellike pies. Either coil them in a round pan or place them side by side in a rectangular pan. Bake for 45 minutes to 1 hour, or until golden brown.

Let cool a little before serving. Eggplant pie can be eaten warm or cold. It can also be frozen and reheated.

Note: When baked in a clay dish, the pies turn out crisper and more evenly cooked. If you don't want to fry the eggplant, you can brush the slices with olive oil and broil them.

GOATS, ASTYPALAIA.

MAKING
THE MOST
OF
MEAT

When I was young, my mother would start to cook our favorite Sunday dish—lamb or veal and potatoes in lemon sauce—on Saturday afternoons. She used to brown the meat and fry the potatoes on Saturday and then, on Sunday, she finished the dish by simmering the meat and potatoes together. To this day, the smell and taste of this dish brings back the best of my childhood memories, which are linked to leisurely Sundays, days of repose and recreation.

In traditional Greek cooking, meat is not everyday fare. Up until the late 1950s, most families ate meat no more than twice a week—but almost always on Sunday. Greece is a mountainous country, without large plains where cattle can be raised. The few cows that were kept in the villages were used to draw plows. People ate mostly lamb, kid, or pork.

As part of traditions that go back to ancient Greece, we roast lamb for the biggest religious or family feasts: Easter, weddings, engagements, and christenings; on Christmas we eat pork. Our forefathers divided the best pieces of sacrificed lambs among the priests and the gentry, while the common people ate the innards. Today, Greeks can afford all kinds of meat, but we still like to eat the innards and practically every other part of the animal, including the head.

Because meat was always expensive, we have found ways to extend our meat dishes by adding vegetables, homemade pastas, or grains. Nutritionists today think that the best way to eat meat is to consume small amounts of it with a lot of vegetables—exactly the way I remember my mother's meat dishes.

MEAT COOKED WITH LEMON, WINE, OR TOMATOES

The strong flavor of the olive oil used in Greek cooking needs to be balanced by the acidity of wine, vinegar, or lemon juice. Adding wine and vinegar when cooking meat goes back to ancient times. When lemon trees were planted in every garden, lemon juice found its way into many dishes, providing its special flavor and aroma.

Tomatoes came quite late to Greece. In what we consider to be the first Greek cookbook—which was a translation of an Italian one, published in 1828 on Syros—tomatoes are called golden apples (from the Italian *pomodoro*) and are used in only one or two of the recipes. But they quickly became part of everyday Greek cooking, as their slightly acid flesh complemented the olive oil. Today, Greek cooks have a tendency to overuse tomatoes and sometimes all the other flavors are buried under a thick tomato sauce.

ALMONDS, WALNUTS, AND GARLIC

One of the the most interesting ways to cook meat or poultry is with a garlic sauce. Walnuts are frequently used to thicken garlic sauces, but in some recipes, almonds are used instead. In others, the walnuts and garlic are pounded together in a mortar, much like the traditional *Skordalia,* or Garlic Sauce (page 54), then lightened with chicken stock. The resulting sauce is poured over boiled chicken and the whole dish is baked briefly. In other versions, soaked stale bread is used to thicken the sauce instead of flour, and the garlic is first mixed with vinegar to

make *skordostoumbi,* a light garlicky vinegar sauce that is used to flavor many dishes all over Macedonia. I have even found a recipe from Agrinio (in the central mainland) in which the sauce was flavored with tomatoes and sugar because tomatoes and vinegar made the sauce much too acidic.

In the early twentieth century, when Tselementes, a very talented Greek cook from Istanbul, wrote the first truly serious book about refined Greek cooking—applying as many of the rules of French cuisine as he

SHEEP BEING TRANSPORTED TO AN UNINHABITED ISLAND FOR GRAZING, NEAR ASTYPALAIA.

could—a new version of chicken in a creamy white sauce appeared and was quickly adopted by the upper and middle classes. It was called *kotopoulo milanesa* (Milanese chicken), although it has nothing to do with Milan. To prepare it, the chicken was boiled, then rice was cooked in its broth and a thick béchamel sauce—or *crema,* as we call it—was poured over the chicken and rice. Although neither the garlic, vinegar, or walnuts is present in *kotopoulo milanesa,* the texture and presentation are very similar to Chicken in White Garlic Sauce (*Kotopoulo Maskouli,* page 173), and I believe Tselementes had that dish in mind when he decided to discard such vulgarities as garlic and vinegar and replace them with the smooth béchamel sauce.

Veal and Potatoes in Lemon Sauce

MOSHARI LEMONATO
ME PATATES

This is my mother's *Lemonato,* the best I have ever tasted. Although this dish is commonly cooked at home all over Greece, it is rarely included in cookbooks.

One of my aunts used to make this with no other liquid but lemon juice, and her version was also delicious. But it contained no potatoes, which I think is a great disadvantage because the best part of *Lemonato* is the potatoes.

In any case, the secret of this dish's success it to keep the heat really low and to simmer the veal for hours.

2 large onions, sliced
½ cup olive oil
2 pounds boneless veal round or
   shank, in a tied rolled roast
1 cup dry white wine
½ cup water
1 tablespoon sugar
1 cup lemon juice
3 cloves garlic, minced
1 pound medium potatoes, quartered
Sea salt and freshly ground pepper

SERVES 4-6

In a heavy nonstick pan, sauté the onions in most of the olive oil over medium heat until transparent, about 3 minutes. Add the veal and brown on all sides. Pour in the wine, bring to a boil and boil for a few minutes, then add the water, sugar, lemon juice, and garlic. Simmer for 30 to 45 minutes, adding more water if needed.

While the veal is simmering, heat the remaining small amount of oil in a heavy skillet and fry the potatoes until they are golden brown. Don't worry about cooking them through because they will finish cooking with the veal.

Remove the meat from the pan and carefully slice it. Return the meat slices to the pan, season with salt and pepper, and continue simmering for another hour, adding a little water from time to time as needed.

Add the potatoes to the pan and simmer for another 30 to 45 minutes, or until the veal is very tender and potatoes are soft. Serve hot.

Note: You can cook lamb using the same method.

Veal in Eggplant Slices

KREAS SE FETES MELINTZANA

This tasty and very attractive dish is always included on the menu of Fatsio, the Athens restaurant that specializes in the cooking of Greek Constantinople.

In some versions of this dish, serving portions of veal or lamb are wrapped with eggplant slices. In others, like the one below, the meat is coarsely chopped and mixed with herbs and spices. Serve this with French fries or egg noodles.

3 pounds eggplants

Sea salt

½ cup olive oil

2 medium onions, chopped

1 pound boneless veal, coarsely chopped with a knife

½ cup dry red wine

½–1 teaspoon minced fresh chili pepper, or ⅓–½ teaspoon dried red pepper flakes

1 teaspoon dried oregano

1 cinnamon stick

½ teaspoon grated nutmeg

1 cup fresh or imported tomato puree (see page 32)

2 cloves garlic, minced

½ cup bread crumbs

3 ripe tomatoes, sliced

8–10 slices kefalotyri or pecorino cheese

SERVES 4

Cut the eggplants into ⅓-inch lengthwise slices. If you are using large, round eggplants, cut each slice in half lengthwise so you end up with strips about 1½ inches wide. Salt the slices and set them aside to drain in a colander for about 30 minutes.

In a deep, heavy skillet, warm 4 tablespoons olive oil and sauté the onions until soft, about 4 minutes. Add the veal and brown until all the liquid has evaporated. Pour in the wine and add the chili pepper, ½ teaspoon oregano, cinnamon stick, and nutmeg and season with salt. Bring to a boil and simmer for about 2 minutes, then add the tomato puree and garlic. Cook over medium heat until most of the liquid evaporates and the veal is cooked through, about 20 minutes. Discard the cinnamon stick. Taste, adjust the seasonings, and add the bread crumbs. Set the mixture aside to cool.

Preheat the broiler. Rinse and wipe the eggplant slices dry with paper towels, brush generously with olive oil on both sides, and lay as many slices in your largest broiling pan as it can hold. Broil the slices 2 to 3 inches from the heat until golden brown, about 6 minutes. Turn over and broil on the other side. Remove carefully from the pan and let cool on paper towels.

Preheat the oven to 375° F. On a cutting board or plate, form a cross with 2 eggplant slices and place about 2 tablespoons of veal mixture in the center. Wrap the veal with the eggplant slices, then carefully lift the parcel into an oiled glass or earthenware ovenproof pan. Repeat until all the eggplant slices and veal are used.

Place a tomato slice on top of each eggplant parcel. Brush with olive oil, sprinkle with a little oregano, and place a slice of cheese on top. Secure with a toothpick and bake for 20 to 30 minutes, or until the cheese melts and the stuffing is bubbling. Serve hot.

Lamb and Artichokes in Egg-Lemon Sauce

ARNI ME AGINARES
AVGOLEMONO

Arni me avgolemono is probably the most sophisticated combination of meat and vegetables one can find in Greek cuisine. This delicate sauce, with its distinctive lemony flavor, complements the taste of the lamb magnificently. As with all Greek meat dishes, you can substitute any kind of meat—beef, veal, pork, even chicken —when making this dish, but I think that lamb tastes the best.

Greeks frequently make this dish in winter with romaine lettuce or chicory, but I think it is at its best when you use artichokes, although they are more complicated to prepare. During fava bean season, you can add fresh, young fava beans in their pods. Their taste complements the flavor of the artichokes beautifully.

In the villages, *Arni me avgolemono* is made with wild greens. Try it with lettuce, endive, or even spinach, although Greeks never use spinach in this dish. Just wash the greens and add them to the lamb five to ten minutes before it is finished. You can also try a pork and celery *avgolemono,* or you can substitute fried zucchini for the artichokes.

1 whole lemon and the juice of
    2 lemons
7 small artichokes, about 2½ inches
    in diameter
½ cup olive oil
3 pounds boneless shoulder of lamb,
    cut into serving portions, or lamb
    shanks
1 medium onion, chopped
½ cup dry white wine
5–6 sprigs dill
10 scallions
3 medium carrots, cut in 2-inch pieces
Sea salt
Minced fresh chili pepper or freshly
    ground pepper to taste

LAMB AND ARTICHOKES
IN EGG-LEMON SAUCE, NEAR THE
MONUMENT OF LYSICRATES,
PLAKA, ATHENS.

Pour about 4 cups of water into a nonreactive bowl and add the lemon juice. Cut the whole lemon in half. Remove the outer hard leaves of each artichoke with a sharp knife and continue snapping off leaves until you are left with a soft cone formed by the inner leaves and the heart.

Rub the cut surfaces of the artichokes with the lemon halves to prevent discoloration. Cut off the green tops of the cones and, with a teaspoon, remove the chokes. Halve the artichokes and after rubbing the cut surfaces with the lemon, place them in the lemon water.

Pour the oil into a large saucepan and brown the lamb on all sides over high heat. Add the onion and reduce the heat. Pour in the wine and simmer for 10 to 15 minutes.

Chop the dill and reserve some to garnish the finished dish. Chop the scallions and remove the artichokes from the lemon water, reserving 1 cup of the water. Add the scallions, dill, artichokes, and carrots to the saucepan. Season with salt and minced chili pepper, if using. If not, season with freshly ground pepper.

(continued)

AVGOLEMONO SAUCE

2 eggs
Juice of 2 lemons
Sea salt and pepper

SERVES 6–8

Add the reserved lemon water and continue simmering for about 45 minutes, or until the artichokes, carrots, and lamb are tender. Add a little more water during the cooking, if needed. Strain the very hot liquid from the saucepan. You should have about 1½ to 2 cups; if more, boil briefly to reduce it.

Just before serving, prepare the sauce. Beat the eggs in a bowl and add the lemon juice. Carefully add the hot cooking liquid to the egg mixture, whisking vigorously and continuously. Place over very low heat, taking great care not to scramble the eggs. When sauce has thickened, taste and season with salt and pepper if needed.

Transfer the meat, artichokes, and carrots to a hot serving plate and pour the sauce over. Sprinkle with chopped dill and serve immediately.

Note: The egg and lemon sauce in its classic form, as described above, is quite tricky to make. The juices from the pan should be just under the boiling point, and they must be added very carefully to the egg mixture to make it thicken evenly. The sauce cannot be reheated.

You can also make a sturdier version of the sauce with cornstarch. Place the cooking liquids in a saucepan and add 2 teaspoons cornstarch dissolved in 2 tablespoons of cold water. Add the beaten eggs with the lemon and whisk over low heat until the sauce thickens. This version can be reheated without curdling.

Variation: To make Lamb and Zucchini with Egg-Lemon Sauce, trim 3 pounds of zucchini, cut them in half lengthwise, and cut into 3-inch pieces. Salt them and drain in a colander for 1 hour. Add them with the scallions and dill after the lamb has cooked for 30 minutes. You won't need to add water. Cook for another 30 minutes, or until the zucchini and lamb are tender. Proceed as above.

Lamb Roasted in Oiled Parchment

ARNI STO HARTI, KLEFTIKO

This is a contemporary version of *kleftiko* lamb, a famous dish in which lamb was roasted in its skin, buried in the hot embers of a fire that was set in a hole in the ground and covered loosely with dirt. This method was developed by the Kleftes, the Greek guerrillas who fought against the Turks in the eighteenth century. They roasted their lamb this way so that neither its aroma nor the smoke of the fire would betray their hideout.

Many variations of *Kleftiko* can be found today throughout Greece, some containing vegetables (zucchini, eggplant, peppers) and even tomatoes.

Usually you will find *Arni Kleftiko* cooked in one big parcel, but I have found that individual packets are easier to serve. And it's easier to open the small parcels without spilling the precious sauce. Serve this with rice or oven-baked potatoes with oregano and lemon.

If you are using a gas oven, pay special attention because the parchment can catch fire.

⅓ cup olive oil

Juice of 1 lemon

1 tablespoon dried oregano

1 tablespoon thyme

4 cloves garlic, minced

Freshly ground black pepper

2 pounds boneless leg of lamb, cut
    into 4 serving portions

Sea salt

4 slices kefalotyri, pecorino, or other
    sharp hard cheese

SERVES 4

In a bowl, mix the olive oil with the lemon juice, herbs, garlic, and pepper. Add the lamb to the mixture and turn to coat on all sides. Cover and marinate for at least 3 hours or overnight in the refrigerator.

Preheat the oven to 375° F.

Cut eight 14-inch square pieces of parchment paper. Lay 2 pieces of parchment on the table, place a piece of lamb on them without wiping off the marinade, and season with a little salt on both sides. (Be stingy with the salt because the cheese is usually very salty.)

Place a slice of cheese on the lamb and pour a teaspoon of marinade on top. Fold the part of the paper nearest you over the lamb and cheese, and cover with the opposite side. Tuck the 2 sides under the lamb, and secure the packet by tying with a piece of string. Continue with remaining lamb and parchment paper.

Lightly oil a baking dish and place the lamb packages in it. Place the baking dish in the oven and bake for 45 minutes to 1 hour, lowering the heat to 350° F. after 20 minutes.

Cut the strings, lift the packets out of the baking dish, and undo the papers to reveal the contents. Be careful not to spill the sauce. Serve each portion in its parchment wrapper, piping hot.

Roasted Lamb with Pasta

GIOUVETSI

Any kind of meat or poultry can be used to make *Giouvetsi*, but I prefer lamb. One can also use any kind of pasta (spaghetti, elbow macaroni, penne), but Greeks generally use *kritharaki*, the rice-shaped pasta that Americans call orzo.

This dish is best when made with fresh, ripe tomatoes and when eaten piping hot, sprinkled with freshly grated mizithra, the hard and tangy Greek goat's milk cheese.

3 pounds boneless shoulder or
    leg of lamb
Juice of 1 lemon
Sea salt and freshly ground pepper to
    taste
4–5 cloves garlic
1 cup olive oil
3–4 cups chicken stock
1 medium onion, minced
1 small fresh chili pepper, minced
3½ cups chopped fresh or canned
    tomatoes
1 teaspoon sugar
Sea salt
2 cinnamon sticks
1 pound orzo
1 cup grated mizithra or other tangy
    hard cheese

SERVES 4–5

Preheat the oven to 475° F.

Rub the lamb with the lemon juice, salt, and freshly ground pepper. Peel 3 cloves of garlic and cut each clove in half lengthwise. Cut slits into the flesh on all sides of the lamb and insert the garlic halves.

Place the lamb in a deep earthenware baking dish and brush it with olive oil. Roast for 10 to 15 minutes, then reduce the oven temperature to 350° F. and continue roasting for 30 to 40 minutes more, or until almost done, basting frequently with the pan juices. If there isn't enough juice, use a little chicken stock.

In the meantime, make the tomato sauce. Heat the remaining oil in a skillet and sauté the onion over low heat until soft. Peel and mince the remaining garlic and add it to the onion. When soft, add the chili pepper, chopped tomatoes, sugar, salt, and cinnamon sticks. Cook for 5 minutes.

Transfer the lamb to a heated dish and cover with aluminum foil to keep warm.

Pour the boiling tomato sauce into the baking dish and stir to mix with the cooking juices. Add 2 cups chicken stock and the orzo and stir again. Return to the oven and cook for 25 minutes, stirring occasionally because the pasta tends to stick, until the orzo is cooked al dente and has absorbed most of the pan juices. Add more chicken stock, if necessary.

When the pasta is almost cooked, remove the cinnamon sticks and place the lamb on top of the orzo. Baste with the tomato sauce, then return to the oven and continue roasting until the orzo is cooked to your taste.

Serve immediately, sprinkled with the cheese.

Note: The exact cooking time and the amount of liquid the pasta needs depend on the brand used.

ROASTED LAMB WITH PASTA
SERVED WITH GRATED MIZITHRA,
AND A LAMB AND VEGETABLE STEW.

Easter Lamb Soup

MAGIRITSA

Magiritsa is made with the parts of the lamb not used for the spit-roasted Easter lamb, which is usually very small (about 20 pounds). In the classic recipe, all the innards—heart, lungs, and so forth—go into the pot, but they do not really contribute to the taste. The flavor of the stock comes from the boiled head and neck, and the soup gets its distinctive taste from scallions, fresh dill, and the egg-and-lemon mixture.

There are lots of different *magiritsa* recipes. A friend described to me the one her family prepared in Halki, a small island that is part of the Dodecanese. In her family's version, no innards were used because, in Halki as in all the Dodecanese, they do not roast the lamb on the spit but instead stuff it with rice and the innards. So in Halki's *magiritsa*, many lambs' heads were boiled to make a very tasty stock, to which egg and lemon sauce is added at the end. The heads were not boned, but as they cooked for many hours, even their bones became soft. Each member of the family got one head and ate it with the broth. No scallions or dill were added to that *magiritsa*.

My recipe for Easter soup was given to me by my cousin's wife, Katy Kremezi, whose mother came from Smyrna (Izmir) in Asia Minor.

Head, neck, some intestines, and
  liver of a young lamb or 3 pounds
  lamb bones
2 large onions, halved
Sea salt
½ cup olive oil
2 cups finely chopped scallions
1 small chili pepper, minced, or
  freshly ground pepper to taste
1½ cups chopped fresh dill
2 eggs
Juice of 1½–2 lemons

SERVES 6–8

Wash the lamb head and neck thoroughly and place in a pot with the onions. Cover with cold water, season with salt, and simmer for about 1 hour, skimming the surface several times.

Cut the intestines into several pieces and wash thoroughly under running water. If you like, slice them open so you can wash them more easily. In a separate pan, bring some salted water to a boil and add the intestines. Blanch for 2 minutes, then remove with a skimmer and discard the water. Chop the intestines finely. You don't need more than 1 cup of chopped intestines.

The head and neck are done when the meat falls from the bones. Remove them from the pot. Using a sharp knife, cut open the head and separate the meat from the bones. Remove the meat from the neck and cut all the meat into small pieces. Strain the stock and discard the onions. Let the stock cool and remove the fat. (Up to this point, the preparations can be made a day ahead. You can refrigerate the meat and the stock, making it easier to skim off the fat.)

To finish the soup, wash the liver well and cut it into small cubes. In a skillet, heat the olive oil and sauté the liver with the scal-

EASTER LAMB SOUP WITH
RED-PAINTED EASTER EGGS.

lions and chili pepper, if using. Add the finely chopped meat and intestines, together with 1 cup of the dill, and turn a few times with a wooden spoon. Transfer the mixture to a pot and add the stock plus an equal amount of water, and bring to a boil. Reduce the heat and simmer for 12 to 15 minutes. Taste and add more pepper and salt if needed.

Beat the eggs in a large bowl with about 2 spoonfuls of water and the juice of 1 lemon. Slowly add cupfuls of the hot soup to the bowl, beating continuously with the whisk. When the egg mixture is very hot, pour it slowly into the pot, stirring well, over very low heat, to prevent curdling. Taste and add more lemon juice if needed. Sprinkle with the rest of the dill, and serve immediately.

Note: Some people add ½ to 1 cup short-grain rice to the soup.

If you hate the taste of boiled lamb, you can make an equally tasty *magiritsa* with chicken livers and chicken stock. There is even a meatless *magiritsa*. Sauté the scallions and dill, adding a few chopped leaves of romaine lettuce. Pour in water or stock and simmer for 10 to 15 minutes. Make the egg and lemon mixture as described above and serve.

Lamb and Vegetables Baked in an Unglazed Clay Pot

ARNI STAMNAS

Unglazed clay jars, used by women to bring water from the village fountain, are called *stamna*. The story goes that some women fed their sons or husbands who were guerrillas in the mountains by leaving a water jar filled with food near the fountain. During the night the men came secretly and collected it.

LAMB AND VEGETABLES BAKED IN AN UNGLAZED CLAY POT, IN TERSANA, CHANIA, CRETE.

Since the water jar has only a small opening, tiny pieces of meat and vegetables were inserted in the jar, which was then sealed with dough and baked.

This version of *Arni Stamnas* was given to me by Electra Kalamboka, from Kavalla in northern Greece.

2 pounds boneless leg of lamb, cut
    into 1-inch cubes
½ cup olive oil
½–1 teaspoon minced fresh chili
    pepper, or ⅓–½ teaspoon dried
    red pepper flakes
3 medium onions, sliced
1 bay leaf, crushed
1 tablespoon dried oregano
1 teaspoon dried thyme
Sea salt
3 medium eggplants, cut into
    1-inch cubes
3 green bell peppers, seeded and
    cut into strips
4 cloves garlic, minced
2 medium potatoes, cut into
    1-inch cubes
1 cup strained fresh tomato puree or
    2 tablespoons tomato paste diluted
    in ⅓ cup warm water

SERVES 6

In a large bowl, mix the lamb with the olive oil, chili pepper, onions, bay leaf, oregano, and thyme. Cover and set aside for 2 to 3 hours or overnight in the refrigerator.

Preheat the oven to 425° F.

Salt the eggplant and place in a colander to drain for about 30 minutes. Rinse and wipe dry with paper towels.

Add the eggplant, bell peppers, garlic, and potatoes to the marinated lamb along with the tomato puree. Season with salt and place in an unglazed clay pot. Cover and bake for 30 minutes. Reduce the heat to 375° F., toss carefully, and bake for another 1½ to 2 hours, or until the lamb is very tender. Serve immediately.

Chopped Meat Rolls in Tomato Sauce with Green Olives

SOUTZOUKAKIA ME ELIES

Soutzoukakia is a classic Greek dish. It is sometimes called *Soutzoukakia Smyrneika* because the recipe is believed to have originated in Smyrna, the old Greek city in Asia Minor that is called Izmir today.

There are many varieties of *Soutzoukakia,* especially in the north of Greece, where one can find similar chopped meat rolls spiced with cumin, grilled over a charcoal fire, and served with plain or garlic-flavored yogurt. Serve these with French fries, mashed potatoes, or rice.

To appreciate this dish, you have to like cumin. My father could not stand it, so my mother cooked *Soutzoukakia* without cumin, adding more oregano.

Modern Greek cooks usually omit the olives in the sauce, but they are included in very old recipes.

3 thick slices stale bread
2 pounds lean ground beef
½ cup chopped onion
4 cloves garlic, chopped finely
1 teaspoon ground cumin
½ teaspoon dried oregano
¼ cup dry red wine
1 egg, lightly beaten
2 tablespoons olive oil
Sea salt and freshly ground pepper
Oil for frying

SAUCE

½ cup olive oil
1 medium onion, chopped finely
3 cups fresh tomato puree or
    good-quality canned
2 bay leaves
1 teaspoon sugar
1½ cups pitted green olives
Sea salt and pepper, if desired

Remove the crusts from the bread, put slices in a bowl, and cover with water. Let soak for 3 to 5 minutes, then squeeze the excess water from the bread with your hands. Mix the bread with the ground beef, onion, garlic, cumin, oregano, wine, egg, oil, and salt and pepper. Mix thoroughly.

Scoop out tablespoons of the mixture and shape into sausagelike rolls, about 2½ inches long and 1 inch thick.

Heat the oil in a skillet over medium-high heat and fry the rolls until browned on all sides and cooked through, about 10 minutes. Transfer to a plate lined with paper towels to drain.

Heat the oil for the sauce in a nonreactive saucepan over medium heat and sauté the onion until translucent, about 3 minutes. Add the tomato puree, bay leaves, sugar, and olives. Simmer for 15 to 20 minutes.

Taste, and season with salt and pepper if needed. Don't add salt before this point—the olives are usually salty enough.

Transfer the rolls to the sauce and simmer for 10 minutes. Serve hot.

SERVES 6

Meatballs

KEFTEDES

Keftedes (plural for *kefte*) sounds like a Turkish word. As with many Greek dishes, the name was probably given by the Turks, who adopted the dish after they occupied Byzantium. Nevertheless, the name comes from the word *kopto,* the Byzantine term for ground meat.

There are many recipes for *Keftedes.* Practically every cook has a particular mixture of ingredients. The following is a combination of recipes from Macedonia and Thrace, and it's my favorite.

3 tablespoons olive oil

1½ pounds zucchini or other summer
    squash, grated

1½ cups finely chopped onions

1–1½ teaspoons chopped fresh chili
    pepper, or ⅓–½ teaspoon dried
    red pepper flakes

1½ cups bulgur (cracked wheat)

1 cup milk

1¼ pounds lean ground beef

2–3 eggs

3 cloves garlic, minced

½ cup chopped fresh mint

½ cup chopped fresh flat-leaf parsley

3 tablespoons ouzo or dry white wine

1½ cups grated Parmesan or
    kefalotyri cheese

1 tablespoon sea salt or to taste

Flour, for dredging

Olive oil, for frying

SERVES 4–6

In a heavy skillet, heat the olive oil over low heat and sauté the grated zucchini until soft, about 10 minutes. Add the onions and chili pepper and cook, stirring, for 2 more minutes. Remove from the heat and add the bulgur and milk. Stir and let stand for 10 to 15 minutes, or until the wheat absorbs the liquid and becomes soft.

In a large bowl, mix the ground beef with the eggs, garlic, mint, parsley, and ouzo or wine. Stir in the zucchini and bulgur mixture. Add the grated cheese and salt and mix thoroughly. Let the mixture stand for at least 1 hour. You can also prepare it the night before and keep it in the refrigerator.

Take a heaping tablespoon of the mixture in your hand and shape it into a ball. Press down slightly and dredge in flour. Repeat to shape all the *Keftedes.*

When ready to fry, heat olive oil in a large skillet and fry the meatballs until well browned on both sides, about 10 minutes. Transfer to paper towels to drain, then serve hot or cold.

Note: Instead of frying the meatballs, you can broil them. Shape as described and, without dredging them in flour, place in a broiler pan and broil for 15 to 20 minutes, turning once.

You can also make *keftedakia* (smaller meatballs) by using teaspoons of the mixture.

If you want to check the seasoning of the meatballs, cook a teaspoon of the mixture before proceeding.

Meatballs with Leeks

KEFTEDES ME PRASSA

This is a typical winter dish, cooked all over Thessaly, Epirus, and Macedonia. Sometimes potatoes and carrots are added to extend it.

⅓ cup olive oil ·
4 medium leeks, white and tender
 green, sliced into ½-inch
 crosswise pieces
1 cup dry white wine
Sea salt and freshly ground pepper, or
 minced fresh or dried chili pepper
 to taste
Meatballs (page 166)
Flour, for dredging
Avgolemono Sauce (page 158;
 optional)

SERVES 4–6

Pour the olive oil into a heavy, wide sauté pan that will hold the meatballs in one layer, and sauté the leeks until translucent, 3 to 4 minutes. Add the wine and boil for 1 minute. Add salt and pepper.

Dredge the meatballs in flour, shake to rid of excess, and arrange on top of the leeks in the pan. Lower the heat so liquid will just simmer, and cover. Cook for about 20 minutes, adding a little water if needed to keep meatballs moist, and shake the pan from time to time to keep them from sticking.

Prepare the sauce. When ready to serve, pour it over the meatballs. Serve very hot.

Overleaf: CHOPPED MEAT ROLLS
IN TOMATO SAUCE WITH GREEN OLIVES
AND MEATBALLS, ASTYPALAIA.

Chicken with Parsley in Egg-Lemon Sauce

KOTOPOULO ME MAIDANO
AVGOLEMONO

This recipe comes from Macedonia. The success of the dish depends on the quality and freshness of the parsley, which should be Italian flat-leaf—the only kind commonly used in Greece—and of the chicken, which preferably should be free-range. The parsley is used not merely as a garnish, but as a vegetable in its own right, like spinach. Serve this dish with rice cooked in chicken stock.

½ cup olive oil
1 free-range chicken
    (about 2½ pounds), cut into
    serving portions
1 cup dry white wine
Sea salt and minced fresh chili pepper
    or freshly ground pepper to taste
1 cup water
3 pounds fresh flat-leaf parsley,
    washed and drained
10 scallions
Avgolemono Sauce (page 158)
Chopped flat-leaf fresh parsley,
    for garnish

SERVES 4–6

Heat half the oil in a heavy, nonreactive skillet. Sauté the chicken pieces until they are golden all over, about 3 minutes, then pour in the wine and cook for 5 minutes. Add the salt, chili pepper, and water. Simmer for 30 minutes, adding a little more water if needed.

Cut off the leaves and discard most of the stems of the parsley.

In another skillet, heat the remaining oil and sauté the scallions and the parsley. Add them to the chicken and cook for 10 to 15 minutes more.

When the chicken and parsley are tender, arrange the chicken pieces in the center of a hot serving plate and place the parsley around the chicken. Pour the sauce over, garnish with fresh parsley, and serve immediately.

CHICKEN WITH PARSLEY IN EGG-LEMON SAUCE, ASTYPALAIA.

Chicken in White Garlic Sauce

KOTOPOULO MASKOULI

This delicious recipe, given to me by my friend Maria Papadina, comes from Kastoria in Macedonia. Similar recipes can be found in different parts of Greece, in the Peloponnese, and even on the island of Mytilini (Lesbos), where it is called *maskoulo,* or *skordalevria.* Food writer Paula Wolfert told me that *Maskouli* is similar to Circassian chicken, a dish that developed in the Caucasus, but unlike Circassian chicken, *Maskouli* is eaten hot and not cold. (Walnuts and almonds were used by the Persians to thicken sauces.)

Chicken is not the only meat we find cooked this way. In Thrace, it is made with goose, and in the Peloponnese I came across rabbit *maskouli.* I have been told that hare cooked in white wine with this creamy garlic sauce is also delicious.

In Ioannina, the capital of Epirus, in the northwest, I came across crayfish in a similar garlic and walnut sauce (see page 104), while in other parts of the country squash slices are baked in garlic and walnut sauce (page 113).

Serve with rice or egg noodles.

1 free-range chicken (about
   3 pounds), cut into serving pieces
1 bay leaf
1 medium onion, quartered
Sea salt and freshly ground pepper
Flour, for dredging
Oil, for frying
3 tablespoons olive oil
3 tablespoons flour
4–5 cloves garlic
½ cup dry white wine
2 tablespoons red wine vinegar
1 cup ground walnuts
½ cup coarsely crushed almonds

SERVES 4

CHICKEN IN WHITE GARLIC SAUCE
SERVED WITH EGG NOODLES, AT
THE DOMA HOTEL, CHANIA, CRETE.

Place the chicken in a pan and cover with water. Add the bay leaf, onion, and salt and pepper. Bring to a boil, then reduce the heat and simmer for 20 to 30 minutes, or until tender but firm.

Remove the chicken pieces from the pan with a slotted spoon, pass the stock through a fine sieve, and skim off and discard as much fat as possible. Measure the stock; you should have about 3 cups. If it is more, reduce it over high heat. If it is less, add a little water.

Heat some olive oil in a deep skillet. Lightly dredge the chicken with flour and fry until golden brown on all sides. Transfer the fried pieces to paper towels and keep warm.

Discard the frying oil from the skillet and wipe with paper towels. Heat the 3 tablespoons of olive oil over low heat, and whisk in the 3 tablespoons of flour. Continue whisking for about 1 minute, until it begins to froth.

Remove from the heat and add the garlic, reserved stock, wine, vinegar, and walnuts, whisking constantly. Return to the stove and continue whisking over medium heat until the sauce begins to thicken. Taste and add more salt and pepper if necessary.

Arrange the chicken on a heated plate, and pour the sauce over it. Sprinkle with the almonds and serve immediately.

Rabbit and Pearl Onion Stew

KOUNELI STIFADO

A meat stew that contains pearl onions and wine or vinegar is called a *stifado* in Greece. We have many variations of *stifado*, some with tomato sauce and some without. For instance, in the islands you will even find octopus *stifado*. This method is thought to be the ideal way to cook wild hare, but because hare is not very common and everybody loves *stifado*, you are more likely to find rabbit or other meats prepared this way. *Stifado* can be made a day ahead and reheated—it tastes better after the herbs and spices have had time to blend. Serve it with mashed or fried potatoes.

2/3 cup olive oil

1 rabbit (about 3 pounds), cut into
    serving portions

1/2 cup red wine vinegar

1/2 cup sweet red wine, such as
    Mavrodaphne

1 teaspoon sugar

Sea salt

1 fresh chili pepper, minced; or
    freshly ground pepper to taste

5–6 cloves garlic, halved lengthwise

2 bay leaves

1/2 cup dried currants

3–4 allspice berries, or 1/2 teaspoon
    ground allspice

6–8 whole cloves

1 cinnamon stick (optional)

1 cup water

2 1/2 pounds pearl onions, peeled but
    left whole

A few sprigs of flat-leaf parsley,
    chopped

SERVES 4–5

Heat half the oil in a large nonreactive skillet, and sauté the rabbit on all sides until tender, about 6 to 10 minutes. Pour the vinegar and wine into the pan and cook the meat for 3 to 4 minutes over high heat. Add the sugar, salt, chili pepper, garlic, bay leaves, currants, allspice, cloves, and cinnamon stick. Pour in the water and as it starts to boil, lower the heat.

Cut a cross in the root end of each onion. In a separate pan, sauté the onions in the remaining oil until they turn golden brown, about 4 minutes, then add them to the stew, together with their cooking oil.

Simmer the stew, covered, over very low heat for about 1 hour, or until the rabbit and onions are tender. Add a little more water if needed. Serve sprinkled with the chopped parsley.

Note: You can substitute 1 cup chopped fresh tomatoes for the water in this recipe, but in that case, add 1 more teaspoon of sugar. You can also cook the *stifado* in the oven. After sautéing the rabbit and onions, bake it in a covered dish at 375° F. for about 2 to 2 1/2 hours.

Stuffed Hare or Rabbit Braised in Wine

LAGOS GEMISTOS KRASSATOS

In the mountainous region of Epirus, where this recipe comes from, game is fairly common, especially in the fall and early winter.

Stuffing the hare with olives brings us back to an earlier style of cooking, since today olives are quite uncommon in Greek dishes. It's particularly odd to find olives in a recipe from a region that never produced them. I think they were added to make the dish more precious and exotic, much like we add chestnuts to the festive stuffing of turkey or chicken today.

Serve with warm boiled wild greens or spinach.

1 hare or wild rabbit, with innards

MARINADE

Juice of 1 lemon
1 cup red wine vinegar
1 cup water
1 tablespoon dried oregano
4–5 cloves garlic, chopped
Sea salt and 1 tablespoon whole
  black peppercorns
2–3 bay leaves

STUFFING

⅓ cup olive oil
1 medium onion, chopped
1 cup dry red wine
5–6 cloves garlic
1 cup water
1 teaspoon dried oregano
½–1 teaspoon minced fresh chili
  pepper or dried red pepper flakes
½ teaspoon grated nutmeg
1 cup bulgur (cracked wheat)
2 cups small black olives, pitted
Sea salt and freshly ground pepper

Wash and dry the hare or rabbit. Mix all the marinade ingredients and rub the marinade all over the hare and inside its cavity. Place the hare in a large, nonreactive bowl, pot, or deep pan that can just hold it, pour the marinade on top, and cover. Let stand in the refrigerator for 2 to 3 days, turning it at least once a day.

Wash, dry, and chop the liver, heart, and other innards. In a deep, heavy skillet, heat the olive oil over medium heat and sauté the onion until translucent, about 3 minutes. Add the chopped innards and sauté until firm. Pour on the wine and add the garlic, water, oregano, chili pepper, nutmeg, and bulgur. Simmer for 2 to 3 minutes, then add the olives. Remove from the heat and cover. Let stand for 5 to 10 minutes, then taste and season with salt and pepper.

Heat the oven to 350° F.

Remove the hare from the marinade and dry with paper towels. Stuff its cavity and sew up the opening. Place the stuffed hare in a deep pan, preferably with a lid.

Strain the marinade into a saucepan. Reserve the bay leaves but discard everything else in the strainer. Cook the liquid until it is reduced to 1 cup. For the sauce, mix the reduced marinade with the garlic, olive oil, wine, oregano, and salt and pepper. Baste the hare and pour the rest into the pan. Cover with the lid or with 2 layers of aluminum foil and roast for 1½ to 2 hours, basting frequently. Turn the hare over after it has cooked for 1 hour.

SAUCE

5 cloves garlic, quartered

½ cup olive oil

1 cup dry red wine

1 teaspoon dried oregano

Sea salt and freshly ground pepper

~~~~~~~~~~~~~~~~~~~~~~~~~~~~

SERVES 4–6

When done, cut the hare into serving portions and place in a serving dish together with the stuffing. Cover and keep warm.

Discard most of the fat from the sauce, pour some sauce over the meat and stuffing, and present the rest in a sauceboat. Serve immediately.

Note: If you can't get rabbit innards, substitute 3 to 4 chicken livers.

~~~~~~~~~~~~~~~~~~~~~~~~~~~~

Baked Rabbit with Lemon Sauce

KOUNELI PSITO, LEMONATO

My mother was given this recipe by her friend Despina Drakaki, who comes from the island of Paros. Her recipe calls for the rabbit to be roasted on a spit—something that is hard to do without making the rabbit dry—so I bake it, and the result is excellent. This recipe is also excellent with chicken. Serve with French fries.

1 whole rabbit, with innards and
    especially the liver

1 cup dry white wine

1 cup olive oil

3 cloves garlic, minced

1 tablespoon dried oregano

Sea salt and freshly ground pepper

1 lemon

¾ cup lemon juice

~~~~~~~~~~~~~~~~~~~~~~~~~~~~

SERVES 4

Wash and dry the rabbit. In a bowl, mix the wine, olive oil, garlic, oregano, and salt and pepper. Rub the rabbit all over with this marinade, cover, and refrigerate for at least 3 hours or overnight.

Remove the rabbit from the refrigerator at least 1 hour before roasting. Preheat the oven to 425° F.

Place the rabbit's innards and whole lemon in the cavity and close with toothpicks. Place the rabbit in a baking pan, brush all over with marinade, and roast for 15 minutes. Reduce the heat to 400° F., brush again with the marinade, and roast for another 45 minutes, turning the rabbit after about 20 minutes and basting regularly with the marinade.

Remove from the oven and discard the lemon. Keep rabbit warm. Place the innards in a blender with the lemon juice. Blend for a few seconds, then add the cooking liquids and blend for a few seconds again. Taste the mixture and add more salt and pepper if needed.

Cut the rabbit into serving portions and pour the sauce over it. Serve immediately.

Note: If you can't get rabbit innards, substitute 4 chicken livers.

Jellied Pork

PIKTI

Pork is the traditional Christmas meal in Greece. The animals are slaughtered just before the holidays, and the rest of the meat is smoked, preserved in its fat, or made into sausages that can be eaten throughout the winter.

From the leftovers—the head and the feet—a delicious pork aspic is prepared in the Aegean islands, Crete, and Mani. *Pikti*, or *tsiladia* as this dish is also called, is usually served as part of a festive Christmas spread together with baked pork, meat pies, or stuffed chicken. It is part of all formal buffet dinners on Christmas and New Year's eves.

My version is a combination of a traditional recipe from Mani and another from Paros, given to me by Koula Maroupa. I have used capers instead of pickled cucumbers; I find that really good capers, such as the ones from Paros I buy in bulk every year, add a lot to the dish.

If you hate the idea of cooking and boning a pig's head, or you can't find one, use two pig's feet and about two pounds of pork shoulder or ham. But you will be missing a lot because pig's head is delicious.

Serve with potato salad and mayonnaise.

1 small pig's head, and 1–2 pig's feet, about 6 pounds total

3–4 cups dry white wine

3 medium onions, halved, each piece pierced with 1 clove

3 bay leaves

4–5 whole allspice

1–2 dried chili peppers, or ½–1 teaspoon dried red pepper flakes

6 cloves garlic, 3 halved and 3 minced

2 tablespoons capers, drained, plus additional for decoration

⅓ cup good-quality white wine vinegar

Juice of 1 lemon and of 1 Seville orange, or of 2 lemons

2 tablespoons grated orange peel, blanched and dried

Sea salt and freshly ground pepper

1 medium carrot, cooked and cut into thin slices

1 bunch watercress

SERVES 8–10

Wash the meat and place in a large pot. Cover with water and bring to a boil. Discard the water, then pour in a mixture of half water and half white wine to cover. Add the onions, bay leaves, allspice, chili pepper, and halved cloves of garlic. Simmer for about 1½ hours, or until the meat falls from the bones. Add more water if necessary to keep meat covered.

Let cool a little, then bone carefully, discarding bones and cartilage and most of the fat. Cut the meat into small pieces and set aside, covered. You should have about 2 cups meat.

Pass the stock through a fine sieve lined with cheesecloth. You should have 3½ to 4 cups. If you have more, reduce by boiling. Let it cool completely, then place in the refrigerator for 2 to 3 hours.

Remove and discard all the fat from the stock. Heat the stock but do not let it come to a boil. Add the minced garlic, capers, vinegar, half the lemon and orange juices, and orange peel. Taste and season with salt, pepper, and more lemon juice if necessary; the taste must be quite strong and acidic. Add the reserved meat to the stock and let the mixture cool.

Oil a rectangular or round 6-cup mold and decorate with carrot slices, more capers, and some sprigs of watercress. Pour in a little of the stock and place in the freezer for 10 to 15 minutes, or until the stock has set and the carrots, capers, and watercress are held firmly in place. Pour the rest of the mixture into the mold and place in the refrigerator overnight.

Just before serving, briefly dip the mold in a bowl of hot water and invert the mold onto a plate. Decorate with sprigs of watercress and serve.

Pork, Lamb, or Veal Stew with Quinces

KREAS KIDONATO

We know that the ancient Greeks ate quinces—Athenaeus mentions them in his descriptions of sumptuous dinners. Although cooking pork, lamb, or veal with quinces is not very common today, Greeks use the word *kidonati* ("like quinces") to describe potatoes quartered lengthwise. So we can assume that quinces were cut lengthwise and were regularly added to stews before potatoes were introduced to Greece around 1830.

Today, ripe quinces are harvested in the fall to make spoon sweets and jelly, or to be baked and served with yogurt or cream. But some whole quinces are kept to be used later in the winter. In Greek villages, quinces traditionally were stored in linen chests, giving a very pleasant fragrance to the sheets and tablecloths.

Kidonato is a dish prepared mostly by Greeks who lived in Constantinople, now Istanbul, but it can be found in many variations all over Greece. The recipe that follows is my own modification, inspired by dishes I tried in Athens, Macedonia, and Mytilini (Lesbos).

½ cup olive oil or melted butter

1 large onion, coarsely chopped

2 pounds boned lean pork (hamhock, shank, or neck), lamb (leg, shank, shoulder), or veal (rump or round), cut into cubes

1 pound pearl onions, peeled

1 tablespoon whole cloves

1 cup sweet red wine, such as Mavrodaphne

1 cinnamon stick

½–1 teaspoon minced fresh chili pepper, or ⅓–½ teaspoon dried red pepper flakes

Sea salt

½ cup water

3 pounds quinces

Heat 4 to 5 tablespoons olive oil in a deep, heavy skillet and sauté the onion and meat until golden brown all over, about 5 minutes. Remove the meat from the skillet with a slotted spoon.

Pierce some of the pearl onions with the cloves and sauté briefly in the skillet. Add the meat and pour in the wine. Add the cinnamon stick, chili pepper, and salt. Cook over medium heat for 3 to 5 minutes, then add the water and simmer, covered, for about 30 to 40 minutes, or until meat and onions are half done.

Peel the quinces, cut into quarters, and core and discard the seeds. Cut each quarter in half lengthwise, and sauté in the remaining olive oil or butter.

Preheat the oven to 350° F.

If you are using tomato paste, dilute it in ⅓ cup warm water and pour it over the meat. Bring to a boil and cook for 3 to 4 minutes. (If you are not using tomato paste, make sure there is enough sauce to cover the meat and onions. If not, add a little more wine and water, and boil briefly.) Taste and add more salt and pepper if needed.

2 tablespoons tomato paste plus
1 tablespoon sugar (optional)

2 tablespoons sugar

Transfer the quince pieces, pearl onions, and meat to an oven-proof earthenware or glass pan. Sprinkle the quinces with half the sugar (3 tablespoons in all, if you have used tomato paste) and pour the sauce over. Sprinkle the quinces with the rest of the sugar, cover with a lid or aluminum foil, and bake for 30 to 40 minutes, or until the quinces are tender and caramelized on top. During the cooking, baste the meat and quinces with the sauce.

Serve very hot.

Meat-Stuffed Cabbage Leaves in Egg-Lemon Sauce

LAHANODOLMADES ME KIMA AVGOLEMONO

As we read in Athenaeus, in ancient times boiled cabbage was thought to be a cure for a hangover. My father, who is now eighty-five years old, tells me that during his childhood in Larissa, in the middle of the largest Greek wheat fields, whenever he had digestive problems he was given hot cabbage juice to drink.

Cabbage (*lahano*) is not used in many Greek dishes today, except in Macedonia. We eat it raw, as a salad seasoned with lemon juice and olive oil, and we make *Lahanodolmades*.

Lahanodolmades are best made with cabbage that has been left to marinate for a month in brine and aromatics such as celery, onions, mint, rosemary, and bay leaves. In Macedonia, all cooks keep a large clay jar on their verandas or balconies, in a place sheltered from the sun, where in November they put their cabbages in brine. This marinated cabbage (*armia*) is also used in dishes with chicken or meat, and there are even pies made with it.

Lahanodolmades can also be made with fresh cabbage that has been blanched for eight to ten minutes.

STUFFING

½ **pound ground pork**
½ **pound ground lamb**
½ **pound ground beef**
½ **pound ground lard**
2 **eggs**
5–6 **cloves garlic, minced**
½ **cup chopped fresh dill**
1–1½ **teaspoons minced fresh chili pepper or dried red pepper flakes**
1 **cup short-grain rice**
3 **large carrots, shredded**
½ **cup olive oil**
Sea salt to taste

In a large bowl, thoroughly mix the ground meats and lard, eggs, garlic, dill, chili pepper, rice, carrots, half the olive oil, and salt.

(Be careful not to oversalt if you are using marinated cabbage.) If you are using fresh cabbage, cut a cross in the base and blanch in boiling water for 10 minutes.

Preheat the oven to 375° F.

Carefully separate the cabbage leaves. Remove the tough stems of the cabbage leaves and, along with 2 of the bay leaves, line the bottom of a deep ovenproof glass or earthenware pot with a lid.

Place each remaining fresh or marinated cabbage leaf on a board and put a tablespoon of the stuffing near the bottom of the leaf or the part nearest you. Fold the bottom and 2 sides in to cover the filling, and roll tightly toward the tip of the leaf. Continue with remaining leaves and filling. Place the packages seam side down in the pot, tightly together. After the first layer, add the 2 remaining

CABBAGES AND LEEKS
IN A KASTORIA STREET MARKET.

1 very large or 2 small heads of green
    cabbage, marinated or fresh
4 bay leaves
Juice of 1 large lemon

SAUCE

2 egg yolks
Juice of 1½ lemons
Sea salt and pepper to taste
3 tablespoons finely chopped fresh dill

SERVES 8

bay leaves and continue layering. Place some cabbage leaves on top, add the rest of the oil, the lemon juice, and ½ cup water. Top with an inverted plate and a sheet of aluminum foil. Place lid on pot.

Bake for 1½ hours, then turn off the heat and leave in the oven for another 15 minutes.

Place a stainless-steel bowl over a pot of warm but not boiling water and whisk the egg yolks until thickened. Add the lemon juice and 2 cups of hot cooking liquid from the pot. Taste and add salt and pepper if needed. The sauce must be distinctly sour to complement the sweet flavor of the cabbage and stuffing. Add more lemon juice if necessary. Stir well. Remove the *Lahanodolmades* from the pot and arrange on a warm plate. Spoon the sauce over and sprinkle with dill. Serve immediately.

Note: See note on page 158 for easier sauce preparation. If you want to make a lighter version of this dish, omit the lard and use 1 pound of lean ground beef and 3 tablespoons of thick yogurt.

Moussaka

My original thought was to leave out what is probably the most famous Greek dish. Although many people think it is a Greek classic, moussaka was, in fact, probably the invention of some educated Turkish chef inspired to use béchamel— a well-known French sauce—as the topping for an eggplant and meat casserole.

In restaurants all over Greece one finds versions of moussaka that are usually too oily, with so much béchamel that it forms a top layer almost as thick as the vegetables and meat. So it becomes the dominant taste. My version includes potatoes and peppers, and only a little meat. It can even be made without béchamel, which is the way I tend to prefer this dish.

My mother always used a bottom layer of thinly sliced potatoes in her moussaka. But you will find that some people like to omit this. You can also make moussaka with zucchini or even artichokes instead of eggplant, but the taste cannot be compared with moussaka made with eggplant.

Don't expect to cut perfect square pieces. Moussaka should be juicy, with the consistency of a gratin.

2–3 medium eggplants
Sea salt
3 large green bell peppers
Olive oil, for broiling and frying
1 very large or 2 smaller potatoes,
   thinly sliced

MEAT AND TOMATO SAUCE

¾ pound lean lamb, cut in very small
   cubes or strips
2 large onions, coarsely chopped
   (about 2 cups)
1 large green bell pepper, diced
1½ teaspoons minced fresh chili
   pepper, or to taste
½ cup dry red wine
5 large tomatoes, peeled and diced
   (about 2½ cups)
4 large garlic cloves, minced
½ cup dark raisins
1 tablespoon sea salt or to taste

Cut off the stems of the eggplants and peel in strips, leaving roughly half the skin on. Cut across into ⅓-inch slices, salt well on both sides, and leave in a colander for at least 35 minutes to drain and rid of bitterness.

Cut the peppers in halves or thirds lengthwise to obtain flat pieces. Discard the stems and seeds, then place peppers under the broiler, skin side up. Roast for about 10 minutes, or until the skin is blistered and black. Remove from the oven, place in a bowl, and cover with plastic wrap or aluminum foil. Let stand for about 10 to 15 minutes, then peel.

Rinse the eggplant slices under running water and pat dry with paper towels. Brush both sides with olive oil, and broil, turning once, for about 10 to 15 minutes, or until both sides are golden.

Heat the olive oil in a nonreactive frying pan and fry the potatoes over high heat for 3 to 4 minutes, until just soft. Remove with a ladle and arrange in a layer on the bottom of a clay or glass baking dish (about 15½ × 10½ inches, preferably oval). It doesn't matter if some gaps are left between slices.

In the oil in which you have fried the potatoes, sauté the lamb briefly. Add the onions, bell pepper, and chili pepper and sauté over medium heat until the onion is translucent, about 3 minutes. Add the wine and cook for about 2 minutes. Add the tomatoes and simmer for 25 to 30 minutes, or until the lamb is tender, adding a little water if necessary to keep mixture moist.

BÉCHAMEL

6 tablespoons (¾ stick) margarine
6 tablespoons all-purpose flour
3½ cups cold skim milk
Sea salt and white pepper to taste
Grated nutmeg
1 cup grated Gruyère cheese

SERVES 8–10

As the sauce is simmering, prepare the béchamel. In a saucepan, using a wire whisk, mix the margarine with the flour over moderate heat. Continue whisking vigorously until the mixture begins to froth. Remove from the heat, and continue whisking for 30 seconds. Pour in the cold milk, stirring constantly, and place again over moderate heat. Season with salt, pepper, and nutmeg. Continue whisking until thickened. Remove from the heat and stir in half the cheese. Let cool slightly.

Ten minutes before the lamb and tomato sauce is finished, add the garlic and raisins. Taste and add salt and chili pepper if needed. The sauce should be strongly flavored.

Preheat the oven to 375° F.

To assemble, arrange the eggplant slices on top of the potatoes. Spoon the meat and about half the tomato sauce over the vegetables. Cover with the grilled peppers and pour in the rest of the tomato sauce. Spoon the béchamel on top and spread evenly. Sprinkle with the rest of the cheese.

Place on the bottom rack of the oven and bake for 1 hour. Check after 45 minutes; if the top is turning brown, cover loosely with aluminum foil for the rest of the cooking time.

Let cool on a rack for at least 25 to 30 minutes before serving.

Note: The raisins are used to sweeten the tomato sauce, and can be replaced with a little sugar.

As this is a time-consuming dish, you might want to prepare the vegetables and the meat sauce a day in advance.

Variation: To make moussaka without béchamel, use the same ingredients, minus the béchamel and instead add 2 peeled and sliced tomatoes, ½ cup bread crumbs, and ½ cup grated gruyère cheese. Proceed as above, but instead of the béchamel, arrange the tomato slices on top. Sprinkle with the bread crumbs and add the cheese. This version of moussaka is better eaten cold or at room temperature.

Zucchini and Vine Leaves Stuffed with Meat

KOLOKITHIA KAI
DOLMADES AMBELOFILLA

Zucchini stuffed with ground meat is a common dish in Greece. In early summer, in Crete, in Peloponnese, and also in the villages on the outskirts of Athens, stuffed vine leaves are added to the stuffed zucchini. The combination produces a much tastier dish.

The recipe that follows was given to me by Mary Belba, a journalist friend whose family lived in Vrilissia, a village in the north of Athens. Once a farming community where all kinds of vegetables and fruits were grown and chicken, sheep, and goats were raised, Vrilissia is now another Athens suburb, filling rapidly with expensive apartment buildings. But Mary's family has kept a large garden and her parents still grow some fruits, including plums and quinces.

If using frozen vine leaves, let them thaw for 20 to 30 minutes. Frozen leaves usually need no boiling, neither do fresh young leaves. But if you are using vine leaves in brine, rinse them in running water and blanch them for 2 to 3 minutes. Set aside.

Wash and dry the zucchini and cut in half crosswise. Cut a slice from both cut ends and reserve. With either a grapefruit spoon or a melon baller, scoop out the zucchini, leaving a thin shell. Chop the pulp; you should have 1½ cups.

In a skillet, warm 3 tablespoons olive oil and fry the zucchini shells, turning them on all sides, until they turn golden. Cool on paper towels.

4 large zucchini, about 1½ pounds

35–40 fresh or frozen vine leaves
(see page 138)

½ cup olive oil

2 medium onions, finely chopped

¾ pound ground beef

1 cup dry white or red wine

6 tablespoons short-grain rice

½–1 teaspoon minced fresh chili
pepper, or ⅓–½ teaspoon dried
red pepper flakes

½ teaspoon grated nutmeg

Sea salt to taste

1½ cups chopped fresh flat-leaf
parsley

3 tablespoons pine nuts

1½ cups warm water

Juice of 1 lemon

Avgolemono Sauce (page 158)

SERVES 6–8

In the same skillet, sauté the onions until soft, about 5 minutes. Add the meat and stir a few times. Pour in the wine and boil over high heat for 2 to 3 minutes. Reduce the heat and add the chopped zucchini, rice, chili pepper, nutmeg, and salt. Simmer for 2 to 3 minutes, then remove from the heat. Add the parsley and pine nuts, and stir well.

Preheat the oven to 375° F.

Line a 9-inch lidded earthenware pot with vine leaves and some of the zucchini pulp. Stuff the zucchini with a teaspoon until full but not mounded and cap the tops with the reserved slices so that they won't empty when you lay them sideways in the pot.

Place each vine leaf on a wooden board, shiny side down, with its stem toward you. Put a teaspoon of the remaining stuffing near the bottom of the leaf, fold the bottom and 2 sides in to cover the filling, and roll tightly toward the tip of the leaf.

Place the rolls among the stuffed zucchini, fitting tightly one against the other in the pot to fill it. Top the pot with the warm water and lemon juice, and place a plate on top so the rolls will stay in place during cooking. Cover the pot with its lid.

Cook in the oven for 1 to 1½ hours, or until the zucchini and vine leaves are tender. Check during cooking to see if a little more water is needed.

Let the stuffed vegetables cool a little before serving, accompanied with sauce.

VINE LEAVES
PACKED IN A JAR,
WITHOUT BRINE.

Quail with Rice

ORTIKIA PILAFI

Quail is the only game one can find in Greek markets year-round. These birds come from game farms on the island of Zante and are very tasty. But like all game birds, they have only a little meat, so we supplement them with something substantial, like rice.

This recipe is my version of one of my mother's dishes.

½ cup olive oil

3 medium onions, chopped

4–6 quail, with giblets or
    3–4 chicken livers, chopped

1 cup sweet red wine, such as
    Mavrodaphne

1½ cups fresh or good-quality canned
    tomato puree (see page 32)

½ teaspoon grated nutmeg

½–1 teaspoon minced fresh chili
    pepper, or ⅓–½ teaspoon dried
    red pepper flakes

1 cinnamon stick

1½ cups long-grain rice

½ cup dry white wine

1½–2 cups chicken stock, warmed

Sea salt and freshly ground pepper

SERVES 4–6

In a heavy skillet that can hold all the quail, heat half the oil and sauté the onions until tender, about 10 minutes. Add the quail and sauté on all sides until lightly browned, about 5 minutes. Pour in the red wine and cook for about 2 to 3 minutes more. Add the tomato puree, nutmeg, chili pepper, and cinnamon stick. Bring to a boil and simmer for 15 to 20 minutes. (You may prepare the dish up to this point well in advance.) Set aside.

About 20 minutes before serving, bring the pan with the quail to a simmer. Heat the rest of the olive oil in a separate pan and sauté the giblets until firm, about 5 minutes. Add the rice and stir a few times. Pour in the white wine, stir well, and add 1½ cups of stock. Stir, then transfer to the pan with the quail.

Season with salt and simmer, covered, for 10 to 15 minutes, adding more stock if needed a little at a time, until the rice is cooked but firm—moist, like an Italian risotto. Taste and season with salt and pepper if needed.

Discard the cinnamon stick and serve immediately.

OLIVE GROVE, LESBOS.

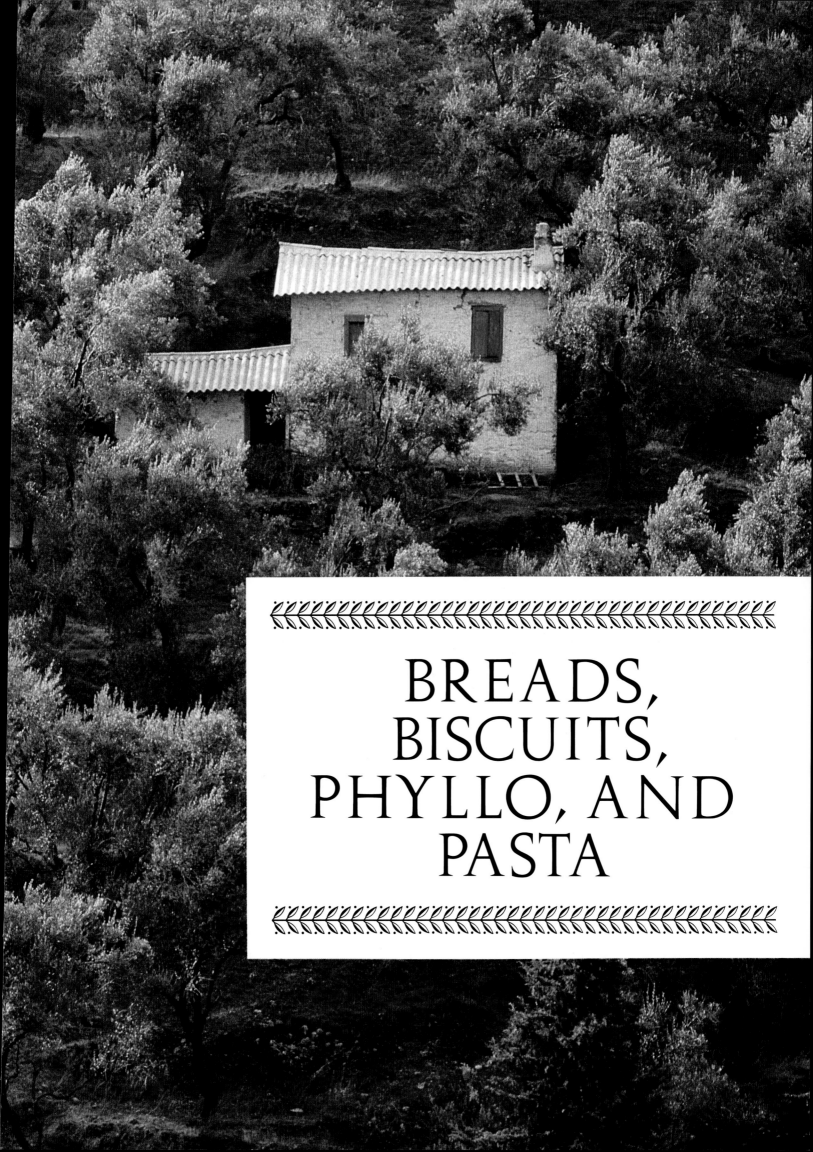

BREADS, BISCUITS, PHYLLO, AND PASTA

I know of no other culture in which bread plays such an important role at all stages of people's lives. Bread is so much linked with our existence that, instead of saying that a person is about to pass away, we say "his bread is finished" or "he has eaten all his bread." In many parts of Greece there are special breads that are baked when a woman is expecting a baby, others to celebrate the arrival of the child, still others for the christening, for the child's birthday, and for when a boy turns twenty-one. There are special breads for people in love; there are engagement breads, marriage breads—different ones for the bride, the groom, and the in-laws—breads for a person's name day, breads that chase away illness, breads for the dead.

THRESHING WHEAT, SANTORINI.

Bread was, up until very recently, the chief element of the Greek diet. We say "I work to earn my bread," and we really mean it. Greeks have long supplemented their simple and meager meals with bread, dipping large pieces in the sauce to satisfy their hunger. Older people, especially those who have lived through the horrible starvation winters during the German occupation of 1941–42, have such strong feelings about bread that they believe it to be sacrilege to throw it away.

In many parts of Greece bread is considered magical and sacred, and it is believed to have powers to keep away evil spirits. Pregnant women traditionally sleep with a piece of bread under their pillows.

There are many traditions that surround bread making, different in each part of the country. Most deal with the rising of the bread and probably have their roots in antiquity. For instance, village women still bake bread using a sourdough starter—the way it has been done for centuries. As people who have tried this method know, sourdough starters can be unpredictable. You can never be certain if and how much the dough will rise. Some believe that you will have success if the liquid in the starter is holy water blessed on Good Friday or on the Day of the Cross in September.

In some parts of Greece, people believe that if a sprig of basil used by the priest to sprinkle holy water on the congregation is included in the sourdough, the bread will rise without fail. On special occasions—engagements, marriages, and so forth —when the bread absolutely must succeed, people seek the help of women *me heri* (with the hand)—women known to bake successfully, perhaps using some special tricks. In some parts of Greece, people believe that if a virgin starts the dough, the bread will be successful. In fact, the mother of a groom sometimes tests the character of her future daughter-in-law by asking her to make bread.

Homemade bread is usually formed into large, round loaves (*karveli*), but can also be shaped in long loaves (*frantzola*). Loaves destined for the church are always round, stamped with a special wooden bread stamp that contains the words *Iisus Khristos Nika* (Jesus Christ Triumphs). There used to be an unwritten law that in dividing and distributing the bread after the blessing, the priest should use only his hands, never a knife to cut it.

Festive breads are formed into braids (*plexouda*), crowns (*kouloura*), crowns with a cross of dough on top, or braided crowns. In the region of Rethymnon on Crete, they even have breads shaped into five-pointed stars (*pentothelitiko*)—the star of Solomon—which are believed to have magical powers to cure all illnesses.

There is a special kind of bread, called *fanouropsomo*, believed to help people find lost things and also make their wishes come true.

In many parts of Greece, especially in Crete and the villages of Attica, the bread baked for special occasions is heavily decorated with pieces of unleavened dough shaped as flowers, leaves, birds, and even people. Today, this bread is frequently sold as souvenirs.

Loaves of bread are often sliced while still warm and placed in a slow oven for up to seven hours, until they have dried completely and become rusks (*paximadia*). These rusks will keep for many months. Savory rusks are briefly dipped in water and eaten with cheese, while sweet ones accompany coffee and sweet wine.

PHYLLO

It is amazing to watch the women of Metsovo and the other villages in Epirus roll phyllo on the special round boards they keep in their kitchens for this purpose.

With their thin, long rolling pins they manage to produce perfect paper-thin sheets of phyllo with such ease that you might think that anybody could do it (see photographs on page 149). However, to make ordinary phyllo—which contains just flour and water—requires special skill and considerable experience. For everyday use, it is better to rely on commercial phyllo. There are many varieties available in the United States. I would suggest you search out and use the thicker version—which is available in Middle Eastern groceries—for all savory pies and for baklava. If you want to make your own phyllo, I have included a much easier recipe in this chapter, which can be executed successfully even by beginners.

HOMEMADE PASTAS

Trahana is the most important Greek version of pasta. Scholars have studied the origins of this staple food, common in the Balkan countries as well as Turkey, but its origins are lost in antiquity. We know that the word *trahana* comes from the Turkish *tarhana,* which is a similar homemade pasta. *Trahana* is made with flour, semolina, or bulgur and milk or sour milk, with some other additions.

In a paper delivered to the 1989 Oxford Symposium on Food and Cookery, food historian Maria Johnson states that *trahana* might have come from China, brought to Greece by Turkish peoples in the tenth century. Others think that it is a Turkish invention. But food historian Charles Perry insists that the word *tarkahana* was first found in the works of a Persian poet of the fourteenth or fifteenth century, and meant a kind of barley bread.

As my contribution, I would like to add that what in the rest of Greece is called sour *trahana* in Crete is called *ksinohondros.* The word *ksino* means "sour" and *hondros* was the name for coarsely ground wheat in ancient Greek. *Hondros* is mentioned in Athenaeus as a gruel, sometimes mixed with honey and sometimes cooked together with meat—exactly the way we cook *trahana* today.

There are other kinds of homemade Greek pasta as well. *Hilopites* are small squares cut from a sheet of egg noodle dough. The Pontians—the Greeks who lived near the Black Sea—brought back to Greece some very interesting recipes for stuffed pasta, including one stuffed with feta cheese (see page 210).

Greeks love spaghetti with tomato or meat sauce, but our recipes for the dish cannot compare with Italian ones. The traditional way of serving spaghetti entails first sprinkling it with cheese, pouring the sauce over it, and then pouring sizzling hot browned butter over everything at the last moment.

Sourdough Starter

All homemade Greek breads use sourdough starter instead of yeast for leavening. In the villages, women keep the starter from one week to the next and hardly ever start from scratch. There is always a neighbor to lend you some. But if you were to start from the beginning, this is the simplest way to do it.

2 packages (2 tablespoons) active
   dry yeast
3½ cups warm water
2 tablespoons honey or sugar
3 cups all-purpose flour

MAKES ABOUT 3 CUPS

In a bowl, dissolve the yeast in ½ cup warm water and add the honey or sugar. Stir well. Add the rest of the warm water and the flour, and stir to obtain a thick mixture. Cover with a damp cheesecloth and let ferment for 4 to 5 days in a warm place in the kitchen. The mixture will froth and rise at first. Then it will appear to separate, forming a light brown liquid on top that smells sour. The starter is then ready to use.

Place it in a jar or plastic bowl with a lid, cover, and store in the refrigerator. To use, stir well and measure out the amount you need for each recipe. For every cup of sourdough you use, replenish the starter by stirring in 1 cup of flour and ⅔ cup warm water. Every week, feed the sourdough with at least 3 tablespoons of water and an equal amount of flour, even if you have not used any.

Note: To prepare the batter for sourdough bread (*prozymi*), you do what in Greek is called *piano prozymi*, or "rub the sourdough." The night before baking, stir starter and measure 1 cup (or amount specified in recipe). Place in a large bowl and stir in 1 cup warm water and 1½ cups of flour. Cover loosely and let stand overnight in a warm draft-free spot. The next morning, batter will be frothy and ready to use.

Country Bread

PSOMI HORIATICO

Horiatico is usually made with a combination of wheat and barley flour. Bread called *horiatico* can be found in bakeries all over the country, in many different varieties: with whole wheat flour, sometimes with a little cornmeal, which makes it yellow; with or without sesame seeds; and so forth. This bread is supposed to imitate the homemade bread still found in many villages, but the taste and texture of the store-bought version is completely different.

The homemade version, which is always made with a sourdough starter, is heavier and more moist, usually scented with aniseed to balance the sourness of the dough. Its crumb is as tasty as its crust, unlike the commercial product. This homemade bread keeps well for three to five days, even for a week, and it is fabulous when toasted.

The recipe was given to me by Sofia Kapetanakou, who comes from the western Peloponnese. Although Sofia has lived in Athens for more than twenty years, she still bakes bread every week because neither she nor her husband nor their 17-year-old son will eat the tasteless commercial variety.

If you can, bake the bread in clay pans. If you don't want to use sourdough starter, substitute active dry yeast; see *Note*.

1 cup Sourdough Starter (page 193)
2–2½ cups warm water
3½–4 cups all-purpose flour
½ cup whole barley flour
1 cup whole wheat flour
1 cup cornmeal
1½ tablespoons sea salt
1 teaspoon aniseed, ground in
  a mortar
1 teaspoon powdered *mahlep*
  (page 36)
Olive oil, for brushing the pans

MAKES ONE 8-INCH ROUND BREAD
AND ONE 9-INCH LOAF

The night before you plan to bake, mix the starter with 1 cup warm water and 1½ cups all-purpose flour and set aside, covered, in a warm place. The mixture will be light and frothy the next morning.

Warm a large bowl, then add the remaining flours, cornmeal, salt, aniseed, and *mahlep*. Make a well in the center and pour in the starter batter and warm water.

Start bringing flour toward the center until mixed with the liquids. Start kneading, sprinkling the dough with flour if it is too sticky, or wetting your hands with warm water if it is too hard and dry. The whole wheat and barley flours make this dough a little sticky at the beginning, so it needs a little more kneading than ordinary bread dough. After working it for 10 to 15 minutes, the dough becomes smooth and shiny. (The mixture can also easily be worked with a hand-held mixer equipped with a dough hook.)

Cut off one-third of the dough with a knife and shape it into a ball. Place in a well-oiled 8-inch round pan. With the remaining dough, form a loaf and place in a well-oiled 9-inch loaf pan. Brush breads with olive oil, cover with plastic wrap, and place in a warm place until doubled in size, about 1½ hours.

Remove plastic wrap and increase oven temperature to 375° F. Bake loaves for 50 minutes, or until lightly golden on top. Invert pans and remove breads. Return to the oven, bottom sides up, and bake another 5 minutes, or until golden and hollow-sounding when tapped. Let cool on a rack.

Note: Alternatively, use 2 packages active dry yeast instead of sourdough starter. Dissolve yeast in 1 cup warm water, then stir into flour and warm water mixture in bowl. Let the shaped loaves rise for 2 to 2½ hours in a warm place, but not the oven. Preheat the oven to 375° F. and bake for 40 minutes.

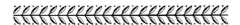

Festive Bread

PROSFORO

Prosforo is the bread taken to church to be blessed by the priests in special ceremonies called *artoklassia* (cutting of the bread). After the blessing, the round loaves are cut into small pieces and each member of the congregation gets one.

Prosforo is decorated by being stamped with a special wooden seal before baking, and it is sometimes brushed with water and sprinkled with glazing sugar while still warm.

½ cup **Sourdough Starter** (page 193)
2 cups **warm water**
4 cups **all-purpose flour**
1 cup **cornmeal**
1 cup **fine semolina**
1 teaspoon **sea salt**
2–4 tablespoons **sugar**, or to taste
1 teaspoon ground *mastic* (page 36)
1 teaspoon ground **cinnamon**
½ cup *mastic*-scented spirit (page 38) or **ouzo**
Olive oil, for brushing the pans
Confectioners' sugar (optional)

MAKES TWO 9-INCH ROUND LOAVES

The night before you want to bake, combine the starter with 1 cup warm water and ½ cup flour. Stir and set it aside, covered.

The next morning, combine the remaining flour with the cornmeal, semolina, salt, sugar, *mastic,* and cinnamon in a large bowl. Make a well in the center and pour in the starter mixture, *mastic* spirit or ouzo, and remaining warm water. Start bringing flour to the center until all the liquids are absorbed.

Start kneading the dough, adding more flour if it is too sticky or wetting your hands with warm water if it is too hard. Knead for 7 to 10 minutes, or until the dough is smooth and silky. (Alternatively, you can work the dough in a food processor or with a hand-held mixer fitted with a dough hook.)

Oil two 9-inch round earthenware pans. Cut the dough into 2 parts with a knife and shape each into a ball. Place in the pans, brush tops with a little oil, cover with plastic wrap, and place in a warm place until doubled in size, about 1 hour.

Remove plastic wrap, turn oven to 375° F., and bake for about 50 minutes. Invert pans and remove breads. Return loaves to the oven, bottom side up, to bake another 5 minutes, until golden and hollow-sounding when tapped. Let cool on a rack.

If desired, brush with a little water and sprinkle with confectioners' sugar.

Easter Bread

TSOUREKI

This delicious festive bread was at one time only baked on Easter. Now it is made year round, including the Christmas holidays. It is customary for godmothers to bake one *Tsoureki* for each godchild.

More a cake than a bread, with a texture similar to brioche, *Tsoureki* slices can also be left to dry for five hours in a slow 200° F. oven to become very tasty biscuits. The same dough, with 2 teaspoons *mahleb* and no *mastic,* is shaped into a round flat bread for the New Year's *Vassilopita* (page 44). A coin is hidden in the dough before baking, to bring luck to whoever finds it in his piece.

1 cup Sourdough Starter (page 193)

1 package (1 tablespoon) active
dry yeast

½ cup plus 2 tablespoons warm milk

8–9 cups all-purpose flour

½ cup unsalted butter or margarine

½ cup sugar

2 tablespoons honey

2 tablespoons olive oil

½ cup orange juice

1 teaspoon ground *mastic*
(see page 36)

1 teaspoon ground *mahleb*
(see page 36)

½ teaspoon sea salt

2 tablespoons grated orange zest

4 eggs, 1 separated

MAKES 2 LOAVES

The night before you plan to bake, combine the starter with the yeast, ½ cup warm milk, and 1 cup flour. Stir, cover, and set it aside in a warm place to rise overnight.

The next morning, in a bowl, beat the butter with the sugar and honey. Add the olive oil, orange juice, *mastic, mahleb,* salt, and grated orange zest. Continue beating, adding 3 of the eggs and 1 egg white, one by one. Reserve one egg yolk.

In a large bowl, sift 7 cups of flour and make a well in the center. Pour in the starter and the butter mixtures and stir to form the dough. Knead with your hands for about 10 minutes, adding a little more flour if it is too sticky or some warm milk if it is too hard. When the dough becomes soft and shiny, form it into a ball and let it rise, covered, in an oiled bowl, for about 2 hours.

When the dough is doubled in size, punch down and divide it in thirds. Roll each into a long cord about 1 inch thick and 30 inches long. Cut each cord in half to form 6 cords, with which you will make the 2 braided loaves.

Stick the ends of the 3 ropes together and braid neatly. Repeat with the other 3 cords to form the second loaf. Place on a buttered baking pan and cover. Let rise for another 2 to 3 hours, or until they have doubled in size.

Preheat the oven to 375° F.

Beat the remaining egg yolk with 2 tablespoons of milk, and glaze the loaves. Bake for 40 to 45 minutes, or until golden brown. Let loaves cool on a rack.

Note: If desired, stick a dyed Easter egg in the loaf, forming a ring in one end of the braid. But as the dye dissolves in the dough around the egg, part of this delicious bread will become inedible.

FESTIVE BREADS, SOME WITH
RED-PAINTED EASTER EGGS, PREPARED
BY MRS. PATINIOTIS IN LIVADI,
ASTYPALAIA.

Raisin Bread from Mykonos

MYKONIATIKO TSOUREKI

This much lighter festive bread is a very interesting variety of the traditional raisin bread (*stafidopsomo*). This version comes from Mykonos, and was given to me by Anna Sigala, my neighborhood baker. She got it from her grandmother.

My mother and father hated raisin bread because, for a period during the 1930s, the Greek government made it compulsory for everyone buying any kind of bread to buy some raisin bread, too. The Ministry of Agriculture had bought all the raisins from Corinth to keep the growers satisfied, for political reasons, and then invented this method to get rid of the surplus.

Later on, when this stupid regulation was no longer applied, raisin breads disappeared from the bakeries because no one would buy them. Only recently, more than two generations later, is raisin bread again becoming popular.

1 cup Sourdough Starter (page 193)
8–9 cups all-purpose flour
1½ cups warm water
2 cups cornmeal
1 teaspoon sea salt
1 package (1 tablespoon) active
   dry yeast
2 tablespoons ground *mahleb* or
   1 tablespoon ground *mastic*
   (page 36)
2½ cups orange juice
1 cinnamon stick (about
   2 inches long)
1 tablespoon whole cloves
3 tablespoons honey
1½–2 cups raisins
1 cup coarsely ground walnuts
   (optional)
Olive oil, for brushing the pans
   and dough
3 tablespoons sesame seeds

MAKES 3 LOAVES

The night before you plan to bake, mix the starter with 2 cups flour and 1½ cups warm water. Let stand, covered with plastic wrap, until the next morning.

The next day, in a large bowl, mix the cornmeal with 6 cups flour. Add the salt, yeast, and *mahleb*. In a saucepan, pour the orange juice over the cinnamon stick and cloves and bring to a boil. Remove from the heat and add the honey. Stir to dissolve and let cool a little, then pass it through a fine sieve.

Make a well in the center of the flour mixture, add the cornmeal mixture, and pour in the starter and orange juice mixtures. Start drawing flour toward the liquids until all is mixed. Knead the dough, wetting your hands with warm water if it is too hard or sprinkling with flour if it is too sticky. When smooth and shiny, after 7 to 10 minutes, cut the dough in thirds with a knife. With each piece of dough, make a rectangle about 7 × 11 inches, and sprinkle with one-third of the raisins and the walnuts, if using.

Roll each rectangle to make a loaf, and put it in an oiled 9 × 4½-inch loaf pan. When all 3 breads are in pans, brush with water and sprinkle with sesame seeds.

Place the pans in a warm (120° F.) oven, cover with plastic wrap, and let stand for 1½ hours, or until doubled in size.

Remove the plastic and turn up the oven to 375° F. Bake the bread for 50 minutes. Invert the pans and remove the loaves. Bake bottom side up on oven rack for another 5 to 10 minutes, or until golden and hollow sounding when tapped.

Cool loaves on a rack.

Festive Bread and Rusks from Crete

KRITIKO CHRISTOPSOMO, PENTOTHELITIKO

This very interesting dark bread is seldom found fresh. You are most likely to taste it in a house in Chania or Rethymnon in Crete, in the form of dried rusks served with coffee or the sweet farmer's cheese, anthotyro. They also make a lovely dessert when dipped in sweet wine.

I was told that this dough was used to make *pentothelitiko,* the five-point star-shaped bread that is believed to have the power to heal all illnesses.

1 cup Sourdough Starter (page 193)
1 cup warm water
5½–6 cups all-purpose flour
1½ cups sweet red wine such as
    Mavrodaphne
2 tablespoons honey
1 tablespoon ground cinnamon
1 teaspoon ground cloves
1 cup cornmeal
½ cup fine semolina
1 cup whole wheat flour
1 teaspoon sea salt
1 teaspoon ground *mastic* (optional;
    see page 36)
¼ cup olive oil
Olive oil, for brushing the baking
    sheets and loaves

MAKES ABOUT 50 RUSKS AND
1 LARGE LOAF

FESTIVE BREAD FROM CRETE,
SHAPED INTO A DOUBLE CROWN
TO FORM A FIVE-POINTED STAR.

200

The night before you plan to bake, mix the starter with the warm water and 1½ cups of all-purpose flour. Stir well, cover, and set it aside in a warm place.

The next day, pour the wine into a small saucepan and add the honey, cinnamon, and cloves. Bring to a boil, reduce the heat, and simmer for 2 minutes. Pass mixture through a fine sieve and measure; you should have about 1 cup.

Combine the remaining all-purpose flour with cornmeal, semolina, and whole wheat flour. Add the salt and *mastic* if using and stir.

Make a well in the center of the flour mixture and pour in the starter mixture, wine mixture, and olive oil. Start drawing flour toward the center until it is all mixed with the liquid. Start kneading the dough, sprinkling with flour if it is too sticky or wetting your hands with warm water if it is too hard. (Alternatively, use a hand-held mixer equipped with a dough hook, or a food processor.)

When the dough becomes smooth and shiny, after about 10 to 15 minutes of kneading, roll out on a floured surface, divide in half, and use one piece to shape a crown. Oil a large pan and place crown on it. Divide the remaining dough into fourths, then roll each piece into a sausage 13 inches long. Oil a baking sheet and space loaves to allow for rising. With a sharp knife, make shallow slits on the surface about ⅔ inch apart. Brush with oil. Transfer the pan and baking sheet to a just-warm 120° F. oven, cover loosely with plastic, and let stand for about 1 hour, or until doubled in size.

Without removing the pan and baking sheet from the oven, remove the plastic, turn up the heat to 375° F., and bake the loaves for 40 to 45 minutes. The long loaves will be ready first. Turn the loaves upside down and bake for another 5 minutes, or until they sound hollow when tapped with your fingers. Let cool on a rack.

To make the rusks, let the loaves cool for 15 minutes. Cut the slashed long loaves into slices. Heat the oven to 175° F. Place slices on oven rack and bake for 5 to 6 hours, or until completely dry. Let cool on the rack, and keep in an airtight box.

Overleaf: RUSKS, WHITE BREAD,
FESTIVE BREADS, AND EASTER BREADS
WITH OLD BREAD STAMPS;
WOODEN BREAD TROUGHS AND
PINAKOTI, WOODEN PEELS; FROM THE
ROOF BEAMS HANG CHEESECLOTH
SACKS FILLED WITH *TRAHANA.*

Fried Cheese Bread

TIGANOPSOMO ME TIRI

I tried this delicious bread in a village in the mountains of the Peloponnese some years ago. Stopping at a small coffee house, I spotted a woman in the back shaping her loaves to let them rise. I noticed that she kept a piece of the dough the size of a fist. I asked what she was going to use it for, and she explained that she would make *Tiganopsomo* for her grandson.

The woman used grated onion mixed with oregano and parsley to top the bread before adding the goat cheese. As she explained, this mixture was left over from a stuffing she had prepared earlier. On other occasions she used garlic with peppers or scallions with dill—whatever she had in the house.

I have tried the recipe with different toppings, but onions and oregano without the parsley seems to work best. The quality of the cheese plays a very important role. Semidry goat cheese, like the one made in Epirus (Metsovo or Dodona), works best. A mixture of feta and very sharp pecorino is an acceptable substitute.

1 piece Country Bread dough (page 194), about the size of a large fist
3 tablespoons olive oil, plus a little more for brushing the bread
2 tablespoons grated onion
Freshly ground pepper
½ teaspoon dried oregano
½ cup grated or crumbled cheese

SERVES 1–2

Shape the dough into a ball and let it rise for 1 hour.

Flatten dough to form a large disk about 8 inches in diameter. Let rise again for about 30 minutes.

Preheat the oven to 375° F.

Heat the oil in a large ovenproof skillet. Transfer the flat bread to it and brush with oil. Sprinkle with onion, pepper, and oregano and top with the cheese. Fry the dough over medium heat for 6 to 10 minutes, or until the bottom becomes crisp and brown. Place the skillet in the oven and bake for 10 to 15 minutes, or until the cheese is melted and bubbling.

Let cool a little before serving. It can also be eaten at room temperature.

Homemade Phyllo

The traditional phyllo made by the women of Metsovo contains only flour and water and a very small amount of olive oil. Seeing these women making the paper-thin pastry with their long, thin rolling pins, one would think that there is nothing to it. But that is hardly the case. You must be very nimble-fingered and need lots of practice to be able to achieve the perfect phyllo. So here is an easy alternative. The recipe that follows was given to me by my neighbor Chrissoula Boniakou, who comes from Alexandroúpolis, Macedonia. Even if you cannot make it very thin, this phyllo will make good pies because it has a consistency similar to puff pastry and is suitable for all kinds of fillings.

4 cups bread flour
⅔–1 cup olive oil
½ teaspoon sea salt
1½ tablespoons lemon juice
1 cup water or milk (more if needed)

MAKES FOUR 17 × 13-INCH SHEETS,
ABOUT 1 POUND

Sift the flour into a large bowl and make a well in the center. Add half the oil, salt, lemon juice, and water, and mix the ingredients with a fork. Transfer the dough onto a floured work surface and knead for about 5 minutes, lifting it and throwing it down onto the surface until it becomes smooth and glossy. (You can also make it in a food processor with a dough hook.) Cover the dough with plastic wrap and let it rest in the refrigerator for about 30 minutes.

Roll the dough out on a floured surface until you have a rectangular piece about ⅓ inch thick. Cut it in 6 pieces and brush each piece with olive oil. Place the pieces one on top of another and roll out again until you have a rectangular piece about ⅓ inch thick. Repeat the procedure once more, then cut the last stack into quarters, and roll each piece as thin as possible.

Flour your hands to lift each sheet and stretch it carefully, starting from the center and working outward. If some little holes appear in the process, don't worry, you can patch them as you will place the phyllo loosely in the pan. Leave it to dry for 20 to 30 minutes.

Note: Remember when you are using the phyllo that it dries out easily, so you must work as quickly as possible and cover the sheets with a damp cloth until the moment you use them.

Sour Trahana

KSINOHONDROS

Trahana, a traditional homemade pasta, is prepared in two ways: sweet and sour. The first is made with ordinary milk and the latter with milk that has been left to sour naturally. Eggs and herbs can be added to the basic recipe.

There are many different recipes for *trahana,* some using flour and semolina and some using bulgur, which in the old days was the home-produced wheat ground in stone mills. According to Tassos Mallios, a native of Arcadia in the Peloponnese, who has a small shop in Nauplia producing excellent *trahana,* the type made with bulgur should be boiled so it absorbs more milk or sour milk, while *trahana* made with flour is kneaded, much like bread.

In the Peloponnese, only sweet *trahana* is made with bulgur, and it is cooked with sheep's milk. On Crete, the traditional sour *trahana* is soaked in sour milk overnight or boiled for 5 to 10 minutes. Stone-ground bulgur is not as coarse as commercial, so to compensate, semolina is mixed with the bulgur when making homemade *trahana.*

In Greek villages, *trahana* is stored in cotton sacks that hang from the rafters, but you can keep completely dried *trahana* indefinitely in glass jars.

3 cups whole milk
3 cups plain yogurt
2 tablespoons lemon juice
2½ pounds bulgur (cracked wheat)
1 cup fine semolina
2 tablespoons sea salt
1 teaspoon freshly ground pepper

MAKES ABOUT 4 CUPS

Mix the milk with the yogurt, add the lemon juice, and let stand overnight, covered with a tea towel, to turn sour.

The next day, mix bulgur and semolina in a large pot. Pour in the soured milk and bring to a boil. Reduce the heat and simmer for 5 to 10 minutes, stirring constantly with a wooden spoon. Season with salt and pepper. Away from the heat, let stand for 10 to 15 minutes.

Place half-cup measures of the mixture on a clean sheet or rack to dry. Let dry in the sun or in a very slow oven (175° F.) for 6 to 7 hours, or until completely dry. Either store as pieces or grate in food processor until crumblike. Store in a glass jar. To soften, soak in water for 30 minutes before cooking.

Note: For *trahana* soup, use 2 to 3 tablespoons of *trahana* for each serving. Sauté 1 to 2 cloves of garlic in a saucepan, then add chicken or meat stock or water. Stir in the *trahana,* add salt and pepper, and serve accompanied by garlic croutons.

GRINDING WHEAT IN A STONE HAND MILL AND
SOAKING THE CRACKED WHEAT TO MAKE
KSINOHONDRO, THE SOUR *TRAHANA* FROM CRETE.

Sweet Trahana

TRAHANAS GLYKOS

I was given this recipe by my friend Sofia Kapetanakou.

¾ cup Sourdough Starter (page 193)
6 cups warm milk (see *Note*)
10 cups all-purpose flour
5 cups semolina
2 tablespoons sea salt
4 medium onions, finely grated
1–2 fresh chili peppers, finely minced,
   or ⅓–½ teaspoon dried red pepper
   flakes (optional)

MAKES 12 CUPS

Combine the starter with 3 cups warm milk and 7 cups flour. Let stand in a warm place until doubled in size, about 2 hours.

Combine the 3 remaining cups flour with the semolina in a large bowl. Add the salt, onions, and chili pepper. Pour in the rest of the milk and the starter mixture. Mix well with your hands.

Turn the dough out onto a floured surface and knead until you get a smooth and elastic dough. Add a bit more flour or warm milk if needed. Return dough to a lightly floured bowl and cover with plastic wrap and then with a blanket. Let stand overnight. Make sure that the bowl has enough room for the dough to double.

The next morning, take ½ cupfuls of dough and flatten them to obtain biscuitlike round pieces. Spread clean cloths in a dry place, preferably in the sun, and lay the dough pieces to dry, turning them once. When they are almost dry, after 6 or 7 hours, or less if you left them in the sun, grate the pieces in a food mill, using the large hole disk, to obtain crumblike *trahana*.

Spread the *trahana* on cotton sheets and let dry completely for 1 or 2 days, depending on the humidity in the air. The finished *trahana* must be very hard. The process is shortened considerably if the *trahana* is dried in the sun or in a very low oven (175° F.).

Store in jars, or in cotton sacks if you have a very dry place to hang them.

Note: Instead of milk, you can use soured milk or half milk and half plain yogurt.

Variation: For the days of Lent, try this dairyless version. Substitute 6 cups vegetable juice (tomato, leek, parsley, carrot, bell pepper, and so forth) for the milk. You can also use 6 cups spinach or any other kind of greens (cooked and pureed in the blender).

Astypalaian Yellow (Saffron) Biscuits

NICHOLAS BEHARIS, THE BAKER, WITH THE ASTYPALAIAN WOMEN WHO BAKE THEIR YELLOW EASTER BISCUITS IN HIS SHOP.

KITRINA KOULOURIA ASTYPALITIKA

I first saw these biscuits on Holy Thursday in Astypalaia (an island of the Dodecanese). In a bakery there I saw pan after pan full of yellow biscuits about to be baked for the second time. I thought they were the baker's specialty and asked if I could buy some. To my astonishment I learned that they belonged to the women of the village, who had brought them there to be baked. I was offered one to taste, and tried to figure out what was giving them their strange flavor. I had never seen or tasted anything like those biscuits anywhere in Greece.

The week before Easter it is customary throughout Greece to bake Easter biscuits, but the ones I was familiar with were sweet and contained many eggs. These were savory—I could taste pepper in them—but I could not figure out the rest of the flavors. When I asked, I was told that their main flavoring was saffron.

In the fall, after the first rains, the women of the island climb the rocky hills of Astypalaia in search of the crocus flowers from which they collect about ⅓ ounce of saffron threads—enough to color and flavor the dough made from 28 pounds of flour that they usually bake. Astypalaian women don't like commercial saffron, believing that the saffron gathered from their own hills is best. And, of course, they are right.

As I learned later, these saffron biscuits are found only on this tiny island. In Athenaeus, bread with saffron is described as one of the foods served during ancient symposia, but in modern Greece—although we now cultivate and export a lot of the precious spice—we use hardly any saffron in our cooking.

I believe that this recipe must be a very old one, and that is the reason it contains no sugar. The women of the island keep the tradition and bake a lot of these yellow biscuits every Easter. They send some to their relatives in Athens and keep the rest in large tin boxes to eat with fresh farmer's cheese or with their coffee for the rest of the year.

Adjusting the recipe given to me by Virginia Manolaki for 8 cups of flour was quite an ordeal. Commercial saffron seems to be weaker than the Astypalaian variety, so I had to use more. Finally, I came up with the version that follows, which is very near the real thing. Serve the biscuits with fresh cheese or with coffee.

2 cups milk

1 1/2 teaspoons saffron threads

1 1/2 cups full-fat cottage or farmer cheese, crumbled

1/2 cup (1 stick) butter or margarine

1/2 cup olive oil

1 egg yolk

8–9 cups all-purpose flour

1 teaspoon ground allspice

1 teaspoon ground white pepper

1 teaspoon sea salt

1/2 teaspoon baking powder

2 packages (2 tablespoons) active dry yeast, dissolved in 1/2 cup warm milk

MAKES ABOUT 5 1/2 DOZEN

In a saucepan, warm the milk with the saffron. Simmer until the milk takes on the vivid yellow of the saffron.

In a mixer bowl, beat the cheese with the butter or margarine, olive oil, and egg yolk. Measure the saffron milk (it should be 1 1/2 cups) and add it to the bowl and beat well, also adding 1 to 2 cups of flour.

In a large bowl, mix 6 cups of flour with the allspice, pepper, salt, and baking powder. Make a well in the center and pour in the yeast and saffron mixtures. Start drawing flour to the center and then knead to obtain a smooth dough. If dough is too sticky, add a little more flour; if too tough, sprinkle with a little water or milk. Let dough rest for 1 hour.

Preheat the oven to 400° F.

Take pieces of the dough and roll to make 1/2-inch-thick cords. Cut 8-inch-long pieces of the cord and stick the 2 ends of each piece together, forming small (about 2 1/2 inches in diameter) crowns.

Place in oiled pans, leaving room to expand on all sides. Place in the oven and bake for about 25 minutes. Remove from the oven and let cool, then arrange on the oven racks. Adjust the oven to 175° F. and bake again for 4 to 5 hours, or until completely dry. Remove from the oven and let cool completely.

Place in airtight jars or tins. They keep well for a very long time.

Pasta Stuffed with Feta Cheese

VARENIKA

It is not only the Italians who stuff pasta. The Pontians, Greeks living near the Black Sea, have a lot of very interesting recipes for stuffed pasta. Most of them are stuffed with cheese or chicken, and shaped into many different forms, half-circles being the most simple.

Some Pontians returned to Greece from Turkey at the beginning of this century, but a lot more are coming now from the former Soviet Union. Many live in Macedonia, and they have made quite an impression with their very distinctive dancing, their way of speaking—sometimes using ancient Greek words that only they understand—and, of course, their characteristic cooking.

I don't pretend to be an expert on Pontian cooking, but the little I have learned makes me think that a book should be devoted to their cuisine.

1 cup all-purpose flour
1 cup fine semolina
4½ teaspoons sea salt
⅓ cup olive oil
½–1 cup water

STUFFING

2 cups crumbled soft feta cheese
4 tablespoons finely chopped fresh
    mint, or 2 teaspoons dried
Freshly ground black pepper

1 bunch fresh thyme
1 tablespoon dried oregano

SERVES 6

In a large bowl, mix the flour and semolina with 1½ teaspoons salt.

Make a well in the center and pour the olive oil and water in.

Gradually draw flour from the sides with your fingers until all is mixed with the liquids. If the dough is too dry, wet your hands; if it is too soft, sprinkle with a little more flour.

Knead the dough until smooth and elastic, then shape into a ball, cover with plastic, and let stand for about 1 hour.

In a bowl, mix the feta with the mint and pepper. Set aside.

Flour a work surface lightly and knead the dough a bit more to shape into a ball. Press and roll the ball with a floured rolling pin to make a very thin sheet, about ⅟₁₆ inch.

With a water or wine glass, cut disks about 3½ inches in diameter. Using a teaspoon, place a little stuffing (less than ½ teaspoon) in the center of each disk. Dip one finger into water and wet half the circle edge. Fold the pasta over to cover the stuffing and form half-circles. With your fingers, pinch the edges together to seal them. If you like, turn each stuffed half-circle around your finger to form tortellini.

In a large pot, bring water to a boil, add the remaining 3 teaspoons of salt, the thyme, and oregano. When the water boils vigorously, drop in the pasta. When the water starts to boil again, the pasta should be cooked. Try and, if done, drain the pasta.

GRAPES, METSOVO.

DESSERTS
AND
SWEETS

In the eighth century A.D., long before sugar was introduced to northern Europe, it was already in use as a sweetener in the southern Mediterranean, in Spain, and in Cyprus. Modern Greeks share their love for sweets with their Arab neighbors and with the Turks, who ruled Greece for four hundred years, from the fifteenth to the nineteenth century.

But even before the introduction of sugar, ancient Greeks used honey to prepare sweets similar to the fried dough pastries and the pies we make today, using sesame seeds, pine nuts, almonds, and walnuts.

Dried figs must be the oldest Greek dessert. Dried figs sandwiched with walnuts and sesame seeds were a staple food of the Mycenaean era (thirteenth century B.C.). My friend Maria Frantzi, who grew up on Rhodes, was given dried figs stuffed with walnuts and sesame seed as a snack to eat at school.

All ancient banquets ended with *epidorpio* (desserts), which seem to have consisted of flat wheat or barley cakes with honey, called *plakous*. Today, in Chania, Crete, people still prepare sweets called *plakoundia*, which are small cakes made of fine semolina with butter. Almonds whipped in honey, and all kinds of nuts that were munched after the main meal had ended, were called *tragemata*, another kind of ancient Greek dessert. It is interesting to note that the most popular sweets in Greece today are still made with almonds, walnuts, sesame, and honey.

Greek sweets tend to be much too sweet by American and European standards. We pour syrup over most of our cakes and pies and even dip our biscuits in syrup or honey. On the other hand, there are many interesting sweets and cookies made without butter or eggs, something almost unheard of in French and most other European cuisines. These are the sweets for the days of Lent.

Another large category of Greek sweets is the fruit or vegetable preserves, called spoon sweets. These are not served at the end of meals but, rather, a spoonful is offered with a glass of water or a cup of Greek coffee to guests. They are also enjoyed in the afternoon, the minute one wakes up from the traditional midday siesta, when they are washed down with a glass of cold water. Morello cherry, grated quince, and rolled Seville orange or bergamot peels are the most common spoon sweets, but you will find a great many other fruits—grapes, unripe figs,

pieces of orange, unripe almonds or walnuts together with their green skin and their soft shells, and so forth—made into spoon sweets. Also, vegetables such as small unripe tomatoes, small unripe eggplants, or pieces of pumpkin pierced with almonds are cooked in syrup and made into spoon sweets.

A good cook was judged by her spoon sweets, which should not only taste good but look nice. For that reason in the old Greek cookbooks one finds a lot of strange recipes for keeping the fruits firm as they cook in the syrup, without losing their color. Fruits were dipped in copper sulphide, diluted in water, or even dipped in a weak solution of whitewash.

COFFEE AND *MASTICHA*, THE MASTIC-SCENTED SUGAR SWEET SERVED IN A GLASS OF WATER.

Another category of sweets—the sweet pies or pan sweets (*glyka tapsiou*)—is made using phyllo pastry. After the sweets are baked, syrup is poured over them. In general, these sweets are heavy, owing to the abundance of butter used for brushing the pastry. In my recipes I have tried to use the minimum amount of margarine (or butter and margarine if you like) and sugar by using much less syrup than usual. By turning the pieces upside down, one can still end up with delicious, moist pastries using one-third the usual syrup.

I must say a word about *kolyva*, the sweetened wheat Greeks prepare as a special memorial dish. I have included it in this chapter because it can be a fantastic dessert, although you will never find it in Greece served that way.

And I must add that my favorite dessert is a bowl of thick Greek yogurt with two or three spoonfuls of Morello cherry or other fruit preserve to give it flavor. Try it, and I'm sure you will agree with me.

Fried Pastry Ribbons

KSEROTIGANA

A specialty of Chania, Crete, this delicious sweet is traditionally prepared for weddings and engagements. It is quite easy to make, but it's time consuming, so most families have stopped making *Kserotigana* themselves and order them from one of the two specialty shops that prepare it in Chania. This recipe was given to me by Mrs. Hara Papadaki, owner of the only remaining bell foundry in Chania.

3 cups all-purpose flour
1 teaspoon baking powder
1 teaspoon sea salt
2 tablespoons olive oil
2 tablespoons lemon juice
½–⅔ cup water
Olive and sunflower oil (half and half), for frying

SYRUP

2 cups water
1 cup honey
1 cup sugar
Large piece of orange peel
Large piece of lemon peel

½ cup coarsely ground walnuts and almonds
2 tablespoons sesame seeds (optional)

MAKES ABOUT 30

Sift the flour with the baking powder and salt. Make a well in the center and pour in the olive oil, lemon juice, and water, little by little, kneading to make a firm dough. Cover and let rest for about 1 hour.

Sprinkle a work surface lightly with flour, divide the dough into 2 or 3 parts, and roll out to obtain a rectangular sheet of pastry about ⅛-inch thick. Cut 1½- to 2-inch-wide ribbons that are 10 to 15 inches long.

In a deep skillet or pan, heat about 5 inches of oil to 360° F. Roll the ribbons and pick them up with tongs. As you transfer them to the hot oil, turn the tongs so the ribbons swirl, and deep-fry each one separately until it starts to turn yellow, about 1 minute. Remove from the skillet with a slotted spoon and drain on layers of paper towels.

In a small saucepan, heat the water, honey, and sugar. Add the orange and lemon peel and simmer for a few minutes. Remove from the heat.

Take one *Kserotigano* at a time, place it on a slotted spoon, and dip it in the warm syrup. Remove it immediately and sprinkle with the walnuts, almonds, and sesame seeds.

FRIED PHYLLO RIBBONS,
THE TRADITIONAL
CRETAN WEDDING SWEET,
IN THE DOMA HOTEL,
CHANIA, CRETE.

Baked Quinces

KIDONIA PSITA

In late October, when the first quinces appear in the market, I like to prepare the simplest dessert one can make with them. I bake them and serve them with thick yogurt.

4 quinces, halved and cored
2 tablespoons whole cloves
**½ cup sweet red wine, such as
   Mavrodaphne**
½ cup cherry-flavored liqueur
½ cup sugar
1 teaspoon ground cinnamon

2 cups thick yogurt
**1 cup Grated Quince Spoon Sweet
   (page 238; optional)**

SERVES 8

Preheat the oven to 375° F.
Place the halved quinces, cut side down, in an ovenproof glass or clay dish that is just large enough to contain them. Pierce each quince half with 2 or 3 cloves.

In a bowl, mix the wine, liqueur, sugar, and cinnamon. Stir and pour over the quinces. Bake for about 1½ hours, basting frequently with the juices. Let quinces cool, then serve topped with yogurt and a teaspoon of Grated Quince Spoon Sweet, if you like.

Batter Fritters
with Honey Sauce

LOUKOUMADES

A very simple but great sweet, *Loukoumades* used to be very common all over Greece. Shops that displayed behind their window a pan of bubbling olive oil and a man throwing in it the pieces of batter, with movements similar to those of a mime artist, were not uncommon in Athens as in many other Greek cities. Now unfortunately there are only one or two *loukoumatzidika* in Athens, and I have the feeling that the numerous ones that once existed in Crete and in Macedonia have also decreased rapidly.

Irini, the hardworking wife of Dimitri Organakis, the owner of one of our favorite tavernas in Astypalaia, prepares some of the best *Loukoumades* I have ever tasted. She adds *mastic* and ouzo to the batter and sprinkles the finished fritters with freshly toasted sesame seeds and a little nutmeg and cinnamon. The recipe I give here is my own attempt to recreate Irini's *Loukoumades*.

1 tablespoon active dry yeast
1 cup warm water
2 cups all-purpose flour
⅓ teaspoon sea salt
½–1 teaspoon ground *mastic*
   (see page 36)
2 tablespoons ouzo

HONEY SAUCE

½ cup sugar
½ cup water
1 cup honey, preferably
   thyme-scented

Olive and sunflower oil, for frying
Ground cinnamon
Toasted sesame seeds
Grated nutmeg

MAKES 20–25

Dissolve the yeast in ½ cup warm water; let sit 10 minutes. In a large bowl, mix the flour and salt with the yeast, *mastic*, ouzo, and remaining water. Stir well with a wooden spoon to make a thick but pourable batter. Let stand for about 2 hours, or until it doubles in size.

In a saucepan, mix the sugar with the water and the honey. Bring to a boil briefly and simmer for about 10 minutes.

Heat about 4 inches of oil in a deep, heavy skillet (or use more oil in a deep-fryer). Take a handful of batter in one hand, make a fist, and, with your other hand, hold a wet spoon on the opening between your thumb and index finger. Squeeze your fist and collect in the spoon the spherical piece of dough that will come out. Drop it into the skillet. Dip the spoon in a glass of water and proceed, the same way, until all the batter is used. *Loukoumades* will puff up and rise to the surface. Remove them with a slotted spoon when they become golden brown and drain on paper towels.

Transfer to a serving plate while still hot, pour the honey sauce over them, and sprinkle with cinnamon, toasted sesame seeds, and a little nutmeg. Serve immediately.

Fried Pastry Squares from Ithaca

DIPLES ITHAKIS

Using a pastry similar to the one used to make *Kserotigana* (page 214), Greeks in the rest of the country make *Diples*—square or rectangular pieces of dough that are rolled, fried, and served with honey sauce. I was not going to include a recipe for *Diples* until my friend Maria Haritopoulou was kind enough to give me the handwritten book of recipes her aunt Xanthipi from Ithaca gave her when she got married. In it I found this magnificent recipe, which I must share with you.

Diples can be eaten warm or at room temperature, and they keep well for a week (if you can keep your hands away from them).

4–5 cups all-purpose flour

1 teaspoon sea salt

½ cup (1 stick) margarine or butter

3 eggs

Zest and juice of 2 oranges (1 cup plus 1 tablespoon)

3 tablespoons brandy

HONEY SYRUP

2 cups honey, preferably thyme-scented

1 cup water

1 cup sugar

Olive oil, for deep-frying

1 cup coarsely ground walnuts

In a bowl, sift 4 cups of flour with the salt and mix in the margarine or butter, rubbing it with your fingers until you obtain a mixture that looks like bread crumbs.

In a separate bowl, beat the eggs lightly and add them to the flour mixture, together with the orange zest, juice, and brandy. Knead well, adding a little water or flour if needed, then turn the dough out onto a floured surface. Knead as you would bread dough, adding more flour if it is too sticky, until you obtain a smooth dough. Cover with plastic wrap and refrigerate for 10 to 15 minutes.

In a saucepan, mix the honey with the water and sugar. Bring to a boil and simmer for 5 to 10 minutes.

Heat the oil to 360° F. Take a fist-size piece of the dough and roll out on a floured surface to make phyllo about ⅓-inch thick, or thinner. Using a pastry wheel, cut the dough into rectangles, squares, diamonds, or other shapes you like and deep-fry in batches until golden, about 1 minute. Drain on paper towels and transfer to a plate. Pour some of the syrup over each layer of *Diples* and sprinkle with the walnuts.

MAKES 25–30 7 × 3½-INCH SQUARES

SEMOLINA SWEET (page 240),
BATTER FRITTERS WITH HONEY SAUCE (page 217),
AND FRIED PASTRY SQUARES FROM ITHACA,
IN THE AVEROFF-TOSITSA HOUSE, METSOVO.

Walnut and Almond Cookies

MOSKOPUNGIA

Here is an almond cookie that includes walnuts. The recipe is from Rhodes and was given to me by Maria Frantzi.

2 cups coarsely ground walnuts
1 cup blanched and ground almonds
½ cup granulated sugar
1 small nutmeg, freshly grated
1 cup stale bread crumbs
½–¾ cup orange flower water
Confectioners' sugar

MAKES ABOUT 50

In a bowl, mix well the walnuts, almonds, sugar, nutmeg, and bread crumbs. Knead with your fingers, adding orange flower water little by little to form a smooth dough.

Preheat the oven to 350° F.

Line a baking sheet with greased paper. Take tablespoonfuls of dough, wet your fingers with orange flower water, and shape the cookies to 2½-inch crescents. Place on the sheet and bake for about 20 minutes, or until firm on the outside but still soft inside. Let cool slightly, then remove from the paper by wetting the paper attached to the cookies with a brush. Sprinkle with a little orange flower water and sift confectioners' sugar over to cover them completely.

TRANSPORTING FRESH CANE,
ASTYPALAIA.

Honey Cookies

MELOMAKARONA

The traditional Greek Christmas cookies, *Melomakarona* are believed to have originated in antiquity. They are also called *phoenikia,* and their name suggests that they probably came from the Phoenicians, a people who lived on the Mediterranean shore of the Middle East where Lebanon is today and who had extensive trade with ancient Greeks. My mother's *Melomakarona* are the best I have tasted, and this is her recipe. She insists on letting the finished biscuits cool overnight before dipping them briefly in the syrup. That way they remain crunchy. Most commercial or homemade *Melomakarona* are very soggy.

In many contemporary households, butter is used instead of the olive oil called for in the old recipes, changing their taste completely—ruining it, in my opinion.

1¼ cups light olive oil
⅓ cup sugar
1 cup fresh orange juice
3–4 cups all-purpose flour
2½ teaspoons baking powder
½ cup brandy
1½ cups fine semolina
Grated rinds of 1 orange and 1 lemon
1 teaspoon ground cloves
½ teaspoon ground cinnamon

SYRUP

1 cup sugar
1 cup honey
2 cups water
1 large piece of orange peel
1 large piece of lemon peel

1 cup coarsely ground walnuts
2 teaspoons finely ground cloves

MAKES ABOUT 50

Using an electric mixer, beat the olive oil with the sugar. Add the orange juice. In a separate bowl, mix 2 cups flour with the baking powder, and add to the oil and orange mixture. Beat with the electric mixer adding the brandy, semolina, orange and lemon peel, cloves, and cinnamon. Turn the mixture out onto a floured surface and start kneading, adding more flour, to obtain a soft and elastic dough. Let stand for 20 to 30 minutes, covered with plastic wrap.

Preheat the oven to 350° F.

Take tablespoonfuls of dough and shape into oval cookies about 2½ inches long. Press them on the top with the back of a fork to mark them with horizontal lines. Place on an oiled cookie sheet and bake for about 25 minutes. Let cool on a rack overnight.

The next day make the honey syrup. In a saucepan, mix the sugar, honey, and water and bring to a boil. Add the orange and lemon peels and simmer for 10 minutes. Remove from the heat.

Place 2 or 3 cookies on a large slotted spoon and dip them in the syrup. Don't let them soak in it; they should absorb only a little syrup, and remain crunchy. Place layers of honey-dipped *Melomakarona* on a serving dish. Mix the walnuts with the ground cloves, and sprinkle over the cookies. Let cool completely before serving. They keep well for about 10 days.

Overleaf: HONEY COOKIES, THE TRADITIONAL CHRISTMAS SWEET.

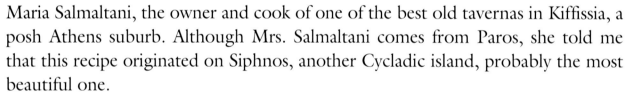

Almond Biscuits from Siphnos

AMYGDALOTA SIFNEIKA

There are many varieties of *amygdalota*. In some, the ground almonds are mixed with flour, butter, or eggs and baked. In others, the cookies are not baked at all; the almonds are mixed with rosewater, then shaped and left to dry a little before being dredged in confectioners' sugar.

Almond cookies that use no butter or eggs are one of our many Lenten sweets, which Greeks prepare especially on Clean Monday, the first day of Lent.

This recipe was given to me by Mrs. Maria Salmaltani, the owner and cook of one of the best old tavernas in Kiffissia, a posh Athens suburb. Although Mrs. Salmaltani comes from Paros, she told me that this recipe originated on Siphnos, another Cycladic island, probably the most beautiful one.

1 pound shelled almonds, blanched, dried well, and finely ground in a food processor (about 2½ cups ground)
1½–2 cups granulated sugar
½ cup water
1–2 tablespoons orange flower water, plus more to wet fingers as you shape the biscuits
Confectioners' sugar, for sprinkling

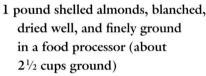

MAKES ABOUT 50

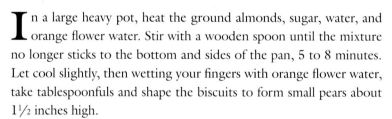

In a large heavy pot, heat the ground almonds, sugar, water, and orange flower water. Stir with a wooden spoon until the mixture no longer sticks to the bottom and sides of the pan, 5 to 8 minutes. Let cool slightly, then wetting your fingers with orange flower water, take tablespoonfuls and shape the biscuits to form small pears about 1½ inches high.

Sprinkle the biscuits with confectioners' sugar until they are completely covered.

Note: Keep the mixture covered while you work because it dries out quickly.

Walnut Cake with Eggs

KARYDOPITA ME AVGA

This wonderful dessert is halfway between a soufflé and a cake. It is a traditional dish from the Peloponnese; this recipe was given to me by my friend Sofia Kapetanakou. In her version, one egg, one tablespoon of sugar, and one tablespoon of semolina were used for each tablespoon of walnuts. I have reduced the number of egg yolks and the amount of sugar, and I can assure you it tastes even better.

5 eggs, separated
¼ cup sugar
¼ cup fine semolina
5 tablespoons bread crumbs
6 tablespoons ground walnuts
1 teaspoon baking powder
½ teaspoon ground cinnamon
⅓ teaspoon ground cloves
⅓ cup brandy

SYRUP

1 cup water
½ cup sugar

Preheat the oven to 375° F. Oil a loaf pan.

In a large bowl, beat the egg yolks with the sugar. In another bowl, beat the egg whites until stiff. Mix the semolina, bread crumbs, walnuts, baking powder, cinnamon, and cloves and add them to the yolks. Stir well and pour in the brandy. Fold whites into the yolk mixture and pour into loaf pan. Bake for about 30 minutes, or until a tester inserted in the center comes out clean.

While cake is baking, make the syrup. Boil the water with the sugar for 8 to 10 minutes.

As soon as the cake is done, pour the syrup over it. Let cool and serve.

SERVES 8

Walnut Cake for Lent

KARYDOPITA NISTISIMI

The Greeks have numerous walnut and almond cakes, but we rarely serve them the way English and Americans serve theirs. Ours are real sweets, eaten with a spoon, because syrup is poured over them.

As with many of Greek dishes, there are two different varieties of walnut cake: one for Lent without eggs and butter, and a festive one with plenty of eggs. This recipe was given to me by Vali Manouilidi.

1 teaspoon baking soda
¼ cup brandy
1 cup fine semolina
1 cup coarsely chopped walnuts
½ cup sugar
½ cup olive oil
½ cup fresh orange juice
1 teaspoon baking powder
1 teaspoon ground cinnamon
½ teaspoon ground cloves

SYRUP

½ cup sugar
1 cup water

½ cup apricot jam (optional)
2 tablespoons water

Preheat the oven to 375° F. Oil a round (9- or 10-inch) cake pan. Dissolve the baking soda in the brandy. In a large bowl mix all the remaining cake ingredients well, add the brandy mixture, and stir with a wooden spoon. Pour the mixture into the cake pan and bake for about 35 minutes, or until a toothpick inserted in the center comes out clean.

While the cake bakes, make the syrup. Mix the sugar with the water, bring to a boil, and boil for 10 minutes.

As soon as the cake is done, remove from the oven and pour the syrup over it. Let it cool.

Over very low heat, mix the jam with 2 tablespoons water, stirring constantly. Spoon the jam over the cake, and spread it evenly. Serve in the pan.

SERVES 8–10

Easter Cheese and Saffron Pies from Astypalaia

LAMBROPITES

Although they don't contain sugar, I included these very unusual festive cheese pies with the sweets because Greeks eat them as desserts. As with the Yellow Biscuits (page 208), the Astypalaian cheese pies contain saffron, something you will not find in any other part of Greece. In Paula Wolfert's book *Mediterranean Cooking*, I found a description of very similar pies from Sardinia.

The original recipe, which called for sourdough starter as well as baking powder in the pastry, was given to me by Virginia Manolaki. This is my adaptation, which uses only baking powder.

PASTRY

4 cups all-purpose flour
1½ teaspoons baking powder
½ teaspoon sea salt
½ teaspoon ground aniseed
⅓ cup butter or margarine, melted
1–1½ cups milk

FILLING

⅔ teaspoon saffron threads
1 tablespoon water
2½ cups fresh full-fat farmer cheese
2 eggs
½ teaspoon ground cinnamon
⅓ teaspoon ground allspice

1 egg plus 2 tablespoons milk, beaten
    together, for brushing
Sesame seeds, for sprinkling on top

Sift the flour with the baking powder, salt, and aniseed. Make a well in the center and pour in the melted butter or margarine. Rub with your fingers to form fine crumbs. Add the milk little by little, and start kneading to form a rather hard dough. Let rest for 30 minutes.

Simmer the saffron threads in the water in a small skillet until they have dissolved. Mix the cheese with the eggs, cinnamon, and allspice, then add the saffron.

Preheat the oven to 375° F.

Sprinkle your work surface lightly with flour and roll out the dough until it is about ⅛-inch thick. Cut 4- to 5-inch circles or 5-inch squares and place 1 heaping tablespoon of filling in the center of each. Using a spoon or fork, spread the filling so that it covers about two-thirds of the pastry, leaving about ⅔ inch of pastry at the edge. Turn the edges of the pastry inward and press lightly with your finger to form a crown of pastry all round the filling.

Oil a baking sheet and transfer the pies to it, brush with the milk and egg mixture, sprinkle with the sesame seeds, and bake for 15 to 20 minutes, or until golden. Let cool on a rack before serving.

MAKES ABOUT 35

Sweet Cheese Pies from Crete

MYZITHROPITES KRITIS

Mizithra is a fresh, full-fat farmer cheese found all over Greece in the spring and early summer, when there is plenty of grass in the hills for the semi-wild sheep and goats to eat and their milk is suitable for this delicate and delicious cheese.

Mizithra (or anthotyro as it is called in Crete, or chlori as it is called in Astypalaia), is usually eaten very fresh, even before it has cooled completely, with honey and biscuits. It is also used to make small sweet or savory pies. On many islands these pies are a traditional Easter sweet. There are, of course, many varieties of *Myzithropites:* the ones made in Astypalaia have a breadlike pastry that is left to rise before it is baked. But the best *Myzithropites* are the ones made in Crete and on Karpathos, another island of the southern Aegean.

The recipe that follows was given to me by Mrs. Maria Salmaltani, the owner and cook of one of the best old tavernas in Kiffissia, a prosperous Athens suburb.

PASTRY

2 cups all-purpose flour
1 teaspoon sea salt
¼ cup olive oil
Zest of 1 orange
½–⅔ cup fresh orange juice

FILLING

1½ cups fresh full-fat farmer cheese
2 tablespoons sugar
Zest of 1 orange

2 tablespoons milk and 1 egg yolk,
    beaten together, for brushing
    the pies

Mix the flour and salt and make a well in the center. Pour in the olive oil and orange zest and rub with your fingers to form fine crumbs. Add the orange juice little by little, and start kneading to form a soft and elastic dough. Let it rest for about 1 hour.

Preheat the oven to 375° F.

Mix the cheese, sugar, and orange zest with a fork.

Sprinkle your work surface with flour, and roll the dough out with the rolling pin. Cut 4- to 5-inch disks or squares, and place 1 heaping tablespoon of filling in the center of each. Using a spoon, spread the filling so that it covers about two-thirds of the area, leaving about ⅔ inch of pastry around. Turn the edge of the pastry inward and press slightly with your finger to form a crown of pastry all round the filling. Transfer the *Myzithropites* to an oiled pan, brush with the milk and egg mixture, and bake for 20 to 25 minutes, or until golden.

Let cool on a rack before serving.

MAKES ABOUT 20

Lenten Filled Cookies

SKALTSOUNIA

These delicious half-circle shaped cookies, covered with confectioners' sugar and filled with dried fruits and nuts, are sold in all Greek bakeries during the forty days of Lent preceding Easter.

The following recipe comes from Crete, where these cookies are also called *stafidota* (with golden raisins).

PASTRY

¼ cup granulated sugar
½–1 cup fresh orange juice
Zest of 1 orange
3 tablespoons brandy
⅓ cup olive oil
1 teaspoon baking powder
Zest of ½ lemon
3 cups all-purpose flour

FILLING

½ cup golden raisins
⅓ cup coarsely ground almonds
⅓ cup coarsely ground walnuts
Zests of ½ orange and ½ lemon
½ teaspoon ground cinnamon
½ teaspoon ground cloves
2 tablespoons brandy
1 tablespoon orange juice

Confectioners' sugar

MAKES ABOUT 50

In a bowl, dissolve the sugar in ½ cup orange juice, then mix with the orange zest, brandy, and olive oil. Add the baking powder, lemon zest, and flour little by little to form a soft dough, adding a little more orange juice if needed. Let it rest while you prepare the filling.

In another bowl, mix the raisins with the almonds, walnuts, zests, cinnamon, and cloves. Add the brandy and orange juice and mix well.

Preheat the oven to 375° F.

Flatten the dough with your hands and roll it out into a ⅛-inch-thick sheet, stretching it with your hands. Cut 4-inch circles and place a teaspoon of filling in the center of each. Fold the pastry over to cover the filling and press the edges with your fingers to seal. Oil a baking sheet and place the cookies on it. Bake for 20 to 25 minutes, or until golden. Let cool on a rack, then sprinkle with confectioners' sugar.

Boiled Sweetened Wheat

KOLYVA

Some people say that *kolyva* was the Christian version of sacrificial food, in contrast to the pagan custom of slaughtering animals to please the gods. Others will tell you that *kolyva* (in ancient Greek the word meant "small coin" or "small golden weight," as well as "small cakes") is the continuation of the mixture of grains (*polysporia*) symbolically offered by ancient Greeks to some of their gods, especially Demeter (Ceres), the goddess of agriculture.

THE GOOD THURSDAY MASS, ASTYPALAIA.

In any case, *kolyva* is one of the traditional symbolic sweets prepared only to mark nine days, forty days, one year, and so on from some beloved person's death. We also make them for All Souls' Day (the first Saturday of the forty days of Lent and the Saturday before Pentecost) as well as on some important saints' days. *Kolyva* are traditionally brought to the church to be blessed, and then distributed among the parishioners as well as the relations and friends of the deceased.

In Athens and the other big cities, most women don't cook their *kolyva* at home anymore, but have them made by professionals who cover the wheat with a thick sugar paste and make elaborate decorations, using silver-coated almonds and dragées. After blessing, portions of *kolyva* are handed, in small white paper bags, to the people attending the memorial service, with the sign of the cross and the name of the deceased printed on the bags.

In Mount Athos, the secluded community of monasteries in Macedonia, the monks prepare magnificent decorations for their *kolyva*, producing fabulous ephemeral pictures of their patron saints. Unfortunately I have seen only pictures of these extraordinary colored sugar icons because no women are permitted to visit Mount Athos.

The recipe that follows was given to me by Koula Maroupa, from Paros. Instead of throwing away the excellent cooking liquid, Koula pours it into individual bowls, and after it cools, places it in the refrigerator. It becomes a delicious jelly, full of vital nutrients. Served sprinkled with cinnamon and a little confectioners' sugar, it can be an unusual dessert.

If pomegranates are in season, a cup of their seeds is a tasty addition. For Greeks, this fruit symbolizes fertility, and we feel we must add it to *kolyva "gia to kalo"* (for good luck).

2½ cups wheatberries

1 teaspoon sea salt

2 bay leaves

2 cinnamon sticks

1 teaspoon whole cloves

¾–1 cup all-purpose flour

1½ cups blanched and coarsely chopped almonds

1½ cup coarsely chopped walnuts

¾ cup sesame seeds, toasted and lightly pounded in a mortar

1 cup golden raisins

1 cup dried currants

1 cup pomegranate seeds (optional)

½ cup finely chopped fresh flat-leaf parsley

1½ teaspoons ground cinnamon

1½ cups confectioners' sugar

Confectioners' sugar and whole blanched almonds, for garnish

SERVES ABOUT 30

Rinse the wheatberries in a colander and place in a large pot. Cover with water and add the salt and bay leaves. Tie the cinnamon sticks and cloves in a piece of cheesecloth and place in the pot. Bring to a boil, reduce the heat, and simmer for about 1½ hours, or until cooked but still chewy. Don't let it overcook. During cooking, stir occasionally with a wooden spoon, and add more water if necessary. Drain the cooked wheat, reserving the liquid, and discard the bay leaves and spices.

Sprinkle the wheatberries with cold water and drain. Spread them on thick linen or cotton towels and leave to dry for 5 to 6 hours or overnight.

In a skillet over low heat, lightly brown the flour.

In a large bowl, mix the cooked wheat with the almonds, walnuts, sesame seeds, golden raisins, currants, pomegranate seeds, parsley, and cinnamon, using your fingers. (Up to this point, the mixture can be kept for 1 day in the refrigerator.)

Just before serving, add the confectioners' sugar and toasted flour to the wheat mixture, mix well with your fingers, and arrange on a large plate or tray lined with a doily.

Press the wheat mixture with your hands to form a smooth mound. Sprinkle with confectioners' sugar, and form a cross with the whole almonds over the top.

Serve spoonfuls on individual plates or, as it is done in Greece, in small paper bags or paper napkins.

Sour Cherry Preserve

VISSINO GLYKO

Sour cherries used to be the symbol of summer. During the few weeks in July when they appeared in the market, you could spot parties of women wearing plastic aprons, sitting around a table in the yards of old Athenian houses with their sleeves rolled up, a hairpin in hand, pitting cherries, and covered in juice up to their elbows.

It was customary for each woman to make at least 2 pounds of *Vissino* and some syrup for *vissinada,* a traditional beverage made by diluting a little cherry syrup in icy cold water. Considering how messy and time-consuming this work can be, I'm amazed how many housewives still prepare it today. If you use a cherry pitter, the whole operation of pitting the cherries becomes much quicker. But purists insist that you should stick to the hairpin our mothers used because the pitter makes two holes and squeezes too much juice out of the fruit.

Another problem is the thickening of the syrup. There are many different secrets on how much sugar you should use per pound of fruit, if you should add water and how much, if you must add lemon juice and how much, and so on. And as the sugar thermometer is hardly known in Greece, all sorts of empirical methods were used to determine if the sour cherries and syrup were ready to be bottled. The most common one was to put a few drops of syrup in a glass with water.

COPPER JUG, METSOVO.

If they did not dissolve completely, but stayed at the bottom of the glass in a consistency similar to that of a thick glue, the syrup was thick enough.

An old expression—uncommon today—asked a bad-tempered woman: "What is the matter with you? Your *vissino* didn't thicken?" (*Den sou edesse to vissino?*)

The recipe that follows was given to me by Vali Manouilides, but I have reduced the amount of sugar. Of course I pitted the cherries with a pitter, which Vali insisted I shouldn't.

2 pounds fresh sour cherries
5 cups sugar
1½ tablespoon lemon juice

MAKES 3–3½ CUPS

Wash the cherries under running water, discarding the overripe or damaged ones, then drain in a colander.

Cover your table with a plastic sheet or a thick layer of old newspapers, roll up your sleeves, and wear a large apron. Place a pan in front of you to collect the pits, and especially the precious cherry juices, as you pit the cherries with a cherry pitter. After you have pitted them all, arrange a layer of cherries in a large nonreactive pot. Sprinkle a layer of sugar over them, add another layer of cherries, and continue until all have been used.

Strain the pits from the juices in the pan and pour the juices over the cherries. Rinse the pits with 5 tablespoons of water and pour that liquid into the pan. Cover and keep in the refrigerator overnight.

The next day, bring the cherries and their juices to a boil, skimming off as much of the pink foam as you can. Boil for about 20 minutes, then add the lemon juice. Continue to boil over high heat for another 10 minutes, then check with a sugar thermometer. It should be 205° to 220° F. If not, continue cooking a little longer. If you have no sugar thermometer, pour a few drops of syrup onto a plate, wait for them to cool, and test with your finger to see if they are as thick as you like.

Pour the cherries and enough syrup to cover them into clean, sterilized jars while the syrup is still very hot, and close the lid. Pour the surplus syrup into another jar or a clean sterilized bottle and cover. Store in a dark cold place for up to 1 year, but not in the refrigerator because it may crystallize.

To serve, place a teaspoon on a little plate alongside a glass of cold water. Or use as topping for thick Greek yogurt or ice cream.

Note: To make sour cherry drink (*vissinada*), pour 2 or 3 tablespoons of the syrup in a glass, add water and some ice cubes, stir, and serve.

Rolled Seville Orange or Bergamot Spoon Sweet

NERANTZI OR PERGAMONTO GLYKO

As a child I used to help my aunt Katina Patinioti grate and thread the rolled orange peels, as if to make a strange necklace. Maybe because I had taken part in making it, this bittersweet spoon sweet was always my favorite.

It was usually made with the Seville oranges we picked from the trees that line the streets of Athens, but now, owing to pollution, we go to the suburbs for our bitter oranges, which are never sold in the markets because everyone who wants them can pick them from the trees.

Using the same method, we also make spoon sweets from bergamot, the fragrant fruits that resemble large lemons, used mostly by the English to flavor Earl Gray tea.

With unripe walnut-size Seville oranges, another spoon sweet is made called *nerantzaki prassino*. It is usually tough and does not compare to the spoon sweet made from ripe fruit.

In this recipe you need only the peels, but the juice of Seville oranges can be used in Jellied Pork (page 178), so you may want to squeeze the oranges, pass the juice through a sieve, and freeze it. I know of no use for bergamot juice.

10 Seville oranges or 8 bergamots or oranges

3–3½ cups sugar

3 cups water

MAKES 1–1½ QUARTS

Wash and dry the fruits. Grate each all around with a very fine grater to get rid of the outer, very bitter layer of the peel. With a sharp knife, slit the skin lengthwise in 8 places and pull each piece of skin from the fruit. Be careful not to break the pieces.

Roll each piece, grated side out. Prick it with a trussing needle threaded with cotton string, and thread it on the string (see photograph) to secure it. After threading about 20 pieces, cut the string, leaving about 4 or 5 inches at each end. Tie the ends, and set aside until you finish with all the pieces of peel.

In a large pot, bring about 3 or 4 quarts of water to a boil. Blanch the rolled peels for about 5 minutes, then remove from the boiling water with a slotted spoon and drop into large bowl filled with cold water. Leave for about 2 hours, change the water, and leave another 2 to 3 hours; change the water again and leave for another 2 to 3 hours. Remove from the water and let the strings dry completely on kitchen towels.

In a pot, dissolve the sugar in the water and heat to the boiling point. When it starts to boil, place the rolled peels in the pot and

cook until just tender, about 15 minutes. Remove with a slotted spoon and let the peels cool on a plate.

Boil the syrup until a sugar thermometer reaches 220° F. Cut and discard the strings, and drop the peels in the syrup to boil for 1 more minute.

Pack clean sterilized jars tightly with the rolled peels, pour very hot syrup over them, and cover the jars with their lids. Store in a cool place—not in the refrigerator. Serve 1 to 2 rolls on a small plate with a glass of ice water.

COFFEE, GRATED QUINCE SPOON SWEET,
AND TWO KINDS OF COOKIES, METSOVO.

Grated Quince
Spoon Sweet

KYDONI GLYKO

Bright yellow quinces appear on the markets in October. Greeks love to eat them baked for dessert (page 216) or cooked with meat (page 180). But as a spoon sweet they are at their best.

All traditional Greek households used to have a curved bronze grater with large holes, made especially for quinces. If you don't have one you can either cut strips with a chef's knife or grate the flesh coarsely with a food processor. A regular grater is not suitable for the job.

As quinces contain enough pectin, it is not necessary to use lemon to thicken the syrup. Nevertheless, lemon is used here to prevent discoloration.

3 pounds quinces
4 cups water
3 tablespoons lemon juice
5 cups sugar
1 cup Greek thyme honey or
    1 additional cup sugar
1 sprig rose geranium, or
    ½ lemon peel

MAKES ABOUT 1 QUART

Wash, dry, and with a very sharp knife, peel 1 quince. Cut it in quarters and discard the core and seeds. With a chef's knife, julienne the quince pieces about the size of matchstick potatoes. Or you can grate the quince pieces coarsely with a food processor.

Put the quince strips in a large pot, then add 1½ cups cold water and half the lemon juice. Grate the rest of the quinces. When you have grated all of them, add them to the pot, bring the pot to a boil, cover, and cook until they start to become tender, 20 or 30 minutes.

Add the sugar and honey and the remaining cold water and continue cooking over high heat until tender, about 30 minutes. Add the rest of the lemon juice after 15 minutes of cooking, along with the rose geranium or lemon peel.

Test with a sugar thermometer; when 220° F., remove from the heat. Fill clean sterilized jars and cover with their lids. Store in a cool place. Serve 2 teaspoons on a small plate with a glass of ice water, or spoon 1 or 2 teaspoons over plain yogurt or vanilla ice cream.

Yogurt with Spicy Quince Preserve

KYDONIGLYKO PIKANTIKO

I tried this delicious dessert in Chania, Crete, in the spectacular dining room of the Doma Hotel. The owner, Ioanna Koutsoudaki, told me that she got the idea from an old recipe, probably one that originated in Turkey.

1½ cups Grated Quince Spoon Sweet
    (page 238)
2 teaspoons grated fresh ginger
1 teaspoon ground allspice
1 teaspoon grated nutmeg
4 cups thick Greek yogurt
½ cup coarsely chopped almonds
Ground cinnamon

SERVES 4

Mix the spoon sweet with the ginger, allspice, and nutmeg and stir well.

Spoon about 1 cup yogurt into each serving bowl, top with 2 or 3 tablespoons of the quince mixture, and sprinkle with almonds and cinnamon.

Semolina Sweet

HALVAS SIMIGDALENIOS

Halva means "sweet" in Turkish, and you will find many different sweets by that name in Greece. Grocer's *halva* is a commercial confection with the main ingredient tahini (sesame seed paste); it is traditionally eaten on Lenten days. *Halva* from Farsala (a town in Thessaly) is a kind of cake made with lots of butter and semolina and flooded with heavy syrup. This third kind of *halva,* which is also called *Halvas Simigdalenios* or *Halvas Politikos* (from Constantinople) is one of the simplest of traditional Greek sweets. Made with semolina, olive oil, and sugar syrup mixed with almonds, walnuts, or pine nuts, this most common *halva* can be made in thirty minutes. It's the dessert we like to prepare when we have unexpected guests.

There are many variations on the basic recipe. This one is my mother's, with some improvements from my sister.

SYRUP

3 cups water
2 cups orange juice
2½ cups sugar
1 cinnamon stick
1 large piece lemon peel
1 tablespoon whole cloves

1 cup olive oil
1 cup fine semolina
1 cup coarse semolina
½ cup blanched and quartered
    almonds
⅓ cup pine nuts

Ground cinnamon

SERVES 16

In a pot, mix the water, orange juice, and sugar, and bring to a boil. Add the cinnamon stick, lemon peel, and cloves. Cook for about 8 minutes, then pass through a fine sieve and discard the cloves and cinnamon stick.

In a heavy pot, heat the olive oil and add the semolinas, almonds, and pine nuts. Stirring constantly with a wooden spoon over medium heat, cook the mixture until the semolina becomes golden brown, about 25 minutes. Remove from the heat.

Very carefully—because it will bubble vigorously—pour the syrup over the semolina, stirring with a wooden spoon. Cover the pot with a kitchen towel and leave for about 10 minutes to absorb the syrup.

Spoon the mixture into a 6-cup mold, and let cool. Unmold onto a plate, sprinkle with cinnamon, and serve.

Note: Halva will keep for 4 to 5 days, well covered.

Rice Pudding

RIZOGALO

I always associate *Rizogalo* with my sister's and my childhood illnesses. Our mother made this delicious rice pudding every time she felt we needed milk for sustenance.

There are two ways to make *Rizogalo:* with and without eggs. I much prefer the latter. The following recipe is my friend Maria Haritopoulou's, and I love its lemony taste. Her method of first cooking the rice in a little water saves you about 15 minutes of constant stirring. If you cook the rice directly in the milk, you must stir constantly because it tends to stick to the bottom of the pan.

For rice pudding, as for all stuffings and soups, we use short-grain rice.

⅓ cup short-grain rice
1 cinnamon stick
2 cups water
6 cups whole milk, or low-fat milk
   plus 2 tablespoons margarine
1¼ tablespoons cornstarch, diluted in
   2 tablespoons cold milk
⅓–½ cup sugar
3–4 egg yolks (optional)
Zest of 1 large lemon (about
   1½ teaspoons)
Ground cinnamon, for sprinkling

SERVES 6–8

Put the rice and cinnamon stick in a saucepan and pour the water over it. Bring to a boil and lower the heat. Simmer for 12 to 15 minutes, or until tender.

Pour the milk over the rice. Add the cornstarch mixture and sugar to the pan. Turn the heat to medium and stir constantly until the mixture thickens, about 15 minutes.

If you are using egg yolks, beat them with a little rice mixture and add to the pan. Stir well. Add the lemon zest and stir well.

Spoon pudding into 6 to 8 individual bowls. Let cool, then refrigerate. Sprinkle with cinnamon and serve.

Note: If you dislike the taste of lemon, substitute vanilla, orange zest, or a few spoonfuls of your favorite liqueur.

Milk Pie

GALATOMBOUREKO

Galatomboureko, like most sweet pies, is not my strong point, so for the best recipes I rely on my friends. This comes from Vali Manouilides, whom I have mentioned on many other occasions and who is one of the best cooks I know.

A good *Galatomboureko* must have a firm but not hard creamy filling and its phyllo should be well moistened with syrup but be crunchy at the same time. Vali's way of sprinkling the top layers with water and then simmering the syrup for a long time and pouring it over the pie when it is very hot makes her version exquisite.

MILK VENDOR, METSOVO.

4 cups milk

½ cup fine semolina

1 cup sugar

⅔ cup margarine or butter

4 eggs

½ teaspoon vanilla extract

1 pound thick commercial phyllo
   dough

About ⅔ cup melted margarine or
   butter, to brush dough

SYRUP

3 cups water

2 cups sugar

½ lemon

SERVES 18–20

In a heavy pot, bring the milk to a boil. Sprinkle in the semolina, whisking constantly over very low heat. Add the sugar, then simmer for 5 to 6 minutes, stirring from time to time. Remove from the heat and add the margarine or butter and the eggs, one by one, stirring. Blend in the vanilla. The mixture will be thick but pourable, like a sauce.

Preheat the oven to 375° F.

Butter a deep 10-inch baking pan and lay in 8 sheets of phyllo, leaving them to hang over the sides of the pan. Brush each sheet generously with melted margarine or butter. Pour the milk mixture over the layers.

Cut the remaining sheets of phyllo about the size of the pan and brush with margarine or butter. Place the buttered sheets on top of the filling, then brush the hanging bottom sheets with margarine and roll them up to seal.

With a very sharp knife or razor blade, score the top diagonally in 2 directions to make diamond-shaped slits on the surface. (This makes it easier to cut later, and also allows the syrup to penetrate the pie.) Sprinkle with a little water and bake for about 1 hour, or until top is lightly brown and filling has set.

The minute you start baking the pie, begin to make the syrup. Simmer the water with the sugar and the ½ lemon for about 1 hour. Remove the lemon half and squeeze the juice into the syrup. Discard the lemon. Pour the syrup over the pie the minute you take it out of the oven. Be careful—the syrup will bubble vigorously and can burn you.

Let cool, and serve, cutting pieces along the slits that you had made before baking the pie.

Rice Pie with Walnuts and Golden Raisins

RIZOPITA ME
KARYDIA KE STAFIDES

This is a Lenten sweet pie that is prepared in Metsovo, but this recipe is my interpretation. Instead of using olive oil, I have used margarine because I think the taste of olive oil is much too strong.

Needless to say, it is infinitely better if the phyllo is homemade.

½ cup short-grain rice
1 tablespoon margarine or light olive oil
2 cups water
1 cup shelled walnuts
1 cup golden raisins
1½ teaspoons ground cinnamon
½ teaspoon ground cloves
4 sheets Homemade Phyllo (page 205), or 1 pound thick commercial phyllo
½–¾ cup melted margarine or light olive oil, for brushing

SYRUP

½ cup sugar
⅔ cup water
2 tablespoons lemon juice
Peel of ½ lemon
1 piece cinnamon stick

SERVES 12–15

Soak the rice for 5 minutes in water to cover. Drain and sauté in the margarine until glistening. Pour in the water and cook over low heat for about 12 minutes, or until it becomes very soft and has absorbed all the water. Turn the cooked rice into a bowl and let cool a little.

Preheat the oven to 375° F.

Mix the walnuts, raisins, cinnamon, and cloves with the rice and stir well.

Brush a 14 × 9½-inch baking pan with margarine and lay in 2 sheets of homemade or 8 sheets of commercial phyllo, brushing each sheet with margarine. Let about 2½ inches of dough hang over the edge of the pan, and trim the rest.

Pour the filling into the pan, smooth it with a spatula, and lay in the remaining sheets of commercial or 2 sheets of homemade phyllo, brushing each sheet with margarine. Trim the top sheets to no more than ½ inch larger than the pan all around. Brush again with margarine, and turn the hanging phyllo inward to seal.

Using a very sharp knife or a razor blade, score the top layers to mark the desired sizes of the pieces you will cut later. Place in the oven, and bake for 1 hour, or until golden brown on top.

After baking for 30 minutes, start preparing the syrup. Place the sugar, water, lemon juice, lemon peel, and cinnamon stick in a saucepan, bring to a boil, and turn down the heat. Simmer until the pie is baked.

The moment you take the pie out of the oven, discard the lemon peel and cinnamon stick, and pour the syrup over the pie. Be very careful—the syrup can bubble vigorously and can burn you. Cover pie with a clean kitchen towel and let cool completely before serving.

This rice pie tastes much better the next day and keeps well for at least a week.

Rolled Baklava with Golden Raisins

BAKLAVAS TYLIKHTOS

Baklava, found in all eastern Mediterranean countries, is probably a refined version of what Aristophanes described in his comedies: baked pastry filled with nuts.

In this more than in any other sweets with phyllo pastry, it is important to use the right kind of pastry—not the very thin kind. Strudel pastry works better, and homemade phyllo is best. Since the filling of Baklava contains nothing more than nuts—and golden raisins, in this recipe—if you use commercial thin phyllo, you will end up needing masses of butter to make it tasty.

The recipe that follows is my lighter interpretation of a rolled Baklava I tasted in Chania, Crete. Instead of flooding it with syrup, as it is the custom in Greece, I found it better to use less, and turn the Baklava in the syrup so the top absorbs some syrup. But this means that you should make Baklava at least one day in advance.

1 cup melted margarine, or a
    combination of margarine
    and butter
1 cup unblanched coarsely ground
    almonds
1 cup coarsely ground walnuts
1 teaspoon ground cinnamon
½ teaspoon ground cloves
1 cup golden raisins
2 tablespoons brandy
4 strudel pastry sheets (approximately
    18 × 17 inches; see Mail-Order
    Sources), or about 1 pound thick
    commercial phyllo dough

SYRUP

1½ cups sugar
1½ cups water
2 tablespoons lemon juice
Peel of ½ lemon
1 cinnamon stick

Brush an 11- or 12-inch round pan with margarine.

In a bowl mix the nuts, cinnamon, cloves, and raisins. Pour in the brandy and knead with your fingers to mix well.

Preheat the oven to 375° F.

Cut one 18 × 17-inch sheet of strudel pastry, or 2 sheets of commercial phyllo, in half to obtain two 18 × 8½-inch rectangles. Brush each sheet with margarine. Put 2 rectangles of commercial phyllo, one on top of the other, or 1 rectangle of strudel dough on a counter. Sprinkle 3 heaping tablespoons of filling on the phyllo. Spread the mixture evenly, leaving 2 inches clear on all sides. Fold the left and right short sides of the phyllo to cover part of the stuffing, brush with margarine, and start to roll the long side tightly as you would a strudel, brushing the outer part of the dough with margarine as you turn it. You will end up with a 14-inch-long cylinder. Place it carefully in the buttered pan, and continue with the rest of the sheets. Place the second roll next to the first, curving it to fit the pan, and continue until you fill it with a coillike shape (see step-by-step photographs of Traditional Greens Pie, page 149).

With a trussing needle, prick the filled rolls in several places. Sprinkle lightly with water and bake for about 1 hour, or until golden brown.

SERVES 10–12

ROLLED BAKLAVA AND
KATAIFI, SERVED HERE WITH
COFFEE AND *TSIKOUDIA*,
CHANIA, CRETE.

After baking for 30 minutes, start preparing the syrup. Place the sugar, water, lemon juice, lemon peel, and cinnamon stick in a saucepan, bring to a boil, and turn the heat down. Simmer for about 30 minutes.

The moment you take the Baklava out of the oven, discard the lemon peel and cinnamon stick and pour the syrup over. Be very careful because the syrup will bubble up and can burn you. Cover with a clean linen towel and let cool completely—for 10 to 12 hours or overnight.

The next day, cut 2-inch pieces of rolled Baklava, and turn them upside down in the pan, so that the top soaks in the syrup. After 3 to 4 hours, the Baklava is ready to be served.

As with rice pie, Baklava is infinitely better 2 to 3 days after it is made. It keeps very well tightly covered for a week.

Note: Using this filling, you can make *Kadaifi* by rolling the filling in shredded kadaifi pastry, available in Greek or Middle Eastern food stores.

Lenten Baklava

The recipe for this excellent and light traditional Baklava was given to me by my sister's mother-in-law, Eleni Margaritouli, from Volos, Thessaly. She is an able cook, and often sends packages of food to both her sons in Athens.

For best results, choose the thickest commercial phyllo you can find.

1 pound walnuts, coarsely chopped
½ pound almonds, blanched and
    coarsely chopped
1 cup dry bread crumbs
3 teaspoons ground cinnamon
1 teaspoon ground cloves
1 teaspoon freshly grated nutmeg
½ cup sugar
About 1½ cups light olive oil
    and sunflower oil (50–50),
    for brushing
1½ pounds thick commercial phyllo

SYRUP

2½ cups sugar
2½ cups water
1 lemon, cut in half

MAKES ABOUT 80 SMALL PIECES

Preheat the oven to 300° F.

In a bowl, mix the walnuts, almonds, bread crumbs, spices, and sugar. Toss well. Brush a 15-inch round pan with oil, and lay in 2 sheets of phyllo. Brush again, and layer in another 2, brush, and layer another 2. Spread some of the nut mixture evenly on top, then layer another 2 sheets. Brush and layer one more sheet. Spread on more nut mixture, and continue layering about 3 sheets between each layer of nuts until you have used all the filling. Layer about 8 sheets on the top, brushing each second sheet with oil. Keep the sheets of phyllo covered while working to prevent drying.

Score the top with a very sharp knife from the center of the pan to the edges like spokes, then cut diagonally in between to form small diamond-shaped pieces. Pour 2 to 3 tablespoons of oil over the top. Bake the Baklava for about 1 hour, or until golden brown.

After baking for 30 minutes, make the syrup. Bring the sugar, water, and lemon to a boil in a saucepan, and simmer over very low heat until syrupy.

As you take the Baklava from the oven, squeeze the lemon halves with a fork and discard them. Pour the syrup over the Baklava very carefully because it will bubble and can burn you. Let stand overnight.

The next day, invert the Baklava into another pan of the same size, and let stand for 3 to 4 hours. Turn again and serve, or cut pieces and store for 7 to 10 days at room temperature.

Grape Must Jelly

MOUSTALEVRIA

From August through October in Greece, one can find fresh sweet grape must (the juice of ripe grapes) with which to make this traditional jelly. The look and taste of the jelly depends on the quality of the must.

But even if you cannot find grape must, you can still make this jelly by passing any kind of grapes through a food mill. To make the juice sweeter, boil it down—the more you reduce it the sweeter it becomes—and add some golden raisins. Pass the resulting juice through the food mill again, then through a fine sieve lined with cheesecloth before making the jelly. The old, complicated way of clarifying the must involved the use of wood ash or—in Crete—a kind of ground limestone. You need not go to this much trouble. If you pass the juice through double cheesecloth, it will be clear enough.

The old rule for *Moustalevria* is to add about 1 cup of fine semolina to every 8 or 9 cups of grape must, boil for about 45 minutes, stirring constantly, and serve in individual plates or bowls. This recipe is my mother's; instead of semolina, she uses cornstarch and flour.

½ cup cornstarch
10 cups clarified concentrated
    grape juice
1 cup all-purpose flour
3–4 tablespoons toasted sesame seeds
1 cup coarsely chopped walnuts
Ground cinnamon

SERVES 8

In a bowl, dissolve the cornstarch in 1 cup of the grape juice, then mix with rest of the must. In a heavy pot, heat the grape juice and, while stirring with a wooden spoon, add the flour, sprinkling it in slowly so it doesn't form lumps. Stir constantly, cooking over low heat, for 35 to 40 minutes, or until the liquid starts to thicken.

Pour into individual bowls or soup plates and let cool completely. Just before serving, sprinkle with the sesame seeds, chopped walnuts, and cinnamon.

The jelly will keep for about a week in the refrigerator.

ACKNOWLEDGMENTS

My most special thanks go to Paula Wolfert. Our joint trip to northern Greece in 1991 was an unforgettable experience. For her enormous help and guidance ever since, I will be forever grateful. I also owe a great debt to my agent, Sarah Jane Freymann. From our first discussions, she understood perfectly what I had in mind and found ways to help me realize it.

I couldn't have achieved anything without my publisher, Leslie Stoker, whose enthusiasm for and absolute trust in the project has never wavered. She is the one who brought Martin Brigdale to the project.

Martin, devoted to his work and to this book, was tireless in his efforts to achieve the perfect picture. During our many trips around Greece, we frequently chose photographic locations that are inaccessible by car. I learned that field photography—and especially food photography on location—requires not only artistic and technical skill, but also endurance, strength, perseverance, resourcefulness, and good humor. Our most valuable ally was Alex Hansen, the assistant photographer, whose poker-faced remarks at many critical moments still make me laugh. We were also very lucky to have the help of the many-talented Louise Pickford—author of *The Inspired Vegetarian*—as our food stylist.

My good fortune continued when the patient and enthusiastic Ann ffolliott became my editor. She coped stoically with my far from perfect English. Even the long-distance communication between Athens and New York didn't seem to stand in the way of our work. I am also grateful for Carole Berglie's careful work with the manuscript.

I owe a debt of gratitude to Joel Avirom for bringing together all the elements and designing such a beautiful book. For their various efforts I also thank Barbara Sturman, Susannah Levy, Wendy Wilson, Hope Koturo, Margaret Orto, and Siobhan McGowan.

I'm endlessly grateful to the women all over Greece—many of them friends—who gave me their recipes and shared with me their cooking tricks these past four years, especially to Vali Manouilidi—surely the best cook in Greece—and Maria Haritopoulou, who was kind enough to give me her own and her aunt's recipes. Also many thanks to Giorgo Papastefanou for showing me his mother's kitchen notebook and to Virginia Manolaki-Angelidi, who deciphered the complicated Astypalaian recipes.

I would also like to express my gratitude to numerous people who helped in many ways: Leonida Vostani, for explaining to me all I would ever have wanted to know about olive oil; Apostolo Bissa, for his valuable information concerning Greek cheeses; Giota Garefi, for sharing with me some of her vast knowledge of Greek wines; and Gianni Kouleli in Santorini and Babi Sitara in Mytilini for showing us the hidden treasures of their islands. My thanks to Niko Stavroulakis for his help and consultation and to my sister, Anna Margaritouli, for her great help in finding the Latin and English names of the different wild greens.

I'm more than grateful to the people who uncomplainingly let us take over their houses during our photographic sessions: Elena Averoff, who let us work in her unbelievably beautiful family home in Metsovo for three days; equally to Dorothy Andrews, in Chania, and Giannis Malinakis in Tersana, Chania. In their houses we shot some of our best pictures. Also to Vassilis and Vivi Mitropoulos in Marathon, Maroula Panagiotou and Vassili Korkolopoulo in Ekali, Roxane Matsa in Kantza, and Alexandra Christou in Astypalaia. Many thanks, also, to the designer Mario Voutsina and the architect Maria Kaltsa for their valuable advice, and to Peggy Zouboulakis for lending us important pieces from her collection to use as props in some photographs.

Last, but not least, I would like to thank my mother, Frossoula, for getting me into the kitchen at a very early age and teaching me all she knew. I also thank my father, Iasson, for his generous support and for relating to me all the fascinating stories of his childhood.

MAIL-ORDER SOURCES

Many Greek ingredients are available in supermarkets and in Greek and Middle Eastern grocery stores.

If you can't locate ingredients, here are some places that provide mail-order service.

For Greek-style Sheep's Milk Yogurt:
Hollow Road Farms
RR 1, Box 93
Stuyvesant, NY 12173
(product list available)

If you want to make your own yogurt, you can get excellent Bulgarian yogurt culture from:

International Yogurt Company
628 North Doheny Drive
Los Angeles, CA 90069
310/274-9917

Mahlep, Mastic, and other Greek ingredients:
Sultan's Delight
25 Croton Avenue
Staten Island, NY 10301
718/720-1557
(catalogue available)

For Aleppo pepper, similar to *Boukovo:*
Shalah Importing Company
270 White Street
Danbury, CT 06810
203/743-4181

For olives and other Greek specialty items:
Peloponnese/The Aegean Trader
2227 Poplar Street
Oakland, CA
415/839-8153
(product list available)

For fresh Greek oregano and other herbs and greens:
Fox Hill Farm
443 W. Michigan Avenue
Parma, Mich. 49269
800/245-4372
FAX: 517/531-3179

For dried Greek oregano and other herbs from Crete:
Dean and Deluca
560 Broadway
New York, NY 10012
212/431-1691

If you have your own garden, seeds for amaranth are available from:

Johnny's Selected Seeds
Foss Hill Road
Albion, Maine 04910
(catalogue available)

Seeds for other specialty greens are available from:
The Cook's Garden
P. O. Box 535
Londonderry, Vermont 05148
802/824-3400
Fax: 802/824-3027
(catalogue available)

Phyllo
Commercial phyllo in the United States is available in many supermarkets. But is it worth seeking out the thicker version that is available in Greek and Middle Eastern markets. For more information about availability, contact:

The manufacturer of Krinos brand phyllo and many other Greek products:
Krinos Foods, Inc.
47-00 Northern Blvd.
Long Island City, New York 11101

The manufacturer of Apollo brand phyllo dough:
Athens Foods
Customer Relations
13600 Snow Road
Cleveland, Ohio 44142
216/676-8500

Strudel dough, which is thicker than commercial phyllo, is available from:
Paprikas Weiss
1546 Second Avenue
New York, NY 10021
212/288-6117
(catalogue available)

To give charcoal grilled foods a Mediterranean flavor, add olive branch briquettes from:
Ultima Foods
3790 Hawthorne Court
Waukegan, Illinois
708/263-8484

If you don't have enough time to make your own stock, try:
Perfect Addition Rich Stock
P. O. Box 8976
Newport Beach, CA 92658
714/640-0220

BIBLIOGRAPHY

History, customs, folklore, and travels

Andre, Jacques. *L' Alimentation et la cuisine a Rome*. Paris: Les belles lettres, 1981.

Athenaeus. *The Deipnosophists*. Loeb Classical Library. Cambridge, Mass.: Harvard University Press, 1971.

Averof-Tositsas, Vangelis. *The Monastery of Saint Nicholas* (in Greek). Athens: Estia, 1973.

Bauman, Helmut. *Greek Flora in Myth, Art and Literature* (in German) Munich: Hirmer, 1982.

Burkert, Walter. *Greek Religion*. Oxford: Blackwell, 1990.

Connell, Christopher. *In the Bee-loud Glade*. Nauplion, Greece: Peloponnesian Folklore Foundation, 1977.

Detienne, Marcel and Jean-Pierre Vernant. *La cuisine du sacrifice en pays grec*. Paris: Gallimard, 1979.

Faure, Paul. *La vie quotidienne en Grèce au temps de la guerre de Troie*. Paris: Hachette, 1977.

Fermor, Patrick Leigh. Mani: *Travels in the Southern Peloponnese*. London: Penguin, 1984.

Fermor, Patrick Leigh. *Roumeli: Travels in Northern Greece*. London: Penguin, 1984.

Flaceliere, Robert. *La vie quotidienne en Grece au siecle de Pericles*. Paris: Hachette, 1959.

Hatzifotis, I. M. *Everyday Life in Mount Athos* (in Greek). Katerini: Tertios, 1989.

Heiser, Charles B., Jr. *Seed to Civilization: The Story of Food*. Cambridge, Mass.: Harvard University Press, 1990.

History of the Greek Nation (in Greek). 16 vols. Athens: Ekdotike Athinon, 1970.

Imellos, Stefanos. "Looking at Food from a Folkloric Point of View" (in Greek). *Yearly Review of the Department of Philosophy*. Athens University. Vol. 28 (1979–1985) pp. 214–46.

Johnson, Maria. "Tarhana: From Steppe to Empire." Oxford Symposium on Food and Cookery, 1989.

Kavadas, Demetrios. *Botanical and Phytological Dictionary with Pictures* (in Greek). Athens, 1938.

Koukoules, *Phaidon. Life and Civilization of the Byzantines* (in Greek). Vol. 5. Athens: Papazissis, 1952.

Lampsas, Giannis. *Dictionary of the Ancient World: Greece-Rome* (in Greek). 6 vols. Athens: Dome, n.d.

Leeming, Margaret. *A History of Food*. London: BBC Publications, 1991.

Liddell and Scott. *Greek-English Lexicon*. Oxford: Oxford University Press, 1968.

Liutprando da Cremona. *Tutte le Opere, La relazione di un' Ambasceria à Costantinopoli*. Rome: Valentino Bompiani, 1945.

Loukatos, Demetrios. *Introduction to Greek Folklore* (in Greek). Athens: Educational Institute of the National Bank of Greece, 1985.

Loukatos, Demetrios. *The Fall* (in Greek). Athens: Filippotis, 1982.

Loukatos, Demetrios. *Christmas and Holidays* (in Greek) Athens: Filippotis, 1984.

Loukatos, Demetrios. *More Winter and Spring Customs* (in Greek). Athens: Filippotis, 1985.

Loukatos, Demetrios. *Summer* (in Greek). Athens: Filippotis, 1981.

Loukopoulos, Demetrios. *Villages and Foods of the Aeolians* (in Greek). First printed in 1925. Athens: Dodoni, 1984.

Megas, Georges. *Greek Feasts* (in Greek). Athens: Odysseas, 1988.

Micha-Lampaki, Aspasia. "The appearance of specific foodstuffs in the traditional weddings of Boeotia" (in Greek). *Society of Boeotian Studies*, Vol. 1b (September 1986).

———. *Bread as Bloodless Offering in Messinia, Peloponnese* (in Greek). Athens: Society of Peloponnesian Studies, 1984.

———. *The Foods of Ancient Greeks, According to the Ancient Comedy Writers* (in Greek). Athens, 1984.

Parke, H. W. *Festivals of the Athenians*. New York: Cornell University Press, 1986.

Perry, Charles. "The Oldest Mediterranean Noodle" *Petit Propos Culinaires 9*. London: Prospect Books, 1981

Pliny the Elder. *Natural History*. London: Penguin, 1991.

Pomeroy, Sarah. *Goddesses, Whores, Wives and Slaves*. London: Hale, 1975.

Siettos, Georges. *Customs During the Feasts* (in Greek). Piraeus, 1985.

Simopoulos, Kyriakos. *Foreign Travellers in Greece 1800–1810* (in Greek). Vol. 3. Athens, 1975.

Sparkes, Brian and Lucy Talcott. *The Pots and Pans of Classical Athens*. Princeton, N.J.: The American School of Classical Studies, 1977.

Stathaki-Koumari, Rodoula. *The Traditional Bread of Rethymnon* (in Greek). Rethymnon: The Rethymnon Museum of History and Folk Tradition, 1983.

Stefopoulos, Andreas. *The Foods of Chryssi, Kastoria* (in Greek). Ioannina: University of Ioannina, 1981.

Tanahill, Reay. *Food in History*. London: Penguin, 1988.

Thesaurus Linguae Graecae (CD ROM) Irvine: University of California, 1987.

Tsotakou-Karaveli, Katherine: *Folkloric Calendar* (in Greek). Athens: Pataki, 1985.

Tritos, Michael. *Metsovo* (in Greek). Athens, 1990.

Tseva, Ageliki. *A Crown of Bread, Full of Ornaments, Is Born* (in Greek). Koropi: Cultural Center A.Tseva, 1983.

Zographos, Demetrios. *History of Greek Agriculture* (in Greek). Athens: Agricultural Bank of Greece, 1976.

Food, Cooking, and Nutrition

Agapios, monk from Crete. *Greek folk medicine, nutrition, and agronomy in the beginning of the 18th century* (in Greek). 1850. Reprint. Athens: Cultura, 1979.

Bauerle, Heidi. *Santorin—Rezepte und Bilder aus der Aegais*. Weil, Germany: Hadecke, 1991.

Blanc, Nicole and Anne Nercessian. *La cuisine Romaine Antique*. Paris: Glenat, Faton 1992.

Chatto, James and W. L. Martin. *A Kitchen in Corfu*. New York: New Amsterdam, 1988.

David, Elizabeth. *A Book of Mediterranean Food*. London: Penguin, 1965.

David, Elizabeth. *Summer Cooking*. London: Dorling Kindersley, 1988.

David Elizabeth. "Mad, mad, despised and dangerous." *Petits Propos Culinaires 9*. London: Prospect Books, 1981.

Davidson, Alan. *Mediterranean Seafood*. Baton Rouge: Louisiana State University Press, 1981.

Edwards, John. *The Roman Cookery of Apicius*. Washington, D.C.: Hartley and Marks, 1984.

Facciola, Stephen. *Cornucopia: A Source Book of Edible Plants*. Vista, Calif.: Kampong Publications, 1990.

Gray, Patience. *Honey from a Weed*. San Francisco: North Point Press, 1990.

Gregoriadou-Vakirtzoglou, Efrosyni. *Traditional and Modern Pontian Cooking* (in Greek). Thessaloniki, 1990.

Halici, Nevin. *Turkish Cookbook*. London: Dorling Kindersley, 1989.

Helldreich, Theodore. *Dictionary of the Common Names of the Plants of Greece* (in Greek). Athens, 1980.

Kochilas, Diane. *The Food and Wine of Greece*. New York: St. Martin's Press, 1990.

Kokkinou, Marigoula and Georgia Kofina. *Lenten Meals and Desserts* (in Greek). Athens: Akritas, 1988.

Lambert-Gocs, Miles. *The Wines of Greece*. London: Faber and Faber, 1990.

Lassalle, George: *East of Orphanides*. London: Kyle Cathie, Ltd., 1991.

Liacouras-Chantiles, Vilma. *The Food of Greece*. New York: Dodd, Mead and Co., 1985.

McGee, Harold. *On Food and Cooking*. London: Harper Collins, 1991.

Michelakis, Nicholas "Olive Oil Quality Improvement in Greece, Past, Present and Future" *Olivae* magazine (June 1992).

Papadimitriou, Elli. *Fish of the Aegean* (in Greek). Athens: Hermes, 1990.

Recipe Club of Saint Paul's Greek Orthodox Cathedral. *The Complete Book of Greek Cooking*. New York: Harper and Row, 1990.

Roden, Claudia. *A New Book of Middle Eastern Food*. London: Penguin, 1963.

Savidi, Lena. 1989 *Calendar with Recipes* (in Greek). Athens: Hermes, 1989.

Senderens, Alain. *Figues sans barbarie*. Paris: Robert Lafont, 1991.

Siesby, Brigit. "The Travels of Dolmades" *Petits Propos Culinaires 5*. London: Prospect Books.

Stavroulakis, Nicholas. *Cookbook of the Jews of Greece*. New York: Cadmus Press, 1986.

Stubbs, Joyce M. *The Home Book of Greek Cookery*. London: Faber and Faber, 1986.

Traditional Greek Recipes (in Greek). 6 vols. Athens: Fytrakis, n.d.

Tselementes, Nicholas. *Cooking and Patisserie Guide* (in Greek) 1920. Reprint. Athens: Fytrakis, 1983.

Wolfert, Paula. *Mediterranean Cooking*. New York: Ecco Press, 1985.

Wolfert, Paula. *World of Food*. New York: Harper and Row, 1988.

Unknown man from Pelion.: *Notebook on Nutrition, Botany and Agriculture* (in Greek) Annotated and edited by G. Sfikas. Athens, 1991.

Unknown man from Syros. *Cooking, translated from Italian* (into Greek) 1828. Reprint. Athens: E.L.I.A., 1988.

CONVERSION CHART

FLOUR

To achieve a near equivalent to American all-purpose flour, use half British plain flour and half strong bread flour. American cake flour can be replaced by British plain flour alone.

SUGAR

American granulated sugar is finer than British granulated, closer to caster sugar, so British cooks should use caster sugar throughout.

YEAST

Quantities of dried yeast (called active dry yeast in the United States) are usually given in number of packages. Each package contains 7 g/ ¼ oz of yeast, which is equivalent to a scant tablespoon.

INGREDIENTS AND EQUIPMENT GLOSSARY

The following ingredients and equipment are basically the same on both sides of the Atlantic, but have different names.

AMERICAN	BRITISH
arugula	rocket
baking soda	bicarbonate of soda
beans (dried)—lima, navy,	
Great Northern	dried white (haricot) beans
bell pepper	sweet pepper (capsicum)
Bibb and Boston lettuce	soft-leaved, round lettuce
broiler/to broil	grill/to grill
cheesecloth	muslin
chile	chilli or chili
eggplant	aubergine
fava bean	broad bean
golden raisins	sultanas
ground beef/pork	minced beef/pork
kitchen towel	tea towel
parchment paper	non-stick baking paper
pearl onion	button or baby onion
romaine lettuce	cos lettuce
scallion	spring onion
shrimp	prawn (varying in size)
skillet	frying pan
tomato puree	sieved tomatoes or pasatta
vanilla bean	vanilla pod
whole milk	homogenized milk
zucchini	courgette

OVEN TEMPERATURES

Consult this chart for the Centigrade and gas mark equivalents for Fahrenheit temperatures.

OVEN	°F	°C	GAS MARK
very cool	250–275	130–140	½–1
cool	300	150	2
warm	325	170	3
moderate	350	180	4
moderately hot	375	190	5
	400	200	6
hot	425	220	7
very hot	450	230	8
	475	250	9

VOLUME EQUIVALENTS

These are not exact equivalents, but have been rounded up or down slightly to make measuring easier.

AMERICAN	METRIC	IMPERIAL
¼ t	1.25 ml	
½ t	2.5 ml	
1 t	5 ml	
½ T (1½ t)	7.5ml	
1 T (3 t)	15 ml	
¼ cup (4 T)	60 ml	2 fl oz
⅓ cup (5 T)	75 ml	2½ fl oz
½ cup (8 T)	125 ml	4 fl oz
⅔ cup (10 T)	150 ml	5 fl oz (¼ pint)
¾ cup (12 T)	175 ml	6 fl oz
1 cup (16 T)	250 ml	8 fl oz
1¼ cups 300 ml	10fl oz (½ pint)	
1½ cups 350 ml	12 fl oz	
1 pint (2 cups)	500 ml	16 fl oz
1 quart (4 cups)	1 litre	1¾ pints

WEIGHT EQUIVALENTS

These are not exact equivalents, but have been rounded up or down slightly to make measuring easier.

AVOIRDUPOIS	METRIC
¼ oz	7 g
½ oz	15 g
1 oz	30 g
2 oz	60g
3 oz	90g
4 oz	115g
5 oz	150 g
6 oz	175 g
7 oz	200g
8 oz	225 g
9 oz	250 g
10 oz	300 g
11 oz	325 g
12 oz	350 g
13 oz	375 g
14 oz	400 g
15 oz	425 g
1 lb	450 g
1 lb 2 oz	500 g
1½ lb	750 g
2 lb	900g
2¼ lb	1 kg
3 lb	1.4 kg
4 lb	1.8 kg
4½ lb	2 kg

INDEX

Designed by Joel Avirom

Composed in Galliard
by Barbara Sturman
at Stewart, Tabori & Chang,
New York, New York.

Printed and bound by
Toppan Printing Company, Ltd.,
Tokyo, Japan.